THE

Fact of a Body

A Murder and a Memoir

~

Alexandria Marzano-Lesnevich

MACMILLAN

First published 2017 by Flatiron Books, New York

First published in the UK 2017 by Macmillan
an imprint of Pan Macmillan
20 New Wharf Road, London N1 9RR
Associated companies throughout the world
www.panmacmillan.com

ISBN 978-1-5098-0562-4

1 3 5 7 9 8 6 4 2

A CIP catalogue record for this book is available from the British Library.

Printed and bound by CPI Group (UK) Ltd, Croydon, CR0 4YY

Visit **www.panmacmillan.com** to read more about all our books
and to buy them. You will also find features, author interviews and
news of any author events, and you can sign up for e-newsletters
so that you're always first to hear about our new releases.

THE Fact of a Body

for my parents

A Note on Source Material

I have reconstructed Ricky Langley's life from a mix of public court documents, transcripts, newspaper articles, and television coverage, and in one case a play that was based on interviews. In that extensive record, there were many instances in which I faced two or more competing facts, and I had to choose one in order to fashion a coherent narrative. In many more instances, I decided to include competing facts, claims, slippages, and ellipses, and to hold those contradictions and absences up to the light. More information on sources is detailed in the "sources consulted" section at the end of this book.

For every event I record here, I have at least one person's statement that it happened and their description of it, or it is a composite event constructed from several different descriptions as detailed in the "sources consulted" section. Wherever I have worked from a transcript, I have edited the dialogue for clarity and pacing. A good portion of the events I write about here occurred publicly and with a great deal of press attention, but I have nonetheless changed some names. The two research trips that form the backbone of the third part of this book were actually many trips that occurred over several years. I have compressed them, but the events depicted on those trips occurred as written.

While I have not invented or altered any facts, relying instead on the documentation I've used as the primary source for this book, at times I have layered my imagination onto the bare-bones record of the past to bring it to life. Where I have done so is made clear in the "sources consulted" section at the end of the book. In all cases, what is offered here is my interpretation of the facts, my rendering, my attempt to piece together this story.

As such, this is a book about what happened, yes, but it is also about what we do with what happened. It is about a murder, it is about my family, it is about other families whose lives were touched by the murder. But more than that, much more than that, it is about how we understand our lives, the past, and each other. To do this, we all make stories.

Legal Note

This work is not authorized or approved by the Louisiana Capital Assistance Center or its clients, and the views expressed by the author do not reflect the views or positions of anyone other than the author. The author's description of any legal proceedings, including her description of the positions of the parties and the circumstances and events of the crimes charged, are drawn solely from the court record, other publicly available information, and her own research.

Prologue

[I]t is always possible that the solution to one mystery will solve another.

—TRUMAN CAPOTE,
IN COLD BLOOD

He was just our Ricky, you know.

—DARLENE LANGLEY,
SISTER OF RICKY LANGLEY

There is a principle in the law called proximate cause, taught to first-year law students through the case *Palsgraf v. Long Island Railroad Co.* A woman stands at one end of a train platform. Picture her: The year is 1924, and Helen Palsgraf is taking her two little girls to Rockaway Beach for the afternoon. The day is very hot, and the brick row house where the girls, their older brother, and their parents live is stuffy. With school out and nothing to do, the girls have been whining all day, and Helen has finally decided to take them to the beach. Perhaps she has buttoned a cotton dress up over her bathing suit and donned a wide-brimmed straw hat to block the sun. Now she leans against one of the station platform supports and fans herself with the hat. A few feet away, the girls play together with a doll one has brought. Helen watches them idly.

At the other end of the platform, thirty feet away, a young man runs to catch the train that is now departing, an express to the Jamaica neighborhood of Queens. Perhaps he has plans to meet his pals there for a night of carousing. They will drink beer; they will listen to a band play; they will dance with pretty girls. Maybe he will even kiss the girl his cousin has told him about, a looker from Connecticut. He is with two other young men, and they all run for the train, but the man we care about carries under his arm a slim package wrapped in newspaper, fifteen inches long.

The train has already begun to leave the station, its large metal wheels turning at an ever-increasing clip, but the man does not want to miss tonight. He runs faster. Can he make it?

The train pulls out. There's a gap between it and the platform now.

The man leaps.

From the train, a conductor leans out to catch his arms and pull him aboard. From the platform, a porter gives him a shove. The man lands safely on the train.

But the package falls—and, when it hits ground, explodes. The package contained fireworks.

The next morning, newspapers report dozens injured. A teenager's hair caught flame. A mother and daughter suffered cuts all over their arms and legs. And at the other end of the platform from the train, a large metal scale used for weighing baggage shook and tottered. The woman standing beneath it, holding a wide straw hat, screamed. The scale fell.

When Mrs. Palsgraf recovers, she sues the railroad for her injuries.

What caused her injuries? Let's start with the scale's falling. This is what in law is called *cause in fact*: If the scale had not fallen, Mrs. Palsgraf would not have been injured.

But there's a problem. Scales don't just fall. The explosion caused the fall.

And explosions don't just happen. The young man's fireworks caused this one.

But fireworks don't just go off. The porter made the young man drop his fireworks by pushing him. Mrs. Palsgraf's injury must be the porter's fault—and thus that of the railroad that employs him.

All of these possible causes are causes in fact. The causes in fact are endless. The idea of proximate cause is a solution. The job of the law is to figure out the source of the story, to assign responsibility. The proximate cause is the one the law says truly matters.

The one that makes the story what it is.

In my memory there is a dark room that stands wide-mouthed as a cave, fluorescent bars weakly aglow in its center. On the walls, rows of leather-bound books stretch to the ceiling, the muted colors of their spines alternating the blue of an old flag, the green of the sea, the red of dried blood. The books are legal registers, the same books in every law firm library in the country that hold case decisions from decades before. Each of them contains countless stories, countless lives, who did what and who was made to pay.

Picture me there. In June of 2003, twenty-five years old. Last week I passed my days hunched in a library carrel that smelled of old wood, where I scribbled six-hour blue book exams to finish my first year of law school at Harvard. Yesterday, I boarded a plane that carried me south to New Orleans, then I disembarked into air that was a hot wet slap. I have come to the South to fight the death penalty by interning with a law firm that represents people accused of murder. I am proud of this work I want to do and also frightened. My knowledge of the law comes only from books, and from the client stories my parents, both lawyers, shared with me as I was growing up. Those were disputes over custody, medical errors or a slip and fall, once a murder, but—nothing like a death penalty case. Nothing like I have been imagining New Orleans, in the midst of a crime wave this summer, will be. On last night's evening news, yellow caution tape stretched tight across a closed door. This morning on Baronne Street, newspaper boxes blasted black headlines of murder. On the library shelves, below the case registers, lie photocopied booklets, each one sheathed in plastic and bound with plastic rings. They detail the steps the state takes for an execution, I know. In this room, lives are defended.

I fidget in my metal folding chair. The brown suit I brought with me is too hot for New Orleans; I can feel the sweat already starting to bead on my forehead. This is where my attention is in this moment: on my clothes and how wrong I feel in them.

A woman strides to the head of the conference table and holds a videocassette up for me and the other interns to see. She is poised, confident, dressed in a simple black skirt and a white shirt that somehow stays crisp in the heat. "This is the taped confession of the man whose retrial we just finished, recorded in 1992," she says. Her accent is thin and British, her hair upswept like a Brontë heroine's. "Nine years ago he was condemned to death, but this time the jury gave him life. Could you please," she says to another lawyer, "get the lights?"

Cause in fact, then: this tape. If I hadn't seen the man's face on the tape—if I hadn't heard him describe what he'd done—he might have stayed just a name to me.

Cause in fact: her showing me the tape. Twelve years have now passed since this day at the law firm, and I want to reach back through the years and tell her no, he isn't my client, he never will be my client, I don't need to see this tape. The child he killed is already dead. The man has already been convicted of murder. Everything that happened has already been done. There's no need for me to see the tape.

Or go back further. Cause in fact: I could have chosen not to come south to this office. I could have chosen never to confront, question, what I believed. I could have allowed my past to remain undisturbed.

What if I'd never gone to law school? What if I'd never found a book about law school on my father's bookshelf one afternoon when I was home sick from school at thirteen? The month I read and reread that book, the month I dreamt my future, a little blond boy knocked on the door of his neighbor's house in Louisiana. The man on the tape answered the door.

I have spent more than ten years now with his story, a story that, had facts gone slightly differently, I might never have found. I have read the transcript of this confession he gave so many times I have lost count, and the transcripts of his other confessions. I know his words better than words I have written. Working backward from the transcripts, I have found the place where he lived and where he killed the little blond boy, and the gas station where he worked and was later arrested. From the transcripts, and by visiting the places in Louisiana where events in the man's life took place, I have imagined his mother, his sisters, the little boy's mother, all the characters from the past. And I have driven the long, lonely road from New Orleans to the Louisiana State Penitentiary, called Angola. I have sat across from this man, the murderer, in a visiting booth, and have looked into the same eyes that are on this tape.

This tape brought me to reexamine everything I believed not only about the law but about my family and my past. I might have wished I'd never seen it. I might have wished that my life could stay in the simpler time before.

She pushes the cassette into the player and steps back. The screen on the old box television flickers. A seated man slowly comes into view. Pale skin, square jaw, jug ears. Thick, round Coke-bottle glasses. An orange jumpsuit. Hands bound in cuffs in his lap.

"State your name," a deep offscreen voice instructs.

"Ricky Langley," the man says.

Part One: Crime

One

The boy wears sweatpants the color of a Louisiana lake. Later, the police report will note them as blue, though in every description his mother gives thereafter she will always insist on calling them aqua or teal. On his feet are the muddy hiking boots every boy wears in this part of the state, perfect for playing in the woods. In one small fist, he grips a BB gun half as tall as he is. The BB gun is the Daisy brand, with a long, brown plastic barrel the boy keeps as shiny as if it were real metal. The only child of a single mother, Jeremy Guillory is used to moving often, sleeping in bedrooms that aren't his. His mother's friends all rent houses along the same dead-end street the landlord calls Watson Road whenever he wants to charge higher rent, though it doesn't really have a name and even the town police department will need directions to find it. Settlers from Iowa named the town after their home state but, wanting a fresh start, pronounced the name *Io-way*, even as they kept the spelling. The town has always been a place people come for new starts, always been a place they can't quite leave the past behind. There, the boy and his mother stay with whoever can pay the electricity bill one month, whoever can keep the gas on the next. Wherever the boy lands, he takes his BB gun with him. It is his most prized possession.

Now it is the first week in February. The leaves are green and lush on the trees, but the temperature dips at night. Lorilei, Jeremy's mother, isn't working. She rented a home just for the two of them—their first—but the electricity's been turned off. Her brother Richard lives in a sprawling house up on the hill, but she isn't staying with Richard. Instead, Lorilei and Jeremy are staying with Lorilei's friend Melissa, Melissa's boyfriend, Michael, and their baby. The baby is two years old, old enough that he wants to play with the boy and screams when he doesn't get his way.

Today the baby is wailing. Jeremy, six years old, just off the yellow school bus home from kindergarten, eats his after-school snack in a hurry, dreaming of getting away from the noise, dreaming of the fun to be had out in the woods.

At the end of the road there is a weathered white house and, behind it, a thatch of woods. The woods are the dense, deciduous, swampy kind, the kind in which rotting leaves mingle with the earth and the ground gives soft way beneath the boy's feet. Though the thatch is very small, with only a single ravine like a scar in the earth, a single place to play war or dream of hiding away forever, these woods are Jeremy's favorite place to play.

He asks his mother for the BB gun. She takes it down from the shelf that keeps it safe from the baby and hands it to him. Jeremy runs out the door. Two children near his age, a boy name Joey and a girl named June, live in the white house by the woods, and though Jeremy likes exploring on his own, it's more fun when Joey can join him. He goes to their door and he knocks.

A man answers. The man wears thick glasses. He has a small head and large jug ears. At twenty-six and only 140 pounds, Ricky Joseph Langley is slight for a grown man—but still much bigger than the boy. He, too, grew up in this town. Now he rents a room from Joey and June's parents, whom he met when he started working with their mother, Pearl, at the Fuel Stop out on the highway. He's supposed to pay Pearl fifty dollars a week, but he's never been able to afford it. He makes up the money in babysitting. Just a few days ago he looked after Joey and Jeremy. He brought them soap when they were in their bath.

"Is Joey here?" Jeremy asks.

"No," Ricky says. "They went fishing." It's true. Joey's father and the boy packed up poles just twenty minutes ago and drove out toward the lake. They'll be gone all afternoon. "They'll be back soon," Ricky says. "You can come in and wait if you like."

Jeremy plays at this house every week. He knows Ricky. Yet he pauses.

"Why don't you come in?" Ricky says again. He opens the door wider and turns away. Jeremy walks over the threshold, carefully props his BB gun against a wall near the entryway, and climbs the stairs to Joey's bedroom. He sits down cross-legged on the floor and begins to play.

Ricky climbs the stairs after him. He wants only to watch Jeremy play—later he will say this, later he will swear to it. But the watching changes something in him, and from this point on it is as if he is in a dream. He walks up behind Jeremy and hooks his forearm around the child's neck, lifting him into the air. Jeremy kicks so hard his boots fall off. Ricky squeezes.

Jeremy stops breathing.

Maybe now Ricky touches him; maybe now he can admit to himself what he's wanted since seeing Jeremy in the bath. Maybe he doesn't. In all that will come from this moment, the three different trials and the three different videotaped confessions and the DNA testing and the serology reports and the bodily fluid reports and the psychiatric testimony and all the sworn sworn sworn truths, no one but Ricky will ever know for certain.

Ricky picks up Jeremy, cradling the boy as if he were simply asleep, and carries him into his own bedroom. He lays him out on the mattress. He covers Jeremy—no, this is a body now; he covers the body—in a blue blanket printed with the cartoon face of Dick Tracy, detective. Then he sits at the edge of the bed and pets the blond hair.

There's a knock on the door downstairs. He goes to answer it. In the entryway stands a young woman. Her hair is the shade of brown that is often a childhood blond.

"Have you seen my son?" When Lorilei asks this, she is three months pregnant.

"Who's your son?" he asks.

"Jeremy," she answers, and Ricky realizes he already knew.

"No," he says, "I haven't seen him."

She sighs. "Well, maybe he's gone to my brother's."

"Maybe," Ricky agrees. "So why don't you come on in? You could use our phone. You could call your brother."

"Thank you." Lorilei steps inside. To her right, propped up against the wall, is a Daisy-brand BB gun, its long brown barrel shiny and smooth.

But she steps to the left. She does not see the gun. He offers her the phone and she dials, looking for her son.

TAPED CONFESSION OF RICKY JOSEPH LANGLEY, 1992

Q: Do you know why you killed Jeremy?

A: No. I ain't, I never even thought I could, I mean, that's the first time.

Q: And what made you decide to do it?

A: I couldn't tell you. I'm still fumblin' with it in my mind, trying to figure out, you know. It's like I know I did it, but yet it's like if, something you read in the newspaper.

Q: Sort of like a dream for you, Ricky?

A: I guess. I couldn't really . . . I don't know how I'm supposed to act.

Q: But you know you did this?

A: Yeah.

Q: Now, you've had problems with kids in the past.

A: Yeah.

Q: You want to tell me about those?

A: It's just, I can't explain. I guess that's my destiny, okay, it's true.

Two

New Jersey, 1983

Nine years before Ricky Langley will kill Jeremy Guillory, when he is still eighteen years old and I am five, my parents buy a gray Victorian house that squats at the top of a hill in the New Jersey town of Tenafly. All around the house the lawns are manicured, but high, reedy grasses surround the gray Victorian, and the wood on one side of the porch has started to rot. The house has been abandoned for six years. The afternoon we move in, the neighbor boy stands in the grass at the side of the porch, watching. Blond hair cut in a kitchen-bowl bob, jeans ripped and bleached like my mother won't let me wear. Behind the boy is a gray stone house, all its windows dark. Sometimes a cat walks up to him, crossing the driveway from his front yard to ours, and he reaches down to scratch its head before the cat saunters off. There seem to be many cats. The boy watches as we make trip after trip into our new house, my two sisters and my brother and I carrying boxes of our stuffed animals, teetering stacks of the large cardboard bricks we'll use to build forts. In this house, my father has told us, we will have a playroom all our own.

Eventually the neighbor boy calls me over. I walk to the railing and squat down. The white posts that line the porch accordion his face like cartoon jail bars.

"What's your name?" he asks.

I tell him.

"You're moving in?"

He looks like he'd be a grade ahead of me, maybe two. I want to say something clever, but "yeah" comes out.

He's chewing on something as he watches me. I catch a flash of pink. Gum. "The dad who used to live here strangled the mom. In the kitchen," he adds.

"Did she die?" I've only recently learned this word.

"No."

He puts his hands in his pockets and watches me, chewing. We're silent for a moment. Then my mother calls.

"Coming," I say.

Later, when I carry a cardboard box of spatulas and bowls into the kitchen, this scene is all I can see: the father pressing his wife backward over the stained orange Formica counters, his hands around her neck, trying to wring the life out of her as if she were a dirty dishrag. When I go to my new school their little girl will turn out to be in my kindergarten class. She'll have light brown hair cut in a pageboy and she'll want to be a dentist and I'll never be able to meet her eyes without wondering whether she watched.

But the school system is a good one, one of the best in the state. The house, marked by its past, is cheap, and with four kids and only my father's salary as a government lawyer, cheap is what my parents need. There's a lawn that unfurls like a carpet and upstairs bedrooms enough for all six of us: my parents will take the large one at the top of the stairs, while my twin brother, Andy, and my littlest sister, Elize, each get a smaller one pushing back into the house. My middle sister, Nicola, and I will share the bedroom farthest from the front. The house's long corridors—perfect for playing catch—make the house seem grand. It was grand once, officers' quarters in the Revolutionary War, when, my father tells me, the neighbor boy's stone house was only the barn. I love imagining horses' heads poking out from the little windows that dot the stone house, the horses' jaws working their hay like the boy chewed his gum.

The big house is in disrepair. The feature in best shape is a wooden staircase that rises steeply out of the entrance foyer. After the officers left the house, my father tells us, a family moved in, then two more generations of families before us. One of those ear-lier fathers built the staircase from a kit out of the Sears Roebuck catalog. It is still well-preserved, shellacked, with its fine turned posts not even dented. A couple of years from now, when we finally get a black mutt with perky ears on the condition that my father be allowed to name him Cowboy, the dog will teethe on the staircase posts. Each time my father will pay to have a man in town with a lathe make a perfect copy of the damaged post. Years from now, when we're adults, my sisters and I will each get a dog of our own, and when we visit my aging parents in this house, each dog in its puppyhood will chew through the posts. Each time my father will go back to the same man with the lathe, then elderly, and painstak-ingly replace each one. As though, having inherited the staircase from the fathers before him, it were his special duty to maintain it.

But the rest of the house has taken a beating. The roof has bald spots where shingles have fallen off like fur from mange. Some of the interior walls have holes, places you can see the house's skeleton beams. Great bubbles of green linoleum rise from the kitchen floor. They crackle when I step on them, but even when I jump I can't make them burst.

My father finds three boys from a nearby architectural college who need cash and aren't afraid of a little sawdust. One of them, Greg, pleases my father by researching how to add gingerbread trim to the house, swirls of two-inch-thick wood he'll cut out and tack to the rooflines, reminding me of icing. Greg has an idea. He will rebuild the house in the style known as Carpenter Gothic, handmade flourishes everywhere.

My father has always loved big dreams, and Greg is suddenly the group leader. Lanky and tan, Greg has a head of curls that turn blonder and blonder in the sun as the summer weeks go by. My twin brother had curls like that as a toddler. Now Andy's hair has turned dark, he favors a crew cut, and when he takes off his shirt at the beach there's a slash all the way across his stomach that I faintly understand and faintly don't. He was sick when we were born; he is sick sometimes now. Even though we aren't unpacked yet, aren't set up in the house, my parents still have a blue duffel bag ready in the upstairs closet for when they have to take him to the hospital, for reasons I don't know but, somehow, know not to ask about. With the crew cut emphasizing the fine bones of his face, and his ribs jutting out over the scar, my brother's white sub-urban sneakers make him look like an adopted refugee from some forgotten war.

But the architect boys are beautiful. Greg scales the pitched peaks of the roof. His friends climb high ladders over the win-dows. They cut through the air like dolphins through water, not slowed by the tape measures and wrenches that dangle from the belt loops of their cutoffs. The tools trail behind them, as though they, like me, can do nothing but follow the boys. In the evenings I watch them from the lawn, the sound of crickets surrounding us. Sometimes when they stay late Greg cuts holes in the top of a jar for me, and when I bring him the fireflies I've caught he praises me. "That's a pretty one," he says. "Isn't its light beautiful?" I love the fireflies' glow so much that once, instead of releasing my catch, I keep the jar on my nightstand. But in the morning the fireflies are just bugs; they don't give off any light.

One day, my father gives Greg a set of keys and claps him on the back. They review clipboard lists the boys suddenly carry, then nod and shake hands in the gravel driveway. My parents pack us all up to visit my mother's relatives in France. By the time we come home, we will have a new home. The house will be wiped clean of its past.

Only one main road leads into Tenafly. It begins on the far end of town from our house, winding leisurely down a large hill. There, the road's banked sides give generous lift to trees that yawn and stretch with plenty of room to bend. Beneath the trees' cano-pies sprawl estates of elaborately landscaped lawns with white-pillared houses and iron gates. Tiny stone bridges arch artificial brooks.

The road narrows. The building that was once the town's high school is now a funeral parlor, classrooms turned into viewing rooms. Next door is the Catholic church. Just past the church lies a set of railroad tracks. The railroad stopped coming through town decades before we moved in; by the time I graduate from college, I will have watched the old station turn from a magazine stand into a hair salon, then into a café that serves ten-dollar organic sandwiches and four-dollar coffees. But as a child I know only to hold my breath as the tracks snag the car tires. Then I touch my finger to the hard glass of the window, lest ghosts find a chink in my connection to the physical world, a way to come in.

The tracks release the car, and from there the town changes. A small downtown appears. A lone apartment building, full of single units, out of place in a town so clearly meant for families. One magnolia tree stands on its lawn, the tree's pale, floppy blossoms beautiful and strange against the oaks and elms of the Northeast. Then lot sizes shrink, only a driveway between houses. A second hill appears, less than half the size of the first. At its top sits our grand Victorian. Past our house the road dips into another town, one with crime ours lacks and school statistics we whisper to each other like warnings.

Three

Louisiana, 1992

The phone line's busy at her brother's house, doesn't stop with the *beep beep beep*. Lorilei's tired. She doesn't want to walk all the way to her brother's. Richard has put a white fence around his yard, as though to separate himself from all the homes that don't have the things he does. Homes like the one Lorilei rents, where she can't even keep the electricity on. The fence, it just gets to her. The gate's on the far side of the house, and to reach their door she has to walk all the way around it, all the way around the pretty yard and the shiny white posts and the toys and bikes his kids have got. But there's nothing else to do, Jeremy's missing, so she thanks the man in the white house for letting her use the phone, zips up her hooded sweatshirt, and walks. By Richard's there's a sidewalk, but here the road ripples up against weeds, a slash in the dirt for a gutter. Lorilei—twenty-nine years old, heavyset even without the pregnancy having begun to show—thrusts her hands into the pockets of her jeans for warmth and bends her head low. Thin sneakers that stick in the February mud, no good for walking. This was supposed to be a quiet night at home, just Melissa and the baby.

The sun spills orange and red streaks across the horizon. It's just before 6:00 p.m. and the street is eerily quiet. House after house she passes has the blinds down, slats pressed together like tight white lips. Behind them, families are sitting down together to dinner. In one yard, a plastic tricycle lies upended, its pedals in the air ready to spin away to nowhere. She taught Jeremy to ride a trike when he was three and the town paper published a photo of the two of them, her hovering over Jeremy, her hands on the hard little moons of his shoulders, both of them grinning into the camera lens. Lorilei Guillory and her son, Jeremy Guillory. Everyone in town knew that last name was hers. That there wasn't a man.

She remembers, suddenly, herself and Richard when they were kids, pedaling into the bend of the road, the hours stretching before them like the bend of the sun.

The hill he lives on is to the west, and in the distance she sees his ranch house. A tire swing for his boy and girl to play on, strung from an oak tree. Richard's toolshed. And a car in the driveway—red, which belongs to Mary, Richard's wife. When she and Mary spoke this morning, Mary said she was going to go grocery shopping this evening and that when Jeremy saw her car pull in he should walk on over and she'd take him. Jeremy had gotten so excited when he heard Lorilei on the phone with her that Lorilei couldn't say no. Hard for her, that Mary's the one with the car and the money, the one who gets to take him shopping. Still, she hopes that means he's there now.

But when Mary answers the door, her lipstick on fresh, Lorilei knows from Mary's blank face that he isn't. She asks anyway.

"Haven't seen him," Mary says. "And I was just getting ready to head out."

That's when Lorilei knows he must be lost.

Ten minutes later she's borrowed Mary's car and driven it to the edge of the woods, the headlights pointed in. It's close to dark now. Jeremy knows to come home before then. When she pulls up, the glint from the car's beams lights the rusted frame of a four-wheeler. Sometimes Jeremy and the Lawson boy, Joey, will sit out here on the frame and fire their BB guns off into the woods for hours. But it's empty now, the woods nothing but quiet. She gets out of the car and leans on the four-wheeler frame. "Jeremy!" she calls. "Jeremy, it's your mama! Can you hear me? Jeremy!"

There's only silence. Not even a bird.

"Jeremy!"

She hears a car pull in behind her. "You all right, Lori?" Terry Lawson, Joey's father, is driving, two of the neighbors with him.

"Jeremy's missing," Lorilei hears herself say. Her voice sounds ragged.

The men grab flashlights from the trunk and head into the woods.

This is where, later, her memory cuts out.

But the tape from the fire department shows that the first call comes in at 6:44 p.m. The caller identifies herself as Lorilei Guillory, the mother of the boy she's reporting missing. The dispatcher takes down her information and promises to send a cruiser out to Iowa. "Io-way," Lorilei says into the phone. "Please. Y'all know where that is?"

"Yes, ma'am. Io-way," the dispatcher replies.

The second call comes in at 6:57 p.m. The caller is a young man, and he says no one's turned up and when are the police coming? The boy's mother just called from his house, but he knows this area's confusing for folks not from around here. "You got two roads out here running right next to each other," he says. "And this one they call Watson Road but it doesn't really got a name. That's the one you want. The house is the white two-story." They'll know it, he says, by the washer in the front yard and the staircase in the back that leads out to the woods. "I'll give y'all the number here," he says, "in case you get yourselves lost."

"I need your name, sir," says the dispatcher.

"Ricky Langley," the caller replies.

That night, Lorilei sits on the front stoop of the white house, and at least one story told of the search for her son includes what happens next. The street is totally dark—no streetlights out this way—but slowly lightens as more and more cruisers arrive. In the distance she can hear the searchers call to one another, a truck engine idle. She knows they're close by but still the sound feels very far away, muffled.

Like how the wet and rotting leaves on the ground in the ravine where Jeremy plays turn everything spongy. He gets so dirty from those leaves, but tonight she must be glad they're soft. She must think of him there, his cheek creased from small twigs as if from a pillow, the way his hair flops in his eyes when he's too sleepy to brush it off. Jeremy sleeps like a puppy on his side, his arms and legs flung out in front of him. His pink mouth open, the little puffs of air. She used to watch him breathe when he was a baby. All new mothers do that, she supposes, but it still felt like a miracle, the way he just kept breathing.

She shakes off the thought. Over the tree line, the search beams make a cat's cradle, and she watches the pattern change. Richard says that in the morning they'll call in helicopters. Why they wouldn't bring them in now, when her boy's out there alone and cold in the dark, she doesn't know.

"Want a drink?" She looks up and the man from the afternoon is standing at the side edge of the porch. It takes her a second to recognize him, the afternoon feels so long ago. Back before everything.

"Ricky, right?" she says.

"Yes, ma'am," he says. He's holding a bottle in one hand and he raises it to her in invitation. Behind him, the darkness of the woods is like a fog. It's as though he stepped from nothingness.

Lorilei doesn't drink. She hasn't had a drink in years. She used to run wild with her drinking, the arrests landing her in the local newspaper, her name a tight "L. Guillory" on the police blotter. But when Jeremy was born she cleaned herself up. She wanted to do right by him. Now there's another baby to think of, three months inside her.

But she's so scared about Jeremy and that bottle looks so good, its amber color glowing in the light. Jeremy's kindergarten went on a class trip to the science museum in Lake Charles today. The same trip she took at his age, and perhaps the drink's warm glow makes her think of the resin fossils she saw then. It's a strange night, Jeremy gone, all the neighbors out and looking, a night outside time. A night that could last forever, suspended like a bug in that amber, Jeremy always out there somewhere, she always on this porch, waiting. All she has to do is make it through this night.

She takes the bottle. There's two inches of liquor. "Thanks," she says.

The first sip is sharp and glass-smooth. It shimmies down inside her, curls up in her belly, warm.

The second sip is sweet. The third.

"Sorry they haven't found your boy," Ricky says. In the glare from the porch light his glasses are opaque.

She doesn't say anything.

"It sounds like people are sure looking," he says.

Lorilei's tired. She doesn't want to talk. So she doesn't. She just leans back against the stoop for a long time, sometimes with her eyes closed when she can't bear the quiet and sometimes with her eyes open when she can't bear the black. The liquor's gone before she knows it. The man stays at the edge of the grass, his hands in his khaki pockets, silent. It's companionable. They could almost be friends.

Later she won't be able to say how long passes before he coughs, a polite sound as if he's afraid to disturb her. "Well," he says then, "I'd better be going back in. I really hope they find him."

Four

New Jersey, 1983

After we're settled into the new house, my father leaves his job as a government lawyer and opens a solo law practice in the nearby town of Teaneck, finding another gray Victorian and renting the first floor as his office. He buys a piece of black lacquer sixteen inches long and eight inches wide and has ANDREW ROBERT LESNEVICH etched into it, followed by the word he worked for: ESQUIRE. The sign will be the first of many. He hangs it over his door and waits for cases to arrive.

Come they eventually do, the parade of the unlucky and unwise that make up any small-town lawyer's work. There's the housewife with the secret fondness for drink who gets behind the wheel and won't admit that her head isn't bobbing only from fatigue. There's the old man who slips on the shopkeeper's icy walk downtown, and the teenage shoplifter whose hands, always so quick, finally fail her. My father's not a gossip; he can be trusted and he likes it this way, one foot in the web of everyone's lives. He is needed, but not too closely. Best of all, he is admired. Years in the Air Force have given him a straight-backed public bearing that allows him to take on others' stories with ease and authority.

Law wasn't his first choice. My father dreamt of flying fighter planes as a boy. His father had been lost at sea in World War II. His mother never went on another date, and his father's naval legacy made a military career feel like a birthright. He had flat feet, he was color-blind, he was six feet four—he would never, after all, be a fighter pilot. But he could play tennis. He joined the Air Force and sat out the Vietnam War at a wooden desk in the tropics, stamping papers over and over and then signing them in triplicate, giving his wrist a workout on the courts beating Army and Navy. When he finished active duty, the question of his future loomed. He had studied geology in college, psychology for a master's. He could resume his studies. Maybe he could become a scientist. Maybe a teacher.

But he didn't want to sit behind a lab bench any more than he wanted to sit behind a desk. If he couldn't be a hotshot pilot he wanted a political stage. He wanted to stand in front of people and have them know that little fatherless Andrew from Cliffside Park, New Jersey, had made it.

When my father reaches this part of the story, one I listen to him tell often, his deep voice grows more insistent, its cadence more punctuated. My father is a storyteller. He tells stories to juries for a living, and he tells them to us around a thick white Formica table so big he found it for a discount; no other family wanted it, he says. We fit perfectly. My father sits on one side of the table, flanked by two of us, my mother on the other side, flanked by two more. The table's edges are curved so Elize, the youngest, just learning to walk, doesn't hurt herself when she bumps into it. Around the table we are his audience and his life is the text. Listening as a child I always imagine that the fork he describes in the road is literal: a one-lane highway somewhere in eastern Missouri, no cars on the road except for his, the yellow cut of headlights through the dark his only guide. It is night, the time for dreams and big decisions, and the velvet sky above is pinpricked with light. From behind the wheel my father sees the road ahead of him split. To his left, the West. A left turn will free him from his mother's clutch. It will save him the depression that has started to haunt him as surely as it does her, from the way his father's death made his tie to her seem fated, his life cast when he was still a baby. Out West is California, where he will have a life as solid and stable as the rocks he once studied. He will be a teacher, yes, but maybe a politician, too. He will feel beloved. He will be happy.

"But instead"—he always comes to this point in the story— "I knew my mother needed me. I took a right turn. I came back to New Jersey. And then I met your mother."

All this from a single turn: his mother, our mother, the four of us children, and now this gray office of his own, where he works in the light of a long metal desk lamp that was once his uncle's. A large bay window looks out onto the porch. Nights that he fails to close the slat blinds, we can stand on that porch and make out the silhouette of his head bent low in the light of the metal lamp. One night, my mother calls the office again and again and, getting no answer, packs us into the car and drives over—a sure sign she's nervous, as my mother, the born-and-bred New Yorker from As-toria, Queens, didn't consent to learn to drive until she was thirty-eight and will never lose the stiffness in her hold on the wheel, her hands locked into the ten o'clock and two o'clock positions as she was taught. Someday, when they have money, she'll use a car ser-vice to take her where she needs to go. But now driving at night is even worse than during the day, and she folds her body to clutch the wheel to her chest as if it were a life preserver.

When we arrive at the office, every window is dark, no sign of my father. "Stay here," my mother says to me and Andy and my sisters. "Stay right here." This is unusual. My parents almost never leave us in the car. Unless my grandparents come and babysit, they almost never leave us anywhere. We have been everywhere with them: into the backs of courtrooms, into fancy restaurants. There's a picture of Andy and me at three years old standing hand in hand on the red velvet steps of the Metropolitan Opera House, me in a white frilly dress and Andy's curls backlit over his pale blue suit. But tonight we stay in the car. It's a warm early fall night and the windows are down. The air's a little sticky, the leaves heavily soft around us. In the glow of a nearby streetlamp, we watch our mother climb the porch steps and press the doorbell. She waits. There's no response. She presses it again. Nothing. She raps on the bay window and calls in—"Drew! Drew!"—her voice growing higher and louder as she repeats his name.

When I am closer to the age at which she stands on the porch than the age at which I sit in the car watching, I'll come back to this moment. Then I'll understand what fears the night held for her. Perhaps he'd finally left the way he threatened to some dark nights, nights that he raged at the choice he'd made on a lonely Missouri road, the choice that had trapped him in this story with us. Nights he sat alone at the white Formica table, drinking off the remainder of the dinner wine he and my mother had opened together, and then opening his own. Those nights he swore we'd be better off without him. Those nights he swore we'd be better off if he were dead.

But this night, as I watch my mother on the porch, and I listen to her call his name and listen to the silence in response, I know only to be afraid that he's dead not by his hand but by fate. He lost his father when he was a baby. He lost the uncle who helped raise him to an early heart attack. Every March, when we kiss his cheek and tell him happy birthday, if he's had some wine he shakes his head and says how surprised he is to still be alive. He repeats this sentence year after year until some part of me, I suppose, grows surprised right along with him.

On this night he finally emerges from the door, and in the light of the streetlamp I watch my mother's face relax into a mix of joy and relief, thankful that they're still in this together. They walk back to the car hand in hand. She's beaming. "Hey, kids," he says. "I fell asleep at my desk." His tie hangs loosened around his neck. He rubs his eyes with his fingers, then he smiles, too. My mother kisses him, presses the keys into his hand. He'll drive us home now. They'll figure out how to get the other car back in the morning.

Grief takes root inside people. But I don't see its mark on my parents at first, not until a bleach-bright summer day nine months later. I am reading my way through my mother's old Nancy Drew hardbacks, proud to have moved on from the picture books she still reads to my little sisters. Today is *The Secret in the Old Attic.* I have climbed the swing set at the bottom of the yard and am lying across the top flat ladder with the book cracked open on my chest, one hand shielding the page from the sun's glare. This position is an experiment. I'm still getting to know our new house, all the nooks I'll read in. But the ladder rungs dig into my back, splinters press through my T-shirt, and I can't get comfortable. We should be done polyurethaning the swing set by now, but we're not. Instead, every Sunday afternoon that my father decides the swing set will be our chore for the day, and my mother dresses us in old OshKosh overalls and gives me, my brother Andy, and my sister Nicola little buckets and brushes of our own, we kids paint the clear gel over our hands instead of the railings. When the gel gets tacky, we press our hands together. Stuck! Then my father marches us into the closet-size bathroom off the kitchen, where I stick my hands under the faucet and wait as he pours from a can of paint thinner. "Rub," he says, and I do, and slowly through the heat and scratch and wet I feel my hands start to unglue, and my skin comes back to me.

That's pleasure, that moment. I keep painting my hands together for the pleasure of his standing behind me, his arms on mine. Even years from now I'll love the metallic smell of paint thinner. And he must love those moments the way I do, because though we make no progress on the swing set, my father doesn't yell. This will be his dearest summer, all of us building this house together.

The lowest rungs already have a coat of shellac, and as I lie up top, their vinegar-sharp smell wafts up to me. The sun burns my legs below my shorts. I scratch at a mosquito bite on my thigh and turn the page. Below me, the yard swells, then dips. It looks nearly flat from up here, but in the distance the gray house rises upward on the hill, its paint still shiny and new. We have the longest yard in the neighborhood. Behind the swing set is an undeveloped patch, sixty feet square, with crab apple trees and a mountain of

rotting grass clippings that sweetly stink. Sometimes I dive on top
of it and feel my face hit the dead grass and the earth give way
beneath me like a cloud. We call the area "the woods," and all our
childhoods, we will conspire to build forts there and hideaways,
though we never will. When my parents get low on cash, they'll sit
around the kitchen table and scheme how they can sell the
woods, but a buyer will never materialize.

As I read, trying to keep the words in focus on the page—I need
glasses, but no one knows this yet—my father mows the lawn with
a red riding mower we call his tractor. He loves the yard almost as
much as he loves the house, and since we moved here he's started
wearing Wrangler jeans that flare out at the bottoms with boots
and a wide-brimmed suede cowboy hat that shields him from the
sun as he cuts neat rows in the grass. A New Jersey cowboy, at
least for now. All my childhood he'll reinvent himself, wriggling
out of a new identity every few years: the opera years, the plaid
golf years, the years when Cole Porter's voice swings through the
house and a white dinner jacket appears. For now, a boom box on
the lawn blares twanging guitars. My brother, Andy, climbs onto
the tire that hangs by a rope from the big oak tree. Though we're
twins, he's a head shorter than me and twenty pounds lighter, so
skinny that strangers gape at him in the supermarket. Now he
flings himself through the center of the swing into a belly flop.

My mother comes running from the house, wailing.

She must have looked out the picture window in her bedroom
just at the moment my brother hit the tire and watched his limbs
drop. She tears across the lawn, barefoot and hysterical, the ties of
her pink bathrobe trailing behind her. She runs for my brother,
who's started to sit up now, not knowing what the problem is yet
understanding he must move his body, but my father catches her
first. He grabs her, stopping her body's tumult, and pins her arms
to her sides. His lips are moving, he's wiping her tears, but I'm too
far away to hear.

I just stare.

I put down my book and sit upright on the swing set. My brother pulls his body out of the tire, stands stock-still beneath the tree, and stares, too.

The scene is wrong. We have never seen my mother cry. My father is the one who sometimes calls us into the bedroom, where we find him lying belly down on my parents' vast bed. He is the one who tells us then that we don't love him, that we want him gone. That we'd be better off if he were dead.

She holds him then, and holds us together. But now she's sobbing.

Eventually she looks up and notices us there, staring. She wipes her eyes. "I'm fine," she calls to us. "I just thought—"

My father cuts her off. "She's fine."

His arm around her shoulder, hers around his waist, they walk back to the house, together.

Five

Louisiana, 1992

As February 8 dawns in Louisiana, a single patrol car sits parked in front of the weathered white house in the town of Iowa. The car belongs to Officer Calton Pitre. A fifteen-year veteran of the Calcasieu Parish Sheriff's Office who'll stay on ten years more, all told serving a quarter of a century as a deputy sheriff in the same clot of southwestern towns where he grew up, Pitre had been sitting in his office in Lake Charles when the call came about the missing boy. Even ten years from now he won't be able to say why the call scared him so much. But he has a little boy himself, Jeremy's age. And those ten years later, when his boy is a teenager, and the lawyers call him up to ask him to testify again, he'll remember Jeremy's name without any prompting. When they found the child he was wearing a little white Fruit of the Loom T-shirt, he'll tell the lawyers. They cut rings out of that shirt to test for semen stains.

His son wore Fruit of the Loom T-shirts, too.

Though his shift was just about to end when the call came, he took it anyway, arriving in Iowa just as the sun set. There were dozens of people in the street. Local parents, but also the fire department from neighboring LeBleu. Fifty or sixty people, and Pitre could see no one was in charge. They didn't have much time. Whatever search they got under way would have to be called off when the sky was fully dark.

The fire department men went into the woods. Pitre went to the white house where the 911 calls had come from—there had been two: the boy's mother, crying, and then, minutes later, a young man who identified himself as a lodger in the house calling back to make sure the dispatcher knew how to find the right street—and asked if he could use the phone.

A woman let him in. It was her house, she said. She showed him where the telephone was and went right back to watching television, half a dozen children sitting cross-legged on the floor in the living room, and in the armchair a young man with brown hair and glasses who turned his head and nodded at him once. They were watching some kind of crime show; Pitre couldn't make it out. He told his supervisor that the search required a command center, a phone line; someone was going to have to take charge. They needed more men. But the supervisor wouldn't commit to anything—wasn't it LeBleu's responsibility out that way? Or Iowa's? Frustrated, Pitre went back out to the street.

Soon he returned and called a second time. The woods were hard terrain. Along the north side of the house was a ravine and what looked like a canal. They needed four-wheelers. Maybe a boat.

The third time Calton Pitre went back to the white house to call his supervisor, he saw the brown-haired man sitting in a recliner, still watching television, and had an idea. "You know the area?" he asked.

"Sure do," the man said.

"Draw me a map?"

The man took the three-by-five spiral pad Pitre offered and carefully penned in the areas around the white house, laying out hash marks for the woods. He made a web of the small backstreets. Drew the route out to Highway 90. "Let me know if you have any trouble with it," the man said.

"Thanks," said Pitre.

TRIAL TRANSCRIPT, 2003

Q: And how did the young man seem to you?

A: He was very calm, he was real calm.

Q: Do you see him in the courtroom?

A: Yes, I do.

Q: Would you point him out and describe what
  he's wearing?

A: Wearing a pair of glasses, light blue shirt
  with a necktie.

Q: Your Honor, let the record indicate that the
  witness has identified the defendant.

The search teams and the cops on the four-wheelers and the fire department found nothing. They needed a dredger for the canal, but that would have to wait until morning. The parents had collected their children and gone home, using the flashlights they'd trained on the woods before to pick their way back across the dark streets, holding each other closer now, even just going through somebody's yard.

Pitre stayed. He kept thinking about the little boy. He had the child's school photograph attached to his clipboard—blond hair, blue eyes, a gap-toothed grin. The uncle, a man named Richard, had given it to him. He sat behind the wheel of his car and flashed the high beams into the woods. Once, twice, three times. Then he stopped and waited. Once, twice, three times again. Wait. The woods were dark, the only movement the ripple of black leaves in the wind. He flashed the beams again. Again. Whenever he thought it was time to go home and get some sleep, he'd imagine the boy's blond head from the photograph against the leaves, the child just starting to awaken from sleep, opening his eyes slowly the way Pitre's son did. That's when the boy would see the flashing lights. That's how he'd know to go toward them. What if Pitre stopped before the boy finally woke up?

But eventually he started nodding off himself. The next day would be a long one. Pitre drove home, kissed his sleeping son, kissed his sleeping wife. Slept.

Now he's back at first light. He sits behind the wheel of the cruiser and sips from his coffee, watching the neighborhood mothers return to help with the search.

The mothers look exhausted, some of them still with their bathrobes on. One woman wears a winter coat buttoned fully over pajama pants and slippers. Word spreads quickly: No news, the Guillory boy is still missing. Fast as an echo comes the answer: He's only lost; he must only be lost. They'll find him. A woman stands where the road meets the grass—where in another part of town, the part with street names, there would be a curb—and shouts to organize the mothers into search teams. Someone else thinks to knock on the door of the white house to find out if there's any coffee left from what the Fuel Stop out on the highway sent over the night before.

No one answers the door at the white house. Ricky and Pearl Lawson, his landlady, have already gotten into Pearl's car. He's due for his shift out at the Fuel Stop, and on the mornings she's scheduled there, too, she drives him. Pearl is a supervisor, sometimes works cashier for the trucks. She's trusted to handle the cash. Ricky does maintenance. Usually there's easy chatter between them, but they're quiet this morning. The morning air is chilly, shrouded in a faint gray mist, and Ricky rubbed his hands as he waited for her to unlock the car. He slid in. He tossed the bag of laundry he has with him into the backseat, and now he stares down at his lap. Pearl won't look at him, either, the two of them like a warring couple this morning.

Last night, as word spread through the neighborhood that a child was missing, and the mothers arrived for the first time, they stood in the street in front of the Lawson house and decided that while they searched, the Lawsons' lodger Ricky would look after their children, like he often looked after Pearl and her husband Terry's two. The children had watched television with Ricky in the living room, and then later gone up to his bedroom to play.

But late last night, after the last child had been collected by her mother and even the police had gone home, only one patrol car still parked in front of the house, periodically lighting up the sky through the windows with its beams, Ricky came downstairs and found Pearl sitting at the kitchen table. He was carrying a plastic basket of laundry. The washer was out in the yard, hooked to the side of the house by a hose. But she looked at him so gravely he stopped and put the basket down. She was in her nightdress already, a cup of tea in front of her. She and Terry slept on a mattress in the living room since Ricky had come to stay. They'd rented him the bedroom.

"You know, Ricky," she said, her voice even and her eyes down, studying her tea, as though she was trying to make her words sound casual, "maybe you'd better leave town for a few days. Just until this blows over."

Pearl knew, Ricky would later swear, that he'd served time for child molestation. She took him in when he was on parole from his sentence in Georgia. They'd met when they were both living in a run-down motel out by the Fuel Stop, paying by the week. Pearl, Terry, and their two kids were all in one room. Ricky didn't know anybody, so he was trying to pay for another all on his own. Pearl and Ricky saw each other on breaks at the Fuel Stop, at the laundry and the ice machines at the motel, and when paying the man at the front desk. One night, as Pearl and Ricky stood in the parking lot just outside the motel doors, she had an idea. She and her husband wanted to rent a house in Iowa. But affording it meant working more, with no one to look after June and Joey. Maybe they could team up.

That was two months ago. And Ricky's never molested the Lawson children. That's a promise he made to himself. A promise he's kept.

Now she's asked him to leave.

So Ricky has a duffel of clean clothes with him this morning, and the laundry sack, too, with the clothes he was wearing the day before, which he'd meant to wash during the night. They pull into the street, and Pearl rolls down her window to nod at Pitre before they drive past the police barricade.

Pitre nods back. He recognizes Pearl. Last night, she'd shown him the phone and coordinated the coffee the Fuel Stop had donated. He recognizes Ricky as the young man who drew the map now pinned to Pitre's clipboard. The sun's still climbing in the sky, tired parents still trickling in, but when enough parents arrive today, Pitre will use the young man's map to organize them into teams. He'll check off sections of the woods as they search. They'll find the child. He's sure of it.

Later, in the evening, when Ricky's finished with his shift at the Fuel Stop, for the first night since he moved in with the Lawsons he doesn't go back to the white house he's so proud to be living in. The first room he feels he can really call his own. The room where now, in the closet, Jeremy Guillory's body stands rigid, wedged in, wrapped in the blue blanket from Ricky's bed, a white trash bag covering his head and shoulders. The hiking boots that fell off while Ricky was strangling him tucked neatly at his feet. The BB gun placed beside him. Ricky had him in there and shut the closet door before the children came into the room. The boy has a sock in his mouth now, a piece of trout line around his neck that Ricky pulled tight. He'd kept making gurgling sounds.

Instead, Ricky gets a ride from his father out to his parents' trailer in another part of Iowa. The trailer park is a wide, flat place, the grass between the lots trampled low. His parents live in a white single-wide. When he was growing up they had a home in the nearby town of Hecker that his father, Alcide, had built, but in the years since, his mother, Bessie's, medical bills had made holding on to that land impossible, and they'd moved into this trailer when Ricky and his younger brother, Jamie, were still living at home. He knocks on the ivory door.

Bessie answers, moving slowly. Twenty years have passed since the doctors amputated her leg, and still she's on one beaten-up crutch. Hard to maneuver around the small space. He nods at her, a quick, stiff acknowledgment, and walks right to the washer and dryer stacked in the far corner of the trailer. Opens the laundry bag. Turns on the washer and stuffs his khakis down into the bottom. The khakis he wore yesterday when he strangled Jeremy. Pours the detergent right on them. They may, or may not, have semen on them. At least until the water hits them.

Only then does Ricky turn back and say hello to Bessie.

It's evening. Bessie's already been drinking for hours. She hoists her body through the tight space to the dining table. She lands heavily, her pink housedress with the little blue flowers puffing out from her ample lap. Alcide clears the bills off the table, then sits, too.

Ricky looks around the dark, dingy little room. He takes in the bills. He takes in the grime crusted on the kitchenette counters, the dishes left in the sink. The lightbulb over the stove that has burned out but has not been replaced. The air smells stale and astringent, a faint sour whiff of Bessie's alcohol. He hates it. He hates it all. He hated it when he lived here and he hates it even more now that he can see what he left.

In the corner is a small television set, placed so it can be seen from both the kitchen table and the brown couch that sits against one wall. It's off but still hot to the touch. Bessie and Alcide watched it all day, knowing Ricky was coming. They have seen the white house where he lives flooded stark and ghostly in the camera lights, have seen the makeshift search headquarters in front. They've heard the reporter say a boy is missing, have seen the child's school photo projected on the screen. When the camera showed the child's mother, she was crying.

Bessie knows Alcide won't say anything about what they've seen. He's not one for words, even less so where his oldest son is concerned. So Bessie will have to be the one to do it. She reaches across the table and takes her son's hand in hers. His hand is cool, slack. He doesn't return her grip. "Ricky," she says, and then pauses.

Ricky waits.

"You didn't have anything to do with that little boy going missing, did you?"

The moment before a mother asks that question, what goes through her mind? Her son has arrived at the trailer door, the son whom, now that he's grown and moved away, she rarely sees anymore. She loves her son. She's loved him since before he was born, since she fought the doctors so he could be born, this child who has had so many problems. This child who has tried to kill himself more times than she can count and has already served two sentences for child molestation. Bessie once told a caseworker she felt she couldn't leave him alone for five minutes without his going and molesting somebody.

Ricky is an adult now. He lives beyond her reach. A boy is missing from the street where he lives.

She asks.

"No," he answers.

The silence she falls into then, is it the sweet and grateful silence of belief? Or is it as black and treacherous as the night now falling outside the trailer door, cloaking the end of the second day of the search in failure and cloaking the dark wet woods and their absence of a body? Does the silence hide as much as the darkness does?

"Betcha the boy's out in the woods," Ricky adds. "They'll find him," he says, and the three of them, the man and woman and the child they conceived, sit together as the second night falls.

Six

New Jersey, 1984

The housedress I have borrowed for Bessie in this scene—pink with tiny blue flowers, a smocked polyester collar with lace appliquéd on it, the dress that puffs out from her lap as she lands heavily in the chair and turns to face her son—is not recorded in any transcript or file. It is my grandmother's dress. When I picture Bessie I imagine my grandmother, these two women will turn out to be linked by so much. In my memory my grandmother wears the dress as she sits on a white wicker bench on the porch of our Victorian house, my grandfather beside her. It is late afternoon on a spring Saturday, the sun still thinking about beginning its descent, the light a shade off from brightness. The gray porch paint glows with the gentle luminescence of a cloudy sky.

We are playing checkers, and it is my turn. I sit on a wicker armchair across from my grandparents, the game board on a table between us. I am red; they are black, and next to me is a small stack of black checkers, the prize for all my kings. Whenever my grandfather moves a piece, my grandmother clucks softly before he can even take his hand off the plastic. "Jimmy—" she says. My grandfather sighs and moves the piece to where I can get it. I wish she'd stop, but I'm also proud I'm winning.

More and more often, my father drives into the city to pick up my grandparents and bring them back to Tenafly to look after us. His law practice is taking off, and suddenly there is a calendar on the wall of my parents' bedroom with dates circled in black Sharpie, and a corkboard with dance and opera tickets pinned to it. While my grandparents and I play checkers, my mother dresses upstairs. Tonight they will see *Tosca*, and from the speakers my father has strung through the house baritone voices swell and bray.

As the sun sets I tire of sitting with my grandparents and leave the porch to walk up the old staircase to my mother's bedroom. My chest is tight; I don't want her to go, don't want to be left with my grandparents for the night. My parents are running late—they're always running late—and my father stands in the hallway outside the bedroom in his white briefs, selecting a tie from the closet rack. In the bedroom my middle sister, Nicola, lies facedown on my parents' bed, watching my mother dress. She shimmies control-top pantyhose up her legs. Never a bra—my mother, flat-chested like I will be, hates bras. Her hair still has rollers in it from the white plastic case on the dresser. Though my mother spent her teenage years taking the train out to Coney Island with a bag containing baby oil she slathered on her skin and a homemade aluminum foil sun reflector to sit behind, and she and Andy both turn nugget-brown as soon as summer begins, my mother's face is unlined. By the time I'm twenty-five I'll have more wrinkles than she will in her fifties. This is the gift of her Italian genes, she says. The gift, she says, that came with the curse of her hair.

Every morning of my childhood she hot-rollers her dark brown hair into the Jackie O. bouffant she adopted as a teenager, the only hairstyle, she swears, that suits her hair's texture. My father is in charge of packing the roller set for trips. My mother claims she ruined her hair with lye as a teenager, trying to get the kink out. Once, on a family trip to Jamaica, I'll sit with her in a beauty shop and see two women laughing to themselves under dryers, looking at us. One of them will come over. "Your mama must've slept with a black man," she'll say to my mother, nodding her head for emphasis.

My mother will laugh. "My father's Italian," she'll say. "Vincent Jimmy Marzano from Astoria, Queens." How much more Italian could you get than that?

The woman will raise her eyebrows and look pointedly at my dark curls. "Well, then *you* must've slept with a black man!" Again my mother will laugh.

Now she stands in front of the chest my father had custom-made for her, its drawers still mostly empty but its size a kind of promise, and selects a necklace he gave her, strings of ebony-black and quartz-pink beads that meet in a large flower at the knot of her throat. She beckons to me, and I come stand behind her. She lifts her hair from her neck and I reach up to hook the necklace's clasp. I am almost as tall as she is. I have her hair, her love of books, her smile. I will grow into her hips, her nose, her determination, her height. When I finish securing the necklace, she turns to me, her eyes shining.

This is a rare night, a magic night. Other nights she dresses alone, without my father in the hall, and my father is off somewhere in the dark, having taken the car and sped squealing out of our gravel driveway. On one of those nights my brother will come into the room and watch her silently while my sister and I lie on the bed. "Who do you love more?" he'll suddenly say. "Daddy or us?" His words will come perilously close to acknowledging what never can be: that there is a choice to be made.

But not tonight. Tonight is beautiful. My mother blots her lipstick. My father knots his tie and smooths his jacket up over his shoulders, then takes her hand. The two of them leave in one breath, a cloud of perfume and aftershave trailing them like a memory.

Later that night now, perhaps ten o'clock. The dark as dark as it will become, the world outside hushed, only the flash of an occasional car's headlights as it passes by the playroom window on its way to a far, unknowable somewhere. My grandmother lies a few feet from the window, on a nubby green sofa bed. At the other side of the doorway to the playroom is the staircase she has just climbed down, after she and my grandfather tucked us into our beds. Now the house is quiet, only the box attic fan whirring in the air and the faint yellow glow of nightlights that line the hallways. The fan must stay on—my father's rule—but in the long wooden room with buckets of our wooden blocks and shelves of comic books, my grandmother shivers. She pulls an afghan around her, pink wool she crocheted for my birth. She and my grandfather went to bed together. But now she's alone.

The stairs groan, the sound of a single step.

The afghan is knitted loosely, the cold air coming through the spaces between its knots and the wool scratchy against her skin. She turns and pulls it tighter. She cannot get warm without my grandfather's body beside her. Every night since they married, they have lain together. Six years from now, my parents will throw them a fiftieth-anniversary party at a restaurant in the city and we will gather to celebrate the sheer accomplishment of the days, of all those accumulated nights. Now she reaches for the Virgin Mary prayer card she keeps tucked near her pillow. The card shows the Blessed Mother's eyes half-closed in peace, her hands pressed together in constancy. On the back of the card is my grandmother's mother's name. Every night since her mother died, decades ago, she has kept this card next to her head. She touches its cool, laminated surface, tells her mother good night. My grandmother knows where she'll go when she dies. She calls that place her truest home.

The stairs groan again, the sound of a body climbing them.

My grandfather wears the hearing aid, not my grandmother. She must hear the stairs, must hear my grandfather's heavy pant as he stands on the step. Does she know where he is going? Does she know what he will do there?

The staircase is still my father's pride. He tells every visitor of its history and keeps the banister at a hard shine. On the wall opposite the banister hang framed photographs of our family, arranged in reverse so that a climb up the stairs is also a climb backward through time: First we smile for the school-day camera in stiff collars and too-tight braids, then we coo on our backs as babies. Then comes my mother, young in pearls and her bouffant, and my father as a little blond-haired boy with his nose pressed to a fence, gazing hungrily beyond the camera's frame. Beneath the pictures, stapled to the steps, is a slice of burgundy carpet that serves as a runner, but it slips perilously while the old wood protests.

The staircase was so loud I could hear its creaks from the back of the house, in the room I shared with Nicola. Listening I pictured my grandfather as he climbed: the way he had to turn his back to the wall of photographs, grip the banister with both hands, and side-shuffle up. How his thick fingers gripped the wood, then the angina that pressed his mouth into a grim line of surprise, his fingers tightening and his arms locked as he breathed into the pain. If he could just bear this one attack, it might be the last. He endures the fact of his old age the same way: by bracing against time's press, always seeming to half-hope that someday he will be returned to himself as a young man with all possibilities ahead.

My grandmother wears housedresses and each night coils her short gray curls onto tight foam rollers she sometimes doesn't bother to remove in the morning. But my grandfather still irons his trousers into a sharp front crease and dons a tweed newsboy cap to match. He keeps his cane polished and ready by the front door for his daily constitutionals. Another year or two from now, still a year before I will walk out of a room whenever my grandfather comes into it, I will wait until they are alone together in my parents' kitchen. Then I will ask them if, old as they are, they have gotten used to the idea of dying.

When I ask this question I am a very serious eight-year-old. I think often of death. I have started to understand that my mother's silence, my father's fits—all of it means that there is something wrong, something about the blue duffel bag they still keep packed for my brother, something the way my sisters' birth announcements hang framed on the wall and the one for me and my brother does not. At times I have the strange, sure feeling that someone is missing.

That can't be right—there are four of us, there have always been four of us. But at times, the thought—death—takes my breath away.

So I ask. Are they used to it yet?

At my question, my grandmother will flinch and flutter her hands in front of her face, as though trying to shoo the thought out of me. But my grandfather meets my eyes, his gaze the same deep brown as my mother's. "No," he will say, calmly. "The fear never goes away."

My grandmother will gasp. She will push her hands on my shoulders, as though by turning me away from him she can turn me away from the knowledge that what he says is true. But I will feel my chest go still, not in fright but in sharp, sudden gratitude to him. The gratitude for having been recognized for who I am, for how seriously I ask the question.

So before my grandfather gets any higher on the staircase, before he climbs his way to our bedrooms, know this: He was not all bad. He was a man who delighted in the power of stories, who when my mother and her brothers were young would take home a projector from his film-cutting job and thrill them by turning their living room into a theater. He knew how to make children laugh and he always had a candy sucker in his pockets or a tin windup dog from the dime store. He was the first artist I ever knew, a painter and a sculptor. He taught me to draw. He taught me what it was to look inward, to be quiet and thoughtful amid the world's clamor. We were alike in this way, he and I. We were alone together in my family in this way. I loved him. In that family way of love, the way that is unquestioned.

As my grandmother lies in her half-empty bed in 1984, and my grandfather pauses on the stairs, there still remains a chance. Maybe tonight, unlike every night that has come before, my grandfather will turn around. He will climb back down the staircase and he will leave my grandmother to a story of her marriage—to a story of her life—that does not include hearing his climb. He will leave me to my childhood bed, and my sister in hers, where we each now lie silent, listening. We both know what we listen for, but we have never said the words out loud.

Or maybe tonight, unlike every other night that has come before, my grandmother will let go of her prayer card, open her eyes, and rise from the bed to walk toward the sound she cannot help but hear—

But no. The stair.

My grandmother in her bed, my sister in hers, me in mine, we listen.

Seven

Louisiana, 1992

Later, Lanelle Trahan, Pearl and Ricky's supervisor at the Fuel Stop, will say that she'd known the night Jeremy disappeared that Ricky was the one who'd done it. She'd been working the register that night, ringing up the extra-large coffees and the scratch tickets and flipping on the diesel pumps for the truckers who climbed down from their cabs to pay in cash, walking a little bowlegged across the station pavement after so many hours on the road. A volunteer firefighter had come in, and as he handed her a crumpled five for a pack of cigarettes and a coffee said, "Got a long night ahead."

"Yeah?" Lanelle said, being friendly.

And the man said yeah, a little boy was missing over on Watson Road in Iowa, and his fire department and another had been called in. Parents from all over the parish were turning up to help, having heard about it on the evening news. "Big search," the man said. "Big. They're bringing in dogs."

Pearl's son, Joey. That's who Lanelle thought of first thing. Whom she assumed was missing. Joey was always playing out in the woods and sometimes Pearl would come in for her shift complaining that he'd gotten himself hurt or lost or worse. God, Lanelle thought, she must be so scared. When time came for her cigarette break Lanelle called up the owner of the Fuel Stop and asked him if she could take some Thermoses of coffee and a couple of sleeves of cups out to the searchers. "I s'pose that'd be all right," he'd said. "Once your shift's over."

So it was ten o'clock, full dark, before Lanelle made it out to Pearl's. A line of patrol cars, their headlights like a sentinel string, blocked the road, but she sidled up to one and rolled down her window—the February night air coming in an uneasy chill—and told the crew-cutted officer inside, barely out of boyhood himself, about the coffee. He let her by.

In the headlights, the paint of the house lit up ghostly white, the places where the paint was dingy and ragged giving it an ominous shape, as if the house were just a skin worn by a creature who lurked underneath. Its back disappeared into the dark woods.

The front door was unlocked, and Lanelle let herself in. Ricky was sweeping the kitchen. "Hi, Ricky," she said, but he just kept up his swift, short strokes. The two of them never did get on. She could hear the television blaring from the living room as she set the Thermoses down on the kitchen table. In the living room, Pearl sat slumped on the worn brown couch, watching television. The white house was on the TV screen, all lit up. Looking at it unsettled Lanelle, as if she were up high looking down at herself on the ground. She sat down next to Pearl. "Pearl," she said gently. "Have they found Joey yet?"

"Joey's not missing," Pearl said. "He's upstairs. Ricky's been looking after the kids. It's a little boy from down the street. Joey's friend."

She went back to staring at the television. Lanelle waited a long moment, but it didn't seem like she was going to say anything more.

If it had been Lanelle's street all lit up with searchlights, you can bet Lanelle would've been out in the street with the others. But Pearl was acting like there was nothing much happening. Lanelle said, "I brought some coffee for the people searching. Boss said we could have it."

"Thanks."

"Well," Lanelle said. "Well, why don't I go take a look upstairs? Check in on Joey and June." Maybe, she thought, the missing boy was just hiding up there. Maybe they were just having themselves a game. Kids that age, when they found a good hide-and-seek spot, sometimes you couldn't get them out.

"That's fine," Pearl said.

So Lanelle got up and did it. The house was laid out kind of funny, Lanelle knew, and to get to the stairs you had to first walk through the bathroom off the kitchen.

TRIAL TRANSCRIPT, 2003

Q: What happened?

A: I went toward where the stairs were and Ricky made a b-line in front of me.

Q: Okay.

A: Made a b-line and got in front of me and would not let me go up the stairs. He told me I could not go up the stairs. He didn't want me up the stairs. And he got mad. When Ricky got mad, you knew when he got mad. I've made him mad before. He would turn beet red and daggers would come out his eyes.

Stop the moment there. Ricky's on the staircase, his eyes blazing, the vein in his forehead sticking out and his face a crimson flare. He spreads his arms to block her, holding the broom straight across, one hand curled around the end like a fist. Lanelle's on the step below him, still in her green Fuel Stop polo, her makeup end-of-the-day tired and her hair smelling faintly of cigarette smoke and diesel fumes.

It's been a long day. She's worked a long shift. She should be at home right now, her feet up, not here at poor Pearl's.

This is when, Lanelle will later say, she *knew*. Something was off about Ricky. Something had been off this whole time. Even if no one would say it.

Lanelle turned around and went to tell Pearl that Ricky wouldn't let her up.

"Aw, that's just Ricky," Pearl said. "He already searched upstairs. He don't mean nothing. Just Ricky being Ricky."

Lanelle knew what she meant. A lifetime of being thought strange could make a man strange. But something didn't sit right.

So Lanelle walked out to the street and tapped on the window of the first patrol car she saw. No command post yet; the cops were doing everything out of the front seats of their cruisers. "Did y'all search Pearl's house?" she said.

"Ma'am?" the officer said.

"This white house," she said. "Right here. Did y'all search it?"

The officer checked his clipboard. "Lady of the house said a Ricky searched it."

"And y'all are satisfied with that?"

"Yes, ma'am."

Later she'd never be able to explain it quite right to herself, why she hadn't just turned around and shoved her way past Ricky and marched upstairs and looked. Sure, later they'd say it would have been too late by then, anyway, that the boy had died immediately, and all there was in that closet—all that Ricky was keeping her from finding—was a body.

But she'd still think about it. For years she'd think about it.

Instead, she told the cops she was there to help and she'd do anything they wanted. They sent her into the woods with the LeBleu fire department, where she stayed late into the night, shining a flashlight on mud-brown leaves that turned reflective in the damp, watching the gleam that came back at her, looking for a color that didn't belong. She walked the edges of the ravine, leaning to peer into it, not really expecting to find a boy, but looking, still looking.

Come morning she was back at the Fuel Stop, cleaning out the Thermoses she'd borrowed. And Ricky was there. All day long, as she passed change back to the truckers and nodded at them, she kept catching herself looking up through the plate-glass windows at the front of the truck stop, watching Ricky as he crossed the lot. It was his face she was looking at. That squinted-up face like a small dog. Did he look normal? Normal, that is, for Ricky? Or did he look like a man with something to hide? And those hands of his—did they look like hands that could hurt a child? It wasn't the kind of thing you could tell anyone about, what she was feeling, but something just didn't sit right.

> TRIAL TRANSCRIPT, 2003
> A: I, myself, when I have company that I don't
>   quite trust, I keep my jewelry in my room. I
>   will lock my door to my room so they don't
>   go into it.
> Q: So you're suspicious?
> A: Right. Because I don't want them going in
>   there, you know, for some reason. I'm hiding
>   my jewelry.
> Q: Okay.
> A: So that set me suspicious to Ricky, him not
>   letting me go upstairs.

She knew what it meant. Ricky had something to hide.

There is no way to know, now, as Lanelle passes back the bills to the truckers, and Pearl wipes down the counters at the Fuel Stop, and Ricky hoists his laundry bag over his shoulder to carry to his folks', that in three months, after Jeremy's body has been found in the closet, after Ricky has been handcuffed and locked up in the parish jail, after the front pages of newspapers all over the state have run the same black-and-white photograph of the bogeyman sex offender who's murdered a little boy, and after the Lawson home has become command central for the police, who have taped the closet and Ricky's bedroom in yellow tape, and, after all of Ricky's belongings from the room have been placed in sealed plastic bags marked EVIDENCE and Jeremy's body has been sealed up and carried off to the morgue, that Terry Lawson—Pearl's husband, Joey and June's father—will take his son, Joey, out for an afternoon motorcycle ride.

No record exists of what Terry Lawson says that afternoon. Maybe he says, "Let's go out to the lake, Son." Maybe "Why don't you come to the store with me, come for a ride?" Maybe "You feeling like ice cream?" He gives the boy his hand and helps him climb up, gets his little legs situated around the bike's body.

Then that motorcycle flies right into the second car of an Amtrak train, killing them both.

The *second* car.

Terry Lawson was steering. His son behind him, hanging on to his waist. Witnesses say that the area was clear—that the train could be seen "for a mile"—and that it blew a loud whistle just before impact. How do you hit the second car of a train? Maybe the first car you don't see coming, and it hits you. But how do you hit the *second* car?

There is so much the people in this story cannot know yet, so much that hovers in the court records still to come. Through the pages of the transcript I watch as Lanelle flips on the pump for another truck and stares at Ricky through the window. I watch as Pearl moves on to refilling the creamers. I watch as Ricky tries to flag down a ride in a passing car.

For three days more, Jeremy's body will stay wedged in the closet as Joey and June play in the hallway across from it. For three days more, Pearl and Terry Lawson will tuck the children into their beds at night and wake them up in the morning and ready them for school, and all the while, Jeremy's body will be there across the hall, standing wrapped in the blue blanket printed with Dick Tracy, his boots and his BB gun placed neatly at his feet.

The grown-ups drink their coffee, the children their morning milk at the table, and in three months' time the father, Terry, will be dead. The boy, Joey, too.

Later, there will be allegations that Terry was molesting June. Nothing ever proved.

I try to study the past, try to read between the lines of its text—to see Terry as he pours himself more coffee and sits down beside the bowls Ricky set out for the children's cereal. Where were his hands last night? He and Pearl gave up their bedroom.

And Pearl, look at her there now, as she opens the refrigerator door and reminds Joey to finish his breakfast. What does she see? What does she see, or what is she able to see? What does she look away from? Did she not know Jeremy's body was there? Three *days*.

Then Terry and Joey die. And Pearl takes June, and disappears.

Eight

New Jersey, 1985

Weeks pass, months, a year. The memory of that strange backward afternoon my mother ran across the lawn crying, and the sound of my grandfather up the stairs at night both sit inside me like a summer cocoon, sheltered up tight against the heat. I'm holding my breath from the inside, trying to keep what's there from igniting.

Each Easter, just before we go to my grandparents' house and sit around their big wooden table for the manicotti my grandfather has made and the thin sheets of beef he's rolled and tied twine around like presents, my parents give us baskets that each have an egg inside. Their shells are white and made of sugar, the sugar along the seams colored and piped like frosting. Inside, they shelter tiny scenes made of sugar, too: a baby chick, cheeping in its nest, or a bunny with a basket. Each scene is a delicate, worked thing. But the shell, though sugar, is not fragile. It's dense and hard.

The silence works like that. It's not fragile. It shields the glittering moments and the confusing ones, too. Such as the times my throat gets parched in the middle of the night and I brave the dark stairs to go down to the kitchen for a glass of water. There, I find my father at the white table. He's got a big glass bowl of potato chips beside him. An empty bottle of wine with another started. Ice cream wrappers litter the ground near his feet. The television blares a news program. He smiles wryly as I enter the room.

"You OK, sweetheart?" he says then.

This is the softest he ever is, so sometimes I tell him. "I had a nightmare," I say. I have been dreaming about witches that come to me in my sleep.

"Go back to bed," he says. "I love you. Come here," he says, and I go to him and kiss his cheek.

He's best like this, sweeter than at any other moments during the day. But I know he won't remember any of it in the morning. In the morning these moments will have blurred and faded into a distant, unreal dream.

The bright solid morning. The morning is the time for action. He buys a new speaker set and wires it through the house so the kitchen's on one control, the living room another, all from a central console. He shines his shoes upstairs and refuses to answer the phone calls from creditors and blares his opera music through the house, sometimes so loudly my ears ache. He and my mother sit at the kitchen table and plan parties, parties that will help people know my father's name in this new town, and my mother teaches me to separate the leaves on a stalk of endive and smear Brie into the center of each, mound sour cream onto a cracker and place a perfect dollop of caviar in the middle. At the parties the grins are toothy and hard and everyone's breath smells like wine.

That summer, my father decides to run for town council. They have T-shirts made for us for the Fourth of July parade: matching red with fuzzy white iron-on lettering that says MY DADDY FOR TOWN COUNCIL. My mother's matches, too, but says DREW. In the picture taken of us at the parade, we stand squinting into the sunlight, our red T-shirts tucked into high-waisted shorts. My sister Nicola waves a tiny American flag. I stand a few feet apart from the family, the sun's sheen off my glasses hiding my eyes. My curls have been cut too short; they frizz around my head. One arm cocked across my chest, I'm not smiling. I cup my arm with my other hand, holding myself together.

I am still and taut as a chrysalis this summer. Do I sense that the silence can't last? Is that what I wait for? Afternoons my father mows the lawn, the air is suddenly thick with fresh green dust from the clippings, the smell pungent and musty, alive and heavy. The waiting feels like that. It crams my lungs. It weighs on my chest.

Then summer swerves and starts its long descent. In the vegetable garden my father has made on the side of the lawn, the basil bolts, tall and tough. The trellises of beans slump pregnant with heavy pods, and the neat rows of lettuce heads swell fat and round. The corn stands straight while the sunflowers bow. From the sunflowers we lop off a head at a time and my mother roasts it flat in the oven until the seeds fill the kitchen with their nutty smell. Each night now what we eat together comes from the garden as we race with bounty, trying to keep ahead of the coming spoilage.

On one of those nights, my mother sits at the end of the picnic table in a white sleeveless shell sweater, her arms tanned. I burn as a kid, but someday when I hit thirty my skin will suddenly tan easily no matter how many times a day I slather on sunscreen, as if claiming itself to her. My father sits opposite her, in a chair we've pulled up to the table. My siblings and I are on the benches, two to each side. The six of us fit neatly around the table. I have started to note this: how we fit perfectly around our belongings, everything spaced for six, and how there is never any extra room. My mother dishes the pasta onto our plates, the pesto sauce, the zucchini spears sprinkled with Parmesan and oregano. The tastes, sweet and bright and sharp, are as steady as devotion: the tastes of last summer, and the summer before that, and the summers to come.

But this time she puts down the serving spoon and looks around the table at us.

How she starts—the words she uses—are lost to me. My father is both the ballast and the break of the house, the jagged rock and the wave that cracks over it, and as a child I am attuned only to what he says and his mood, and never to my steady mother. The dinner table is his to command—his court to teach us about the world, to talk of politics and countries and the values he wants to instill. My mother is quiet. Years will pass before I realize, with the jolt of my own world snapping into view, how smart she is.

"Are you listening?" she says to me that night. "Your father and I have something to tell you."

Such a grave sentence. It wears its seriousness like an alert flag. Something in her voice tells me that whatever she has to say, I don't want it. The air is thick with unspoken words already, I am all full up with my own secret. A clot forms in my throat. Can't she see that the night is a light one, the breeze soft and the setting sun aglow? Vivaldi's violins waft from the speakers my father has strung up in the trees. No one is fighting, my father is not yelling, and my grandparents are far away across the bridge in New York.

Don't ruin this, I think.

"I need a sweater," I say. I snap onto this answer like a prize, my voice triumphant.

"You need it right now?" she says.

"I'm *cold*."

She sighs. "Hurry up, then."

"I'm cold, too," my baby sister, Elize, says.

"Get your sister a sweater," my mother tells me. "Take which-ever ones you see first; it doesn't matter." Her voice is clipped and forced—the strain, I will think later, of trying to hold one more minute when it has already held too long.

The house mushrooms around me into a shadow. In the dark, all I can hear is the same old empty ghost-creaks the walls always make, the sound of them settling down into time, and the con-stant whir of the attic fan, its metal shutters opening and closing at the top of the stairs. I never go up those stairs alone in the dark. I make sure of that. Nights that we have dinner in the kitchen and one of the other kids is using the bathroom there and my mother tells me to go use the one upstairs, I walk out of the kitchen and stand quietly in the dark in the dining room, count slowly to forty, and then come back in. Sometimes I stomp my feet louder and then softer and then louder again, to mimic the coming and going. Sometimes when I return to the white kitchen table, she looks at me and says, "That was quick." Then I wait longer the next time. I just can't tell her why I can't go upstairs.

A few years from now, in fifth grade, I will sit in the school counselor's room. It will be a routine meeting, one done in pairs arranged by the alphabet, and with me in the room will be one of the popular boys: tall, lithe, and tan, able to whip his foot just right into a soccer ball, sending it soaring.

"Are you excited to move to the middle school next year?" the counselor will ask.

The boy will look at her like she's crazy. He already knows he's in his most popular place.

"I'm excited," I pipe up. "There will be so many kids."

She smiles at me.

"I'll be able to disappear," I say.

To disappear is what I dream whenever my grandfather sits down at the edge of my bed. His brown eyes look into mine, then he contorts his face to spit his teeth into the palm of his hand. He holds them out to me. The teeth glisten like a sea creature. He grins, his mouth suddenly a rim of wet pink with a black sopped hole in the middle. "See," he says, though he has shown me this so many times before, "I'm a witch. Don't forget. If you tell I'll always come find you. Always. Even after I'm dead."

I turn my head away and fix my eyes on the yellow skirt of a doll that is also a lamp. Its body illuminates the skirt, dissolving it into a glow of radiant yellow. It burns in the dark room, and as he puts the false teeth on my nightstand, brings his hand to the edge of my nightgown, and lifts the cloth from my suddenly cold legs, I stare into the yellow and will myself into flame, into dissolution. His hand travels up my leg. His other hand undoes his zipper. I stare at the light so hard that around me the air splinters. I feel him tug my underwear down. I feel his fingers. The air splits into molecules. It is cold between my legs again—his hand has moved—and then his hand is back, gripping a thick part of him. He holds my legs apart. He rubs himself against me.

Around me, the molecules spin. I feel myself break apart with them.

I still hate the color yellow.

But as a child, standing barefoot in the dark dining room as, outside, the summer night slowly loses its glow, I am more afraid of what my mother will say. So I go.

I rush up the steps, trying to tune my ears away from the creaks of my climb. I will myself to listen to the fan instead of the stairs. The fan's shutters mouth a slow roar, its breath a cold vacuum beneath. My little sister's bedroom has the feel of an attic, the ceiling slanted; it's really a hallway. I'll have to go through hers to reach mine. The same way my grandfather does when he comes upstairs at night. On her dresser there's a fuzzy sweater of baby-chick yellow, its arms folded behind it like wings. I stop. The feeling of staring at it—its pale yellow in the dark, my willing my body to be still and empty—will last forever. Then I decide: I'll tell my mother I didn't see a sweater at first. I'll tell her I had to search. Behind me is Elize's toddler bed. I can feel the idea of that bed pressing against my back. The knowledge that he, too, stands here. The times I've walked into my sister's room and seen him standing over her. I struggle with my mind to go blank.

Then I've got to run.

From my own bedroom, I snatch a blue sweater, my favorite color. Back through her bedroom, under the fan, down the steps. I fly. I come to a halt in the dark dining room, the wood-slat floor cool and smooth beneath my feet. My body still. In the quiet my breath thuds as loud as the fan.

Stalling, still stalling.

Then I walk outside.

When I step onto the side porch my mother spots me and waves.

"What took you so long?" she calls. "Come sit down!" After the smooth floor the grass feels sharp. It prickles against my feet, the bright outside light coming at me from a place far away. I slide onto the splintered wood of the bench and hand my sister the soft fluff of her sweater. I am in my body but not here, not really.

"Your father and I have something to tell you all," she says.

This can't be about my grandfather. She can't know about that. There's another secret?

"You all had a sister," she says. "Her name was Jacqueline. She was Andrew and Alexandria's triplet." My mother never uses our full first names—my brother is Andy, and I, though I hate it, am Ali—and the words she chooses as much as their meaning tells me how much is wrong. "Do you remember how we said that Andrew and Alexandria were sick when they were born?" Nicola, looking at her as wide-eyed as a student, nods. That's what they tell us when my brother faints: that he was sick when he was little, and that this is just the aftereffect. It's what they tell us when the neighbor suddenly appears to look after us, and my mother pulls the packed blue duffel bag from the closet. "Well, Jacqueline was, too, but she was too sick. Too little. She died when she was five months old."

The strangest feeling comes. I already knew.

Later that night, after my parents have tucked us into bed, I lie awake in the dark in the room I share with Nicola.

"Ali?" she says. Tonight I let her call me that. "Are we going to die, too?"

"No," I say. "Shh, just go to sleep. We aren't going to die."

"But she died."

I consider this. "Yes, but we aren't going to. That's a kind of dying you only do when you're little. We're big now." I am seven and she is five. "We aren't going to die."

As I say this, I realize suddenly that I am lying. That we will, one day. I hope she doesn't know this. I hope she doesn't know about forever.

"Promise?" she says.

"Promise," I say. And my sister is quiet after that. But I lie awake in the dark for a long time. How did I know about the girl?

Nine

Lorilei's the one who leads the police to Ricky Langley, finally. Early Monday morning, her son still missing, the sheriff calls her up at Melissa's house and asks her to come down to the station for questioning. He's kind but firm. They need her to take a lie detector test.

Let's put her in a small room at the police station for this. From the ceiling hangs an overhead cone light like the one my parents had in their kitchen while I was growing up, the cone light that's in every interrogation scene in the movies and that must hover over Ricky Langley when he finally gives his videotaped confession. Lorilei's not a suspect—"No, ma'am, we're not suggesting anything," the taller, burlier cop keeps saying to her—but the truth is they don't have any suspects. Not yet.

The men introduce themselves as Don Dixon, from the FBI field office, and Donald DeLouche, from the Calcasieu Parish Sheriff's Office. "But you can call me 'Lucky,' " the tall man says, taking off his hat and shaking her hand. "Everyone else does."

Some kind of luck, she must think. Where's her boy?

At the table the men's voices are a mixture of gentle and tense. She can't tell if they think she had something to do with Jeremy's disappearance. Likely she's too tired to care what they think. Just bring her back her boy.

"Now, ma'am, I need you to remember everything as careful as possible."

She sighs. "I told the investigators already. I went next door, and then second thing I went to the Lawson house. There's a boy and a girl live over there; Jeremy plays with them sometimes. A man answered the door and he let me use the phone to call my brother."

"Do you know his name?"

It's the first time anyone's asked her that. She didn't then, but she does now. "Ricky Langley," she says.

Lucky stands up, picks his hat up off the table, and walks out. Dixon follows him.

A minute or so later, another cop walks into the room. He's younger than the other two, clean-shaven. He sits down on the chair Lucky left and pulls it up to the table. "Don't you worry about them," he says. "They're just going to check on something. My name's Officer Roberts. Now. You were telling them about the man who answered the door?"

Roberts keeps her there for hours more, going over the day in detail. Sometimes another cop comes in and joins him. Together they retrace every step she took. Finally, they have her go sit in the sheriff's office.

That's where they tell her they've found her boy. He's dead.

Twenty-four hours before, that name, Ricky Langley, wouldn't have meant anything to Lucky and Dixon. But on the morning of Sunday the ninth, as the search continued, the two of them had gone into the woods together to hunt geese. Later, maybe, there'd be hell to pay for their going hunting with a child still missing. Later maybe the whole thing would look a little funny. But the white-fronted geese passed overhead only twice a year, and anyway, the boy was most likely drowned and dead.

Early in the morning, they'd set decoys on flat slab boats they floated slowly forward until they heard the soft squawking of the flock cooing out to the decoys. Then they'd tethered the flats where they were—within good range of where the geese were headed— and dug two chest-high pits into the soft silt on the side of the bank.

Now, as they squatted side by side in their pits, both of them with their hands on their rifles, a Thermos of hot coffee set between them, Dixon stared into the blue-gray vacant sky and said to Lucky, "What do you make of that boy still being missing? You going to keep on with the search?"

The pits were bone-cold. The air too quiet. "Through the day at least," said Lucky. "But they don't need me there." He poured coffee into the plastic top of the Thermos, took a sip. "They're dredging the canal today. The sheriff's office has got it."

"I know it ain't my case," Dixon said, "but I don't think he's in the woods. If he were they'd have found him by now."

"He drowned, I'll bet. Lots of kids drown out that way."

"They'd have found him then, too."

"Maybe," Lucky said. He didn't seem inclined to say more.

Dixon waited a long moment, choosing his words carefully. Then he said, "If y'all don't find his body by morning, the FBI's gonna have to get more involved." Under the Federal Kidnapping Act, adopted after the murder of Charles Lindbergh's baby, after twenty-four hours a presumption kicked in that a missing child had been taken across state lines. Jeremy had been missing thirty-six.

Soon, it wouldn't be Lucky's case anymore.

"I know that," Lucky said.

"They'll take over."

"I know." Lucky fiddled with his gun. Flipped the safety, brought it up to his eyes. No geese yet. He sighted on the target not yet there. "All right. I'll bring the mother in tomorrow."

That night, after Dixon and Lucky had packed in, the long hours in the pits having yielded them nothing, Lucky stopped off at the sheriff's building on his way home. He'd finish some paperwork, he thought. Get ready for the mother in the morning. He was seated at his desk, the single light of his desk lamp illuminating the sheets of paper in a warm yellow glow, when the phone rang. On the line was a probation officer. "Heard about your missing boy," she said. Her voice had a strong twang. "There's a man you should know about out on parole from child molestation in Georgia. Not

my case, really—Georgia never sent the papers—and the last time
I saw him was in December. Then he disappeared."

Plenty of men skipped out on parole. She meant well, he knew,
but this was probably nothing. "What's the last address you have?"

"Let me check," she said. Lucky heard the sound of papers rus-
tling. "He was living with his parents in Iowa." She repeated,
"Iowa. Y'all pronounce it funny, don't you? Says here he's got a
preference for boys six years old or so. How old's your missing
boy?"

Lucky's heart started to pound. "Six."

"You might try to find him," she said. "His name is Ricky
Langley."

When Lucky and Dixon pull into the Fuel Stop parking lot, it's a
little past ten in the morning Monday, the sky a clear, weightless
blue. They've got a warrant for Ricky Langley's arrest for skipping
out on parole in Georgia, the judge's signature barely dry. Dixon
gets out of the car. There's a young man with jug ears riding a tractor, spreading crushed shell across the ground. Dixon waves at him
and motions with his arm to shut off the tractor.

"Get down," he says. He squints at the man. Brown hair, kind
of scrawny, glasses. "I'm Agent Dixon and this is Detective De-
Louche. Are you Ricky Langley?"

"Yes, sir."

Lucky hasn't said anything yet, but now he starts walking straight
at Ricky. "You have the right to remain silent," he says. The dust
from the shell kicks up as he walks. "You have the right to an attorney. If you cannot afford to hire an attorney, one will be provided for you." Ricky doesn't respond and Lucky doesn't stop.
"Do you understand these rights as I have explained them to you?"
He's next to Ricky now.

"Yessir."

"We're going to ask you some questions," Lucky says. "You're
going to come with us."

Ricky goes still as prey caught in a hunting sight. Then he looks down—which, Dixon will later say, helps him know they've got the right guy. Guilty people, when they're getting ready to admit it, look down.

Finally Ricky says, "I got a coat in there."

"Inside the gas station?"

"Yes."

"All right, we'll get it."

Lucky walks back toward the station for the coat and to pull the time cards, which will show what hours Ricky worked the day Jeremy disappeared. Dixon takes Ricky to the cruiser. He'd cuff him right there if he had to, but Ricky comes willingly, a few steps in front of Dixon. The men walk stiffly, each body both sprung and cocked, alert for different reasons. The February air is as cold and dry as an empty room. When they reach the car, Dixon leans down and opens the back passenger seat of the car, motioning for Ricky to slide in. Ricky does. Dixon fixes the seat belt and says, again, "You have the right to remain silent." His voice is hard. Ricky's head pops down again. "You have the right to an attorney." Dixon goes through the whole thing a second time. He needs this arrest to be airtight. "Do you understand these rights as I have explained them to you?"

"Yes," Ricky says. He sounds miserable.

Dixon sits down in the driver's seat. Through the rearview mirror, he looks at Ricky. Dixon takes note, as he's been trained to, of the way Ricky's jugular vein pulses light and fast beneath his lowered chin. The tension in the muscle cords at the sides of the neck. Ricky's hands are balled into fists. He looks like a man holding something in. He looks like a man desperately wishing the moment were not real.

It's time, Dixon decides.

He twists backward in his seat. "Now, Ricky," he says. He can't see Ricky's face, just the top of his head, the mat of his dark hair. "I want you to look me in the eye, man to man."

Ricky doesn't move.

"Man to man, Ricky." Dixon levels his voice, no bullshit. Someone like Ricky, someone who's been thought weird his whole life, an outcast, a guy no one respects, Dixon knows the way to do it is to sound even. Sound like you're taking him serious. "Look me in the eye, Ricky."

For a flickering second Ricky looks up. When Dixon sees his eyes, he knows. Their pupils are as wide as buckshot. Dixon's got him.

"I want you to look me in the eye"—Ricky looks away—"no, I want you to look me in the *eye*, Ricky, and tell me whether you know anything about Jeremy Guillory's disappearance."

A shudder ripples across Ricky's shoulders. Like the rattle a body makes when giving up.

Then, suddenly: "I did it." Ricky exhales. "I did it, I did it, I don't know why I did it but I did it." He drops his head to his hands. Just like that. That simple. Three days, and it's over like that. Done.

"Where's the body?" Dixon says.

"My closet. In my bedroom."

Without a word Dixon turns and exits the car. Shuts and locks the door behind him.

Which leaves Ricky alone in the cruiser, having just confessed to murder.

What does he think of? That night—the night he killed Jeremy—when all of the parents had collected their children and gone home, and Pearl had told him that maybe he should leave town, her face turned down as if she couldn't bear to look at him, and she'd gone to lie next to her husband on the mattress in the living room, Ricky went back up alone to his bedroom in the dark. Joey and June were asleep in their bedrooms across the hall. The house was quiet. Ricky sat on the bed and he listened to the quiet.

It was the first time in hours he'd been alone, the first time since Jeremy had rung the bell that afternoon. He couldn't go to sleep—his heart was too keyed up for that—and he kept thinking of Jeremy. Thinking of how his eyes had been open when Ricky had grabbed him, and how they'd closed, as though on their own. He knew it was impossible, but sitting in his bedroom, knowing the boy was in the closet, he kept thinking he heard breathing. He kept imagining those eyes opening. Someone was watching him.

There was a staircase off the back of his bedroom that led twenty feet straight into the woods. If Ricky wanted to get rid of the body.

But instead, in the middle of the night, he crept downstairs to the kitchen and took a roll of aluminum foil. He taped and foiled his two bedroom windows, so the light was blocked.

He couldn't say who he didn't want to see him, why he needed those windows gone. It was just that he needed the world smaller, closed and tight around him.

That's the feeling that must come back to Ricky now, in the cruiser, the clear bright winter sun beating through the windows, the inside of the car heating up. If the world could just stay this small, suspended. He stays inside the feeling for a long time, he doesn't know how long.

Until Dixon returns and says, "We're going to the house."

For days the street has been crowded with people, with dogs and police troopers and truck hitches for the search boats. But when Dixon and Lucky pull the cruiser up now, the street is empty. Ricky's cuffed in the back, his head still tucked forward.

"This is the house," Lucky says. Dixon knows to stand down. This will be Lucky's case after all. "The boy's in there," Lucky says. It's not a question, but he looks at Ricky anyway.

Ricky raises his head slightly. Nods.

"All right," says Lucky. "Let's go."

Lucky doesn't call an ambulance. He doesn't rush. Later he'll bring this moment up on the witness stand, tell the jury that of course he didn't rush, he knew the child was dead. Repeat it twice, as if he's justifying the decision to himself. It's an odd moment to thorn into him, an odd moment for him to come back to. The boy *was* dead. Rushing wouldn't have mattered any. Lucky could've called an ambulance, he could have run right in, he could even have skipped hunting the day before, and it wouldn't have mattered: Jeremy was dead. Funny where the mind wants to lodge. Funny where it wants to think it can make a difference.

Lucky gets out of the car.

The deputy who shows up with the video camera has pimples on his cheeks, that's how young he is. Or at least that's how I see him now, as I read the transcript. For the next few hours, this man will frame everything recorded through the camera's viewfinder. He is the only person present who doesn't say anything on tape, doesn't react, just records. He is a mystery in this transcript, but—think what he sees. What he's required to take in. I'd rather imagine him new to this; I'd rather think his eyes go wide. I see his skin scraped raw with razor burn and his neck as skinny as a chicken's.

Dixon sizes him up, shakes his head. Already he and the police photographers have been up to the bedroom to photograph the scene. It's fine that the department's started to add video, but they treat it like a shit job for the new cops.

"You ready?" Dixon says. I see him snap on latex gloves and unfold a clear bag marked EVIDENCE. The kid had better have seen a dead body before. The last thing they need is the cameraman getting sick.

"Ready," the boy says. He doesn't sound it.

"I'll get the suspect," Lucky says—his words suddenly formal, now that there's going to be a tape.

When Lucky comes back he's got Ricky beside him, cuffed. Ricky's shuffling along, won't look up. He flat-out stops at the front door. Then he crosses the threshold.

"Roll the tape," Lucky says.

It's on.

"What I want you to do now," Lucky starts, then stops. "What I want you to do now, Jeremy—"

(This little slip, calling Ricky by his victim's name, is the only sign Lucky is nervous. The only sign of how big this moment is for him. Later the transcription clerk will mark it with "[sic].")

"We'll let the cameraman follow you inside and I want you to take me up to the room where this happened and I want you to show him the room and I don't want you to touch anything, OK? I know there's some guns in here and, like I say, I don't want you to touch anything."

Lucky looks expectantly at Ricky.

"Uh-huh," says Ricky.

They go.

It's a tight fit, the three of them walking up the staircase, the cameraman right behind Ricky. The film will be dim on the television screen later, their bodies almost shadows, Ricky's black shirt a spot of dark night in the dusky light. The camera angle makes the ceiling seem lower. The walls tighter. The men climb wordlessly, one crisp step after another. They reach the bedroom.

"In here?" says Lucky.

Ricky nods, then remembers he's supposed to answer out loud. "Yeah."

"You got anything to add before we go in?" Lucky says to Dixon.

"Yeah, gimme a minute," Dixon says. Maybe now that the moment's about to go down, he's got doubts about handing it over to Lucky. This was his find. He's the one who told Lucky to get moving, wasn't he? He's the one who got Ricky to confess. Or maybe he just wants to make sure, again, that the arrest stays airtight. Whatever the reason, he goes through it all again. Says, "Ricky, when you were arrested back up at the gas station and you got in the car with me, did I ever threaten you, or anything like that?"

Ricky shakes his head. Then: "Nuh-uh."

"Was I polite to you?"

"Yeah."

"And I just said, 'Ricky look me in the eyes man to man,' and I advised you of your rights. And everything you said to me was voluntary."

"Yes, sir."

"All right, then." Dixon nods to Lucky. They're ready.

The men step into the room. "Cut the tape," Lucky says, and the boy fumblingly obliges. Then to Ricky: "Show me the closet." Ricky starts to move. "No, don't walk over there. Point at it."

Ricky does.

"The child's in there?" Dixon again. He knows the answer. He was up here before, when Lucky went to get Ricky. But he's watching Ricky now. Watching the small lines of distress that have started to crack through his body.

"Yeah," Ricky says.

"He's just in there, or—"

"I got him in some blankets."

Lucky steps forward and motions for Dixon and Ricky to leave the room. Then he walks to the closet. Its door is white, chipped paint with a dirt crust. It's wide-open. Inside there's a bundle of blankets. Not really in the shape of a body. Just a bundle. He waits until he can feel the cameraman behind him. He nods. The camera starts recording again. Lucky speaks each word carefully and slowly. "It's 3:35 p.m. We are back in the room. The date is February 10, 1992. We are back in the southeast bedroom of Ricky Langley and our photo division has finished taking their still photographs and we are about to remove the blanket or quilt or whatever it is that Ricky Langley advises that he covered the body up with."

He shines a flashlight into the closet. The beam cuts through, touching the bundle with yellow. Then it moves to the side so the camera can see the shape. Lucky steps back into the frame, reaches in. "We are going to put this—it is a Tweety Bird curtains or bedspread I place in this bag."

The tape is awkward from this point on. Lucky narrates every step. He must want so badly to get it right. He lifts layer after layer and each time shows the blanket to the camera before putting it in the bag.

But see that first bag, waiting in the corner to be taped up, the plastic bag with EVIDENCE written right across it, no doubt what's in the bag? It will be mislabeled, and switched with a bag of clothes cut carefully from Jeremy later. See the bag Lucky fills next? It will be mislabeled, too, and combined with a bag that contains nothing of significance.

I've seen a clip of this tape. I've watched Ricky and Lucky and Dixon climb the porch steps of the Lawson house—seen Ricky, with his hands bound, walk to the front door Jeremy had walked through a few days before. The confession that was shown to me at the law firm, the tape that launched me into this story, was filmed right after this, when Dixon and Lucky brought Ricky back to the police station. He looked like a rabbit, his eyes darting, the handcuffs just restraining him locked at the waist. The rest of his words come through the staccato flash-time of memory, as though my body could absorb only in jolts, in gulps with swallowed black in between.

Only the transcript—only looking at it now—settles the memory.

The blue blanket is the last sheet Lucky lifts on the tape. "Covering the lower portion of the victim is a blue bedspread with some figure on it—maybe Dick Tracy with a gun in his hand, multicolored. At this time we are removing it and we see the remainder of our victim."

The camera doesn't linger. It catches the blond hair and then falters in the face of the boy. But on Jeremy's lip right now—too small for the camera to catch, and no one's looking at him that closely, no one wants to look at a body that closely—there is a single dark pubic hair.

When they cut the samples from Jeremy's white T-shirt, the samples Calton Pitre will remember for decades, they'll find semen stains on his shirt. That semen will match Ricky's. But this hair on his lip? It isn't Ricky's. They'll test it twice. Twice the answer will come back: not Ricky's.

Ricky killed Jeremy; that we know for sure. And the pubic hair might have just fallen off a blanket. But those blankets don't belong only to Ricky. There's too many of them. They must be from Joey's and June's beds, too. Maybe the hair could have been transferred to them in the laundry.

But maybe not. Does the hair belong to Terry, who, right this moment, is still alive, has not taken his son for a ride, is out of the house at an unknown location while the police perform their search? Does the hair belong not to the convicted sex predator, the one people now know to fear, but to the father who may secretly be a predator, too?

Lucky keeps narrating. "You can observe a sock which appears to be in the mouth of the victim. Our victim is dressed in a white T-shirt, light blue or turquoise sweatpants with a yellow stripe around the bottom, white socks and the boots that the mother said he was dressed in were here."

Teal. Lorilei describes those sweatpants as teal. Four days ago she lifted them from the dryer and folded them, matching the edges of their waistband together, creasing the small legs into a careful package. She stacked it with that T-shirt. She took the clothes to the dresser she and Jeremy were sharing at Melissa's and she laid the pants down in the bottom drawer, the T-shirt in the drawer above. She laid them down carefully. As if she were laying down a child.

All these clothes Jeremy is wearing—all these pieces of evidence—have history. The evidence holds the life they had together. It holds her love.

"Also, in the corner of the closet," Dixon continues, "you can see the BB gun. Which the mother described as belonging to the victim, Jeremy."

Back in the station, Lorilei brings her head to her hands and sobs.

Ten

New Jersey, 1986

I have only the barest of retellings of this next story to work from—
told to me once by my mother years afterward and never repeated—
with little memory of my own to offer. So let me construct the
story from these traces. It is the year after my mother told us
about Jacqueline. Now we are on the Massachusetts island of Nantucket, where we have rented a house for the summer and have
brought my grandparents with us. Elize is four years old, a doll of a
child, with long blond curls and a kewpie nose. Lately she's been
modeling for the British clothing company owned by friends of my
parents, and she wears, now, one of the white flounced dresses the
company favors. Perhaps she has on the one with the green satin
sash that matches her eyes. It is early evening, and the house bustles
with activity as the adults dress for dinner. My sister has wandered
off, a rare moment alone, and she climbs up on one of the grand
upholstered chairs of the house's formal living room. It was a cap-
tain's home in the island's whaling days, and dark oil portraits of his
long-dead daughters line the walls, each with a dour expression and
a golden name placard screwed beneath her: PRUDENCE VIRTUE
CHASTITY. My sister turns around to look at each of the funny faces
and makes a face back at one of them. She tries to imagine what
she's been told: that each one was once a child, just like she is.

In her fist, she grips a prize recently acquired: a five-dollar bill.

My mother walks in from the kitchen, a glass of red wine in
her hand, her hair still wound around white plastic rollers, her black

dress still unfastened in the back. "There you are!" she says. She sips the wine distractedly. Then, noticing: "Sweetie, where did you get the money?" She must be thinking my sister took it from her open purse or from her dresser drawer. An innocent mistake, cause enough for a gentle lesson.

But: "Grandpa gave it to me" is what my sister says.

"Oh?" my mother asks. She still thinks this will be a sweet story. There is a penny candy store on the island where one cent will buy a single sticky Swedish Fish or a gummy bear, and already my grandfather has taken us there once, and paid a quarter each for us to fill white paper sacks. He indulges us, just as he did my mother and her brothers while they were growing up. He always had candies in his pockets for them. My sister is too little for the tooth fairy, but maybe, my mother reasons, she got the five dollars by fetching his cap for him, or his cane. My mother decides to play along. "And how did you earn that?" she says.

"I sat on his lap," my sister answers.

The whispers that follow are sheathed knives, fierce contained urgency. Voices are not raised; doors stay closed. Behind one, I am questioned, and I know to keep my voice low, that my parents do not want my grandfather, grandmother, or brother to hear. I answer simply. Yes, my grandfather has touched me. Yes, it's been happening for years. They ask more questions—where, what do I remember, what did I see around me—to determine how long. Five years is the answer. I begin to cry. Not because of what happened. But because now my mother knows. Some part of me has been waiting for this—but more of me is terrified. I am convinced that we will all be safe if she just does not know this about her father. I am convinced it is my job to save her from that. That to say out loud that a father is capable of this would be the most terrible thing.

They ask enough questions of me, then my sisters, to determine the loose outline. Then we all go to dinner.

———

Can this be? Can this be right? Can they lead us all to a big round restaurant table laid with a red-and-white-checked cotton tablecloth—the restaurant we go to in these years has my grandfather's name, Vincent's—and pull out a chair for the man about whom they have just learned this? Can they sit across from the woman, his wife, my grandmother, whom they will decide to keep this secret from to protect? How many times during that dinner do they see my grandfather's hands, and wonder what those hands have done?

Or am I mistaking my own interest in the past for theirs? Can my parents sit across from him and never, never imagine the actions that lie behind the words they have been told, never see the story unspool before them?

I know only what happens next: My parents never tell my grandfather what they have learned. They never tell my grandmother, either. They give, somehow, no sign that anything is wrong. We finish the vacation. We go home to the gray Victorian house. My parents stop asking my grandparents to spend the night, and the abuse stops without anyone's saying anything. They arrange the memory as carefully as a script.

And from there, as before, my father drives the big gray Chevrolet across the George Washington Bridge and into the Queens neighborhood where my mother grew up. As before, he pulls in front of the burgundy-awning door of the brick row house where my mother was a child, where my grandfather waits, a newsboy cap on his head, a vinyl jacket pulled around him, ready for his outing. My father holds out his hand to my grandfather and accepts the wooden cane with the other. As before, my father gives the old man his shoulder to lean on, and they creep their way to the car. He hoists my grandfather up over the running boards, then tucks the cane beneath the seat. My father slams the chassis door, walks over to the driver's side. He carries my grandfather back over the bridge to us.

The people in this story still want to believe they can control the past, wipe it clean just as a crime scene is scrubbed. They want to believe that that scene, scrubbed, becomes just a bedroom.

My parents tell me now that they had consulted a psychologist who told them that the best thing they could do for their children was to model unaffectedness. Model that what happened had no impact.

It's not that I don't believe them. Not exactly. But I wonder about the neatness of this advice. It echoes so perfectly, too perfectly, the silences I already know of my parents. The silence about my father's rages. The silence that followed for years about my missing sister. It echoes—but we are not there yet—what happened to my sister's body.

For now, just understand this: They need to leave the past behind.

So in my memory my grandfather is there, sitting like a lump in my throat, in the living room chair at the foot of the stairs. He is there at Christmas, he is there at Easter, he is there when it is just Sunday and my grandmother sits beside him and asks me to play a game of checkers with her, and I do not say that I am too old for checkers. He is there when I am thirteen and wearing my first grown-up dress, black velvet with a deep V-neck halter. He is there when I rise onto my tiptoes and twirl to make the crinoline skirt float up around me. It is his hot breath that leans into my neck and whispers how grown-up I look, how nicely my body fills out the dress. He is there when I am fifteen, and just starting to be angry.

When we left Lorilei she was sitting on the police station bench, her head in her hands, sobbing. She's pregnant with the next child inside her, the boy who'll grow up in his brother's wake.

In the months that follow Ricky's arrest, she'll walk a hard line between her grief and her rage. That one drink on the porch the first night the searchers were out for Jeremy—that will turn into months of drinking, months of drugs. She'll fall back into her old ways and the past will flood out over the present. Inside her, the whole time, will grow the new life, but she won't then be able to nurture it. It will just grow.

One year later there's a newspaper clipping that matches Lorilei's address. Reading it, I see a woman (she refuses to identify herself, but her hair must still be the light brown shade that is often a childhood blond) walk from a house to meet the cops as they step out of their cruiser. She cradles a baby in her arms.

"Y'all don't need to come in," she says.

"Ma'am, we're responding to a suspected domestic incident," the cop says. "A neighbor called."

"Y'all don't need to come in," she repeats. She squints into the sun. Her left eye is already starting to swell. The baby in her arms begins to fuss and she shifts him tighter in to her chest. She's named this boy Cole. He'll have his father's last name. "Look," she says. "If he goes"—she nods back at the house—"I ain't got no other way to pay my bills."

She looks at the cop hard now, in the eyes. "You have a good day," she says firmly. Then she walks back to the house, carrying the baby in her arms.

One more year later, when Ricky is finally sentenced for her son's murder, she doesn't go to the courtroom. She sits in a motel room across the road and waits. Her brother Richard is in the courtroom when the jury gives its decision. Three hours, they've deliberated. Ricky will die for Jeremy's death.

Richard crosses the street back to Lorilei. It's over, he tells her. It's done.

When I began writing this story I thought it was because of the man on the tape. I thought it was because of Ricky. In him I saw my grandfather. I wanted to understand.

But I think now that I write because of Lorilei. Her story didn't end the afternoon that Richard embraced her in the motel room while, across the road, Ricky was led away in handcuffs. Ten years after the first trial, Ricky's death sentence was overturned. He was taken off death row and sent back to Calcasieu Parish to await another trial.

That trial was in 2003. It was the trial that had ended just before I came to Louisiana. That it had just ended was the reason the lawyer showed me the tape.

I have the transcript. Day two of the trial, the prosecution calls Lorilei to the stand. She tells the jury about handing Jeremy his BB gun. "That was the last time I saw him," she says. She catches herself. "I mean—that was the last time I saw him alive." She tells them about going to the Lawson house to search for him. About meeting Ricky. Using the phone.

The prosecutor thanks her. The judge excuses her. She returns to her seat. The trial continues.

But on day four, the defense calls her to the stand.

The jurors must be so confused at this moment. She's the dead boy's mother. She's already testified. They've been looking at pictures of Jeremy's body for days. At one point a juror has broken down crying at the photographs of the body, and the judge has had to stop the trial. Why is the defense calling her?

But she rises and walks to the stand. She knows all about Ricky's life now. She's spent years learning. She sits down in the wooden box, smooths her dress over her hips, and turns in her seat to look at the jury.

"Do you have anything you'd like to say to the jury?" the defense attorney asks. He's a tall, slim Brit. He's been defending Ricky for twenty years.

"Yes," she says. Her voice steady. "I do."

The room must be silent, everyone rapt. Lorilei readies herself. These are the words she's practiced.

"Even though I can hear my child's death cry, I, too, can hear Ricky Langley cry for help."

It's Ricky she testifies for. She tries to keep him alive.

I read her words in the courtroom, and what I see is my father, as he folds his fingers around my grandfather's hand. He feels the weight of my grandfather's hand in his. He lifts, and helps hoist the old man into the car so he can bring him across the bridge. So he can bring him home to us.

I want—I need—to understand.

Part Two: Consequence

Eleven

Arizona and Louisiana, 1964–1965

The year is 1964, and twenty-four-year-old Alcide Langley, the man who will be Ricky's father, steers a station wagon along a highway in Red Rock, Arizona. Maybe to understand is to go back to the beginning, and for Ricky I must start here. I imagine the station wagon my parents had when I was a child, but that was the early 1980s, so subtract, now, the faux-wood paneling, the power steering. Give this family a smaller car, and in the back, five children crammed in, four across, with the baby balanced between her sisters' kneecaps. The car's trunk holds their belongings in cardboard boxes bound with twine; beneath the girls' feet are smaller boxes that make their little legs stretch almost straight out. Beyond the car, out into the distance, rises the eponymous rock, blazing red and orange, more like fire than any horizon that Alcide, born a child of the Louisiana swamp, has ever known. The earth glows as though lit from within.

As though it is scorched and barren. As Alcide drives, he aches for—he senses like a memory behind everything—the lush greens, the hopeful blues, of California. The sight of a palm tree silhouetted against the sky made even his life feel like a movie. He never wanted to leave. But his job at an auto plant, arranged for him by his uncle, was what had allowed him and Bessie to move just outside Los Angeles five years before. That job supported all of them: him, Bessie, and the five children she now turns around in her seat to shush. Alcide lost the job. Without it, there's nothing for them in California.

"Quit that!" Bessie says to Oscar. He's teasing his little sister Darlene again, poking her until she squirms and laughs, and if he keeps it up she'll drop Vicky, the baby balanced between Darlene's and Francis's knees. Oscar, the oldest, is a freckled boy of five, with hair Bessie cut with the aid of a mixing bowl and a gap-toothed, ready grin. Someday a lawyer will hold up his picture next to a photo of another little boy with that smile, and make a point about how similar they look, but not yet—it is still February 28, 1964, and for a few moments, at least, Oscar is still alive. He pokes Darlene one more time in the side, and she says "Mommy!" and the baby laughs. The baby, too, has only a few more minutes to live.

Bessie ignores Darlene. The children will work it out; they always do. She's not happy they're going home, either, but it sure will be easier to have relatives around.

They'll settle in the small clot of towns around Lake Charles, Louisiana—Hecker, LeBleu, Iowa—where Bessie's brother lives and where Alcide's father is buried. Bessie and Alcide courted in these towns. Maybe they necked behind the pecan trees that ring the old graveyard, or laughed together in the gas station's parking lot. They'd both left school after eighth grade, Alcide a local boy and Bessie new in town, from Indiana. He was seventeen, she was sixteen when they tied the knot. They married for love, not for need; Oscar wasn't born until ten months later, the following April. When the local paper ran its annual May announcement of spring births, it listed Bessie and Alcide's son as "Baby boy Langley." They hadn't settled on a name yet, that was how badly they wanted to get this new family right. Finally they chose the name Oscar for the history it had on both sides: Bessie's father's name and the name of the brother Alcide had lost when he was just a boy, dead in a car crash at eighteen. Alcide had been eight at the time. His brother was a god to him. Then a lost one.

A year later, Bessie was pregnant again. This time the baby was a girl and the name Francis came more easily. Darlene the year after that. Then Alcide had finally gotten it in his head that maybe they could try their luck in Los Angeles. Bessie had always wanted to go—she was used to the idea that the sprawl of a country was something you could cross. No more living amid his parents and eight brothers and sisters and their families, roots so strong they bound you. A new life. New adventure.

But it turned out to be harder than they had thought. Lonelier, too. And now there's no choice but to go home with no money, no prospects, Alcide driving the whole way back like a dog with his tail between his legs. For seven hours now, on unrelenting highway, Alcide has been driving. For twenty hours still, he will. Beside him, Bessie rests, and if her seat has a lap belt (which in 1964 has only begun to come standard in the front decks of cars, and are rarely in the back) she has left it undone.

Almost thirty years from now, when the lawyers tell this story at the murder trial of Bessie and Alcide's unborn son, they will move what happens next to the pitch-black middle of the night, as though it is unthinkable in bright midday light. But in 1964 it is two o'clock in the afternoon, and Alcide sweats in the sun. There is no air conditioning, and the air outside the rolled-down windows blows as hot as a heater. Under the windshield, the sun's heat must concentrate and beat down on Alcide. The children need food; the children need clothing; the children need. He cannot give the children what they need. Maybe now the sweat stings his eyes and he reaches one hand up to wipe the sweat away, and this—just this instant, when his hand cups his eyes, when his eyes are not on the road and his hand is not on the wheel—maybe this is how it happens. At the trials, the lawyers will question whether Alcide in this moment was drunk. Does he now have a flask hidden under his seat, a flask that holds liquor he must balance the wheel to gulp down, but that makes all the long hours of giving up—of steering his family right toward giving up—possible? For some acts the heart must be steeled. But as he is about to lose so much, I must find a kinder way to tell this story. Alcide sweats in the heat.

He does not see the bridge abutment.

The car slides off the road and into the abutment. The windshield shatters, throwing the family into the air. Oscar, the only boy, the beloved boy—his head is severed clear off. The baby girl dies. The middle sisters—Francis, Darlene, and Judy—live. Alcide lives; the sisters will have a father. And Bessie, who right now lies unconscious at the bottom of a concrete ditch, is falling into a coma that will keep her in a dark sleep for days to come—but she, too, will live. The sisters will have a mother.

Her hips are smashed. Her pelvis, smashed. In the years to come, she will endure thirty operations on her right leg before the doctors give up and amputate it. Now, while Bessie lies in a coma in an Arizona hospital, Alcide arranges to take the girls back to Louisiana. The same local paper that announced Oscar's birth runs a notice of the crash and a service to be held at a cemetery, ringed in pecan trees, in Jefferson Davis Parish.

At Hebert Cemetery, Alcide buries Oscar and the baby in an unmarked grave at the foot of his father's stone, leaving space for when he dies, and beside him, a space for Bessie. As he stands at the grave and watches his children go into the ground, he must wonder how soon she'll need it. He must square his shoulders and wipe at his eyes and pray to keep the family he's been left with. Then he and the girls move in with Bessie's brother Lyle and his wife, Luann. Lyle and Luann are strict Pentecostal. They don't have indoor plumbing, and decades from now, at the time of the trials, they still won't. They don't play music. They take in children who need help, they're kind like that—but sometimes, with Luann's sternness and the way they keep taking in children even when the cupboards are bare, you never can tell if it's generosity or if it's that God won't give them enough suffering to prove their faith to him, and so they'll arrange privation themselves.

But they're there when Alcide needs them. Soon he has a new job, a long-haul trucking company that will keep him on the road for days at a time. I imagine him that first morning. He rises early and stands outside, ready to go, just after dawn. He'll walk the mile to the pickup spot. It's October; the grass is wet and jungle-wild in the morning dew, the earth more pungently alive than it was even in California. He feels that new smell like a clot of earth in his throat.

He could choke on all that's new. Darlene and Judy follow him outside and stand in front of the house, silent, wide-eyed, watching him the way they've been all morning. Darlene's almost four now and has said little in the past few weeks. Judy's two and keeps asking, *Where's Oscar, where's Mama, I want baby.*

"You girls mind Luann and I'll be back soon," Alcide says. He doesn't say *home*.

Darlene's face twists like she's about to cry.

"Aw, honey, you'll be all right," he says. He rubs at his neck where the collar itches. He's had the flannel shirt for years, but Luann insisted on mending the elbow and starching the collar, and its stiffness is irritating him. In one hand he folds the brim of a new white hat with the trucking company's logo. Flattens it, works it with his fingers, crushes it in a fist, opens it again. "You'll be all right," he repeats.

Then he goes.

To see him standing there on the grass, the sun beating on his broad face, the sweat settling into the folds of his forehead, I work from the picture the local newspaper ran of him and Bessie on their fiftieth wedding anniversary. His face is square, his skin rough, his eyes behind thick glasses are heavy-lidded with age. I try to scrub off time from the picture, erase all that the decades have brought.

But there are parts of the story where the record is so forceful, where what happens is so striking, that the facts overwhelm my imagination.

Such as what happens to Bessie. When she wakes from the coma, she's transferred to Charity Hospital in New Orleans, a three-hour drive from where the girls live with Luann and Lyle in Hecker. It's too far to be close to her babies and too close to be the kind of freeing far that carried her and Alcide to California. It's just stuck, just waiting. In-between time.

There, in the state Bessie wanted so badly to leave, the doctors construct a cast to hold her body. They lay wet strips of plaster in rows from her ankles to the top of her chest, until all of her is imprisoned in stiff white. A hole over her genitals allows waste to exit. Her legs they fix splayed open, with a metal bar running between her ankles that the hospital orderlies will yank to move her. Only her arms are free, and when Luann takes Darlene to see her in the hospital—Darlene is just a child now, but someday she will be the one who rises and walks to the front of the courtroom to tell the story of her family—Bessie is able to lift her arms. "Mama," Darlene says, and Bessie pulls Darlene to her and starts to weep. Darlene will remember that hug forever: the familiar pull of the familiar arms, her mother's familiar love, the alarming tears falling wet on her mother's face and, instead of the soft familiar lap, the cast.

Months pass as Bessie lies in the hospital. One month, two months, three. On her back, in the plaster cast, she stares up at the ceiling. What kind of in-body suffering is she doing alone in this place? What will she have to carry with her later? She stares at the ceiling for so many hours she must start to see patterns in the tiles. The tiles are cracked and have water damage. Sometimes the spindly rust-colored lines must look to her like a clawed hand, sometimes like the striated jasper rocks she used to pick out of the riverbank when she was a child. She loved those rocks when they were wet, when they shined and sparkled in the sunlight. But they always turned dull as they dried.

Encircled by a curtain that hangs on a track around her bed, Bessie is alone. But beyond the curtain the room is full of unseen women. Wards meant for twenty hold forty. Only their moans reach her, seeping through the thin fabric of the curtain.

And the smells. The way rot wheedles in, the awareness of nearby death that creeps up your nostrils, crawls over your skin. Infections pass through, too. Decades from now, a doctor will remember a night eight women died on just one ward, and give thanks that those times are over. But now Bessie is in the middle of them. She can do nothing but lie in her white cocoon and wait. Try not to listen. Try not to smell. In the months she lies here, guards from Angola regularly bring inmates to the hospital. Angola, where her son will someday be an inmate. A buyout scheme: The guards and the technicians and doctors who treat the inmates have been paid to look the other way while they escape. At least once, while Bessie lies in her bed, an inmate is discovered gunfire rings through the hospital. Through the curtain, she must listen.

She knows the sound of approaching steps, can tell when the steps are heavy enough that an orderly's about to poke his head through the curtain and wheel her off to be x-rayed. Sometimes when she hears voices she can't tell if they're real or if her mind's making them up for company. Sometimes the orderlies bring her new drugs, which she swallows still lying on her back on the cot. Drugs for the infections, drugs to help her sleep, drugs for the pain. Mostly, drugs for the pain. The drugs do not take away the pain. When Alcide visits he brings her bottles of liquor, and they keep the curtain closed around them as he unscrews the cap and pours. In the early months, when they still fear one of the nurses will notice, he pours gently, to muffle the sound. Then quickly, once they realize no one will. Carefully he hands the cup to Bessie, who tilts it to swallow. The liquor burns as it enters the body of a woman so malnourished she's losing half her body weight. But it helps.

At Christmas, the doctors let her leave the hospital for a few days. Alcide borrows a pickup for the occasion, and with the orderlies' help gets her lying down in the back on some pillows Luann piled there for her. Luann and Lyle move into the living room and give Bessie and Alcide the bedroom. On the bed she can be eye-level with her girls. At night, Alcide lies down next to her, and the children come, too, and bend over her, in turn, to touch their foreheads to her lips. In those moments, they are all together again as a family—all of them, that is, who are left. The girls go to bed, and Bessie and Alcide lie together in the night. When the year turns to 1965, the family celebrates. Then Bessie returns to the hospital.

For five more months she lies on her back encased in plaster, five more months of the X-rays and the drugs for the infections and the drugs for the pain that do not work and five more months of the whiskey. Her body withers inside the cast, until she weighs less than seventy pounds. She is the size of a child.

But while she gets smaller, the cast tightens. Not everywhere. Only around her midsection.

Bessie is five months pregnant.

> TRIAL TRANSCRIPT, 2003
> Judge: "I know I can't ask questions, but—"
> Defense attorney: "Would you like me to ask the question?"
> Judge: "I just want to know how you get pregnant in that thing."
> Defense attorney: "Judge, I was trying to be delicate and not ask those questions."
> Judge: "I just said what everybody was thinking, you know—what's up?"
> Defense attorney: "Doctor, I believe we've decided to leave it to people's imaginations, have we not?"

In the courtroom, the story is told this way: She is in a body cast. She becomes pregnant.

Ricky grows inside her.

Imagine Bessie's joy when the doctors tell her. Her baby is dead and her boy is dead and the year has brought grief and pain unimaginable and somehow out of all this pain, on one Christmas bed, new life has begun. The doctors had told her she'd never be pregnant again.

This baby is a miracle.

Picture the doctors as they stand by her bed. The white coats they wear, the stethoscopes that hang from their necks, the lives and education they've had. Yes, they know she's happy, but this pregnancy cannot be thought a miracle. She's been on every drug they can give her, many not intended for pregnant women. The fetus is five months along, which means for five months it has grown against the hard plaster of the cast. She's been x-rayed countless times. Those might have killed off the pregnancy, but the fetus survived, and now who knows what it has survived with. "Your pregnancy cannot be carried to term," one doctor says. "It's not safe. Not for you, and not for any child."

"This proves you can get pregnant again," the other reasons with her. "Better to let your body heal now. Better to ready it for another chance."

Perhaps Alcide holds hands with Bessie as they listen, and perhaps between their pressed, complicit palms passes the knowledge of what the doctors may not know: the whiskey. Eight years must pass before *Roe v. Wade,* Charity is a Catholic teaching hospital, and still the doctors insist: This baby cannot be born.

But this mother is not going to let her child go.

So the doctors do what they must, and take a saw to the cast, cutting a wide moon into it to halo Bessie's stomach. Bessie does what a mother must: Inside her cast, she waits. And the baby grows.

On September 11, 1965, they cut Bessie open in one long slash across her abdomen and pull the baby from her. A boy. Seven pounds, two ounces. Ricky Joseph Langley, Bessie names him, the boy who will live in place of the dead son. Alcide and Luann come to the hospital to take him home to where his older sisters wait, giddy, ready to meet their new brother.

Years from now a lawyer will stand in front of twelve jurors and lift a stack of paper made from taping together the pregnancy warnings of all the drugs Bessie took. Then he'll drop the bottom page—and the pages will unfurl all the way to the floor and smack it. Demerol and Codeine. Librium. Atropine, chloral hydrate, Diabex, and Fluothane. Imferon, Lincocin, Luminal. Menadione, Nembutal, and Vistaril. Then all the X-rays.

Years from now, those twelve jurors will sentence the man who is this child to die. He will be sent to live in a small tile cell on a block where five times he will hear guards come to the grate of another man, pull that man from his cell and lead him off down a corridor and into a chamber from which he'll never return. The man who is this child will wait in his cell and listen to the condemned man's footsteps fade down the corridor. The man who is this child will wait to know when it will be his turn.

But none of this, yet. Not in 1965. In 1965, a proud older sister lifts the corner of a blanket and peeks at the brother who is now hers. "Two arms, two legs, five fingers, five toes," Darlene will say years later, remembering this moment.

That baby was perfect. She checked.

Twelve

New Jersey, 1987

I fall in love with the law through objects. The windowsill of my father's office is cluttered with them: a snarled metal wheel-well cover that survived a car crash; a plastic replica of a spine, nicked off-kilter as though by a knife; a pair of bullet casings I roll in my palm like marbles, left behind by bullets that didn't hit my father's client. When my father wins that verdict, the casings disappear from the windowsill. A week or two later, while my parents are in their bedroom dressing to go out, my mother surprises him with a small wrapped box with a ribbon around it. He unties the ribbon, tears off the paper, eases up the lid, and there it is, the trophy he didn't realize was missing: those cracked casings, now encased in gold and mounted on cuff links. She smiles at him, takes his palm in hers, and gently twists his wrist. Carefully, she slides the metal prong through his shirt cuff, then flips up the end, securing my father's cuff with the missed chances of someone else's life.

A decade and a half from now, when I've grown up and followed my parents into the law—when I am still certain that I believe in the law—I'll be assigned to work in the vast intern room of a Louisiana law firm while I wait for an office to become available. The intern room is windowless, situated in the heart of a warren-like building. It holds a cluster of craft tables pressed together, each like the one my mother kept in the playroom for us when I was a child. Each table holds a boxy beige computer that still uses floppy disks. The computers contain a database of legal briefs we'll modify for all the cases that pass through the office.

Against the bookshelves in one corner stands a mannequin that must have been used to illustrate a defendant's position during a shooting death. Now its neck is strung with colorful Mardi Gras beads. The mannequin is black, one arm white, and an intern has posed the arm into a permanently lewd gesture at its crotch. On the floor to my left sits a large cardboard box with its top open, full of folded felt blankets. They're not here for the late nights we some-times spend in the office. They're too hot to be of use in this swampy climate. Instead, intern rumor has it that they were once used to illustrate the smothering death of a child. Working in that room afternoon after afternoon, looking up cases as the Pixies blare from my computer speakers, it will again be the objects that compel me the most. That return me to the feeling of my childhood, to the col-lision between the story and the artifact. Next to the box lies a rep-lica of a white plaster cast in the shape of a woman's torso and legs.

Bessie.

I stare at that cast every day and I remember the cracked casings on my father's wrists that held the story of something long ago. Lying in that cast, immobile and imprisoned—is it possible Bessie wanted to make love to Alcide, that Ricky was born of a desperate attempt at connection, a desperate attempt to regain what was shattered in the crash? Or was it Alcide who wanted it, always a drinker with a temper, now more so after the crash? Was what happened—was what began Ricky—love? Rape? Something hard to define, in between?

When I am twelve, my mother decides to go to law school. Quickly, law spreads everywhere in our house. The bookshelves hold mem-oirs by the hard-charging trial lawyers my father admires. He plays cassettes of their closing statements while he does push-ups on the carpet of the staircase landing, or sits on the steps shining his shoes with a wooden brush. In her early forties now, my mother attends law school not part-time at night but full-time during the day, with students in their early twenties. Evenings, while dinner cooks on the stove, she spreads her books on the white Formica table. They are each three inches thick, with hard burgundy covers. She opens one and leans close to its dictionary-thin pages, licking the pad of her ring finger to turn each page. Sometimes she holds her finger there, and pokes up her head to root for a yellow highlighter she'll use to underscore the text. Then one of our school No. 2 pencils. She marks a note in the margins, sits back and bites the pencil in its middle. I bite my pencils the same way. The house is soon full of pencils nearly splintered at the center. Years later, I remember the waxy taste of the yellow paint, the papery taste of splintered wood, the sharp metallic of the graphite. When dinner's ready, she calls to us. We set our plates on the other end of the table, and while my mother studies, we eat.

My mother has a talent for law, it turns out. She makes good grades and joins moot court. Soon my father takes over dinner, wrapping pork chops in bacon and provolone, griddling them and dousing them with ketchup. We have been raised my mother's way, eating carob instead of chocolate, taught as toddlers that the word *candy* meant bananas topped with plain, unsweetened yogurt—at least until we got to kindergarten and our friends corrected us. The griddled, tangy fat against the cool sweet slip of the ketchup shocks our tongues. That year, my father makes our Halloween costumes, and he throws himself into the job with a newcomer's enthusiasm. With yellow fabric and a staple gun, he turns me into the Cowardly Lion from *The Wizard of Oz*. The television show *ALF,* about a furry brown alien with a porcine nose, is popular that fall, and for my brother my father staples together brown felt and paints a cardboard toilet paper tube into a snout. Next year, the stores will be crowded with ALF costumes, but that year, when the local children line up in the town auditorium on Halloween, the municipal employee serving as the judge walks down the line of children dressed as clowns or in witches' hats, their ninja blacks and their fairy-tale pinks, and pins the blue ribbon on my brother's chest. When we have a school vacation while the law school is in session, it's my father's turn for a break and my mother takes us to class with her—and to the cafeteria. My brother is still frighteningly skinny; anything he wants to eat is cause for celebration, and later we'll all talk about how much we love law school when what we mean is we love macaroni and cheese.

But it's the professors who make an impression on me. I sit with my knees close together in a hard-backed chair at a pull-down desk, impossibly grown-up law students all around me, and stare at a woman with bobbed gray hair who wears a burgundy jacket and skirt. I've never seen a woman in a suit before. Standing in front of an enormous three-part blackboard, she raps the board with the chalk and begins. "Imagine . . ." she instructs the students, and begins to describe a set of circumstances. I don't know yet to call what comes out of her mouth a hypothetical, the quick situations sketched by law professors to teach students to analyze how a principle applies to different circumstances. I recognize it for what it is: a story.

My mother's law school loan money is a windfall. My parents have always loved money, always had the faith that more will appear if they spend it. They take us to the French Caribbean, renting a house at the edge of a cliff. They've miscalculated, it turns out: Dinner the first night costs as much as they've planned for the week. But we are already there, the trip has already begun, and soon the week has the feel of magic.

During the day, we run barefoot on the beach, and try to shimmy up coconut trees, able to scale only a few feet before we tumble back onto the sand, laughing. We collect the fallen coconuts from around the trunks and pitch them into rocks, trying to smash our way to the sweet meat inside. My father has rigged up speakers at the house, and at night he sends French torch songs sailing over the deck. He and my mother hold hands and kiss as they listen to the music. My sisters and I stand on the deck, the shale tile cool against the soles of our feet—for a week, it seems we never have to wear shoes—and take turns twirling, the matching turquoise silk skirts my mother has bought us sliding coolly up our legs, our laughter flying out over the ocean. We are all light and happy and far, far away from home.

The last day, we stand on an airport tarmac waiting for the flight that will carry us home. Back to the Saturdays of my grandparents' arrival, back to my father sitting late into the night at the kitchen table, drinking, or the scrape of his car tires sending gravel spinning off into the dark. I remember a new heaviness in my body, but maybe that's the work of time and my looking back. On the tarmac, the island sunlight ricochets off the parked bodies of silver planes, so bright it stings my eyes.

My brother stands in front of me. He is still thin, still not quite out of the danger woods of our birth, and the crew cut my mother made him get for the trip has only emphasized the shape of his skull, leaving his eyes round and wondering. While we wait, he curls his palms under his chin like paws and juts his lower teeth out. His eyes big, his head small, he makes a perfect chipmunk. My sisters and I laugh. Already he is the entertainer, the one who, sick for so long as a child, now wants only to make others laugh. Next he tells a joke. The setup has seven Chinese brothers in it. For the punch line, one fries in the electric chair.

"What's that?" I ask. I am a proud child and I hate having to ask, but something in the phrase "electric chair" demands that it be known.

"He got the death penalty," my brother says.

By the time I understand his words, I am against the death penalty. Death is what I am afraid of. Death is what my sister was lost to; death is what the grown-ups fear for my brother; death is what I have nightmares of. Through my mother's books and my father's stories, I have begun to think of the Constitution as a document of hope. The law I love can impose death? Never mind the reasons in law books. This is where it starts: with horror. From this moment on, I will always be against the death penalty.

———

For my mother's graduation, my father has a white tent erected in the long sprawl of our backyard. That night darkness envelops the tent, and there's a moment when the band stops playing, the crowd he has invited hushes, and a waiter in a vest emerges from the dark carrying a cake, its top aflame. The waiter sets it on the table with a flourish. My mother's eyes are wet and shiny in the candlelight as she bends, beckoning to us children. Together, we blow out the candles, and what the cake says is suddenly clear: L & M-L. My father, tall and burnished in a tuxedo, squeezes my mother's hand. They will become law partners.

The building they find to rent is at the center of our town, along the railroad tracks, across from the old train station. On the other side of the station is the big Catholic church. A few steps down the block from their new office is the movie theater and a newsstand that sells bubblegum, *Archie* comics, and books of logic games. Around the corner is the one apartment building, where the only magnolia tree blossoms lush every spring. My father takes the third floor for his criminal and malpractice cases. On the second floor, my mother becomes a family lawyer.

I am raised in the law the way other children are raised in religion. When my siblings and I gather around the table for family dinners, we don't bow our heads to say grace. Instead we raise them high and try to catch the words that fly between my parents. The divorce fights she's handling, the battered women she advocates for in those early years when she still takes low-paying work. The medical malpractice cases that pay nothing if he loses, but big—one-third of the verdict—if he wins. A gambler's payday, and one that rewards curiosity. "I like the law because I get to learn a little bit of everything," my father tells me. I recognize something of myself in his words—and something of the way I love the objects on his windowsill.

As a child I learn to write on long legal pads pilfered from my parents' office. I lie on my stomach on the nubby carpet and try to fill the pads' lined pages with my writing. I have invented a character I name Cassie, who lives on the same island we visit every summer and goes to the movies in the same theater. The difference is that Cassie loves a boy, Bobby, and so is unlike me.

I am ten and then eleven and then twelve, and though my friends all talk about boys, I don't have crushes. I think love is foolish and distracting and I alternately pity and scorn my friends when they talk about it. I don't like pop music, because all the songs are about love, and I think most of the preteen magazines at the comic store downstairs are silly, because all they talk about is crushes. It's not just that I feel too tall, too awkward, and too dark, with my frizzy hair in a town of straight blond hair, to think a boy could like me. It's something deeper than that, though I can't say what. How I feel about it is like the answer I give when, a few months after Christmas, my mother asks me what happened to a new stuffed animal. "Shh," I say, and point to a corner of my room. "It's sleeping." When she asks me again a few days later—"Hasn't it woken up by now?"—the answer must come from a place inside me that understands more about my brother than I'll let on. "It's in a coma," I say.

But that's a story my mother tells me later, one that becomes family lore, her face always looking slightly bewildered as she tells it, her tone always a little too light. What I remember from those years is standing next to my bed, the smell of spring grass clippings and the growl of my father's mower coming in through the open window, sunlight that feels far away filtering in through the glass. I climb onto the mattress and stand tall on it, something I'm forbidden to do. I push my bare feet into the soft blanket for balance. I ball my small hands into fists that I jam into my sides, arms cocked out akimbo, imagining myself a fighter, and in this pose I swear allegiance to myself. I'll never fall in love, never do any of that froufrou stuff all the girls I know seem to want. I won't lose my edge. Not ever. I hardly know what I am promising myself except this: a different life. I carry this knowledge of what I am heading for like a secret inside me, a debt privately carried, a future owed.

To hold it doesn't seem strange. All around me are unspoken secrets. Beneath what can be said is still the thrum of a world that belongs only to darkness. My sisters and I do not talk about the nights of the past five years, which have vanished as though they never happened. If at night, my father sometimes wails and throws himself on the bed, I understand that this is a life separate from the one my parents live in their office at the center of town. If at night, when I come down to the kitchen he's not sweet anymore but angry, angry at me or angry at life, and he curses me or tells me he wants to die, I understand that that has not happened, nor have the nights the wheels of his car spin out of the driveway as my mother stands at the front door in her bathrobe and sobs. Always, the next morning, when I find my mother darkening her eyebrows at her vanity table with the bulbs all around that light up her face, she says, "I'm sure your father didn't say that." Or "You must be misremembering." I am, I understand, to be as expressionless as the careful face I arrange for myself when the doorbell rings on Saturday afternoons and it's my grandparents, dropped off on the porch as my father finishes parking the car in the driveway. If at night, sometimes I can't sleep because I watch the crack of light around the door and listen for the creak of the stairs, I know better than to mention this in the morning. At twelve I still wet the bed, and though I don't have the words to say why, if I did I would say that it makes me feel safe. That when I feel the bed all warm and wet around me I know: Nothing will come for me in the night. Nothing will want to. In the morning I scoop up the smelly sheets, fold the mattress cover over the wet parts so they won't touch me, turn my nose away and carry the bundle down to the basement steps, where I can throw it into the air and let it fall to the foot of the steps, where the maid my parents have hired will deal with it. She is the one who, in the morning, cleans up the empty wine bottles and ice cream wrappers my father has left at the kitchen table. Each morning, through careful ministrations taken while my family slumbers upstairs, the house is erased and begins anew.

So maybe this, too, is why I come to love the objects in my father's office: Whatever secret they hold locked inside can't be erased. The evidence is there, solid. Waiting for the future to come looking.

Thirteen

Louisiana, 1965–1983

After the crash, the house the young family makes for itself is a haunted one, but it lasts. Bessie stays in the hospital for months after Ricky's birth. Then she is allowed to come home, and she and Alcide live with Lyle and Luann in their two-bedroom house. Luann tends to the four children, Lyle brings home his pay, and Alcide goes out on the road for his trucking job. Nights he's home, Lyle and Luann sleep in the living room, giving Alcide and Bessie their marital bed. It's a hard arrangement. They were used to living on their own in California. Now Luann has an opinion on everything where the children are concerned, and who can blame her when she's the one raising them? It's all Bessie can do to navigate the house on her crutch, navigate the day through the layers of pain and the shots Luann helps her with. It's easier not to chafe. Bessie's always been wilder than Luann, but now she bends to her Pentecostal ways. No music. No television. No booze. Luann fills the silence by talking of God. She must smell the alcohol on Bessie's breath; she must guess at what Alcide carries back for her from his stops on the road. But Luann tries, too. She bites her lip to keep herself silent, turns her cheek the way the Bible tells her to. The women will never be friends, but in silence they make it through.

It's harder on Alcide, maybe. At twenty-seven, he wants to provide. The care Bessie gets at Charity is subsidized, and the trucking company's good work, but what's left of the bills still eats up

Alcide's pay. They're guests in Lyle's house, barely contributing to their keep. He tries not to let that burn him. He goes silent, too. He waits. Puts aside what money he can. Tells himself they're young still, that there's time ahead for a new beginning. When he stops for coffee on the road, the pamphlets of lots for sale that every truck stop diner has in a rack by the door must catch his eye. He must take the pamphlets to his booth and flip through them as the waitress refills his coffee. "You all right here, hon?" she asks. He nods at her distractedly, peering at the tiny grainy photos of rural lots, his mind already off somewhere else, into an imagined future. Maybe that thirty acres out by Moss Bluff, with long crabgrass and a creek running through the back. For a minute he pictures Bessie sitting by the creek. Not Bessie as she is now, braced against the crutch, her face in the grim line of pain, but Bessie as she was ten years ago, a girl of sixteen with hair the color of river reeds and teeth as bright as her white cotton dress. A smile that always made him remember laughing with his brothers when he was a boy. Or maybe this other ad—a small shotgun house in New Orleans, persuade Bessie to give city living a try. For an instant he has a flash of Bessie's trying to make it from one room to the other with them all in a row like that. He can't know yet that in a few years the doctors will amputate her leg, but even now it is constantly infected, hard for her to walk on. He sighs and puts down the flyer. Swigs back his coffee, feels the dregs' bitter splash against his throat, swallows, puts down the empty mug. Fishes a dime from his pocket, slaps the coin down on the table, stands to go. The doctors say three operations a year are ahead, and already the pain's like a fog over Bessie. Pain or grief, who can say. It'll be a long time before he gets his wife back. If he ever gets his wife back. He puts the trucking company's hat back on and gathers the pamphlets in his fist. Leaves them on the rack, a little crumpled. Let some other man dream.

So it's a relief, it must be, to swing himself up into the cab of his truck, start the great growl of the engine, and ease the truck out of the lot. High in the cab, he lets the miles of black tar clear his mind. No past behind him, no future ahead. Only road. His only responsibility to go forward, clear as the bright white lines of the lane markers. Sometimes, maybe at night when there's no distraction, or maybe when the afternoon sun is high and bright overhead, and the glass windshield again concentrates the heat until he sweats and he feels the hard nubs of the wheel go a little slippery beneath his palms again, sometimes then the crash must come back to him. The hot choked memory dream of that afternoon. His hand reaching up to wipe at his forehead. The concrete rushing at him through the windshield, as though it were the thing hurtling itself toward collision, not him. Not the car. Not his family. Then Bessie's scream. The shock of the impact entered him through the wheel, up through his bones. The smell of burning. His last sight of Oscar.

But Alcide is a pragmatic man, proud of and defined by the way he can keep going. A skill learned young, after his brother's death in the motorcycle crash. A skill he needs now.

So most days, he's all right. He goes on the road; he makes his deliveries; he comes back when he can and he kisses his wife on her forehead and sits in Lyle's house at Lyle's table to eat the meal Lyle's wife has made. When the grief comes, and when what the grief feels like is anger, he takes one of Bessie's whiskey bottles and swallows the silence down. He remembers to kiss his daughters and he remembers to love his broken-down wife and he remembers to hide the empty bottles so Luann won't see. These years are hard, but they have a kind of hope to them. He waits to make his new beginning. He waits to start anew.

Then Ricky turns four, and he can. There's a new baby, Jamie. A son whose life has nothing to do with the crash. The doctors had to cut Bessie open again to pull him out, and Jamie will turn out to be blind in one eye and hard of hearing, but the child is perfection. Two boys, three girls, a raise that puts a little money in his pocket finally. Alcide sends away for the housing kit catalog, and he and Bessie choose the only kit they can afford. It's nothing fancy—four rooms on a foursquare frame, no flourishes—but it will be their home. That fall is clear and bright, good weather for building. He's not naive or reckless enough to think they can move far away. No longer does his head fill with thoughts of California. Someone has to take care of the children through Bessie's operations. But they can get next door, at least. He'll build on Luann and Lyle's lot.

Alcide is still strong—the muscles in his broad shoulders will never leave him—just starting to go soft around the middle from the trucking. He and Lyle work long hours in the sun, laying down the frame for the house, building up the walls. With each wood beam, with each nail he drives through it, he is laying down the bones for their new life.

When I imagine him there, kneeling at the frame of the house, a nail gripped between his teeth, him hammering on a board while the broad sun beats and sweat runs rivulets down his forehead and his back, I see my father, a sawhorse erected in the backyard and one of the house's repairs under way. I hear the din of an old boom box playing a ball game, the batter's hit and the crowd's responding roar. I stand at the edge of the grass, the blades coming up itchy yet soft between my toes, and it's how Ricky would have stood, watching Alcide hammering in the heat. The eldest son. At four, Ricky is a normal-looking child. A little big-eared. A little skinny. But he laughs when Darlene or Judy tickles him. And he's a big brother now.

Ricky pads over to Alcide, who must look up and see his son haloed against the high afternoon light. On the radio Waylon Jennings has just finished crooning a lonesome line, the strum of the guitar fading out to an audience's applause. Ricky's shy around his daddy still. He just stands there, waiting. Alcide has a flash of Oscar at four, the way Oscar used to run to greet him at the door and how he would fall to his knees to catch him and wrestle.

Now Alcide pinches the nail from his teeth and holds it out to Ricky. "You going to help me with this, Son?"

Ricky nods. He bends forward and takes the nail, his face serious and watchful.

"Hold it right there," Alcide says. He gestures to the board. "That's right. Just like that." The child toddles closer.

Alcide brings the hammer down to the nail slowly and taps, careful not to clip Ricky's fingers. "Good, good. Go get the next one, you hear?" He'll have to go back over this later, driving each of the nails deeper into the wood. But for now the sun is high and the beer is cold and the music is good and he's here with his son, his living healthy son. He waits for Ricky to fish another nail from the box. The afternoon could last all day. Alcide wouldn't mind. Let the afternoon last right into a new life.

Alcide pounds the final beams into the frame of the house. He and Lyle dip brushes into sealant to protect the wood from the Louisiana humidity. As they stroke the vinegary liquid over the boards, and the sun begins to sink in the sky, bringing the afternoon to its close, and as Ricky heads back into the house to Bessie's call, how much of the past are they sealing in? How many of the memories Alcide holds have made their way into this house he builds, how much has seeped in through its doors? Think what you will about the drink, about how lately it can't hold back anger, grief slips out of him and blindsides Alcide. Those times he catches himself just as his fist slams into the table, aware, suddenly, of the vein in his forehead, of the rage in his throat, of Ricky cowering in the doorway, small and trembling. Think what you will about the way Bessie sometimes closes herself in the bedroom and sobs, and he doesn't have to ask her why: Oscar's smile ripples through Ricky's, Ricky's voice is an echo. The fact is, the same newspaper that printed the articles about the crash that might have killed this family will print notice of Bessie and Alcide's fiftieth wedding anniversary. A haunted house, maybe. But they survive.

The ghost comes to Ricky in a dream, and Ricky, five years old now, has no choice but to take her hand and follow. Into the night sky they fly, the stars of Orion's Belt and Perseus sparkling above them, the only town Ricky has ever known sleepy and dark below. From this high the roofs are pitched in rows like the tops of crypts in Louisiana graveyards, the distance turning houses for the living as small and perfect as the houses for the dead. The ghost and Ricky fly for what seems like a very long time. Ricky can't see her face, only sense the way her white robes blow in the wind, and though Ricky is scared and tired in the dream he doesn't dare let go of her hand, not with the ground so far away. They fly for a longer time still, the air cold and whistling around them, and on the ground below he sees pink and purple flowers that are somehow lit up even in the dark. He knows they are the flowers his mother remembers from California, the ones she speaks of in her stories of a happier time.

They keep flying.

Then he sees, far below on the ground, a man sitting cross-legged by the side of a highway road, cradling something in his lap as he rocks back and forth over it. His father, Alcide, is a young man, younger than Ricky can remember ever having seen him, with a full, dark head of hair and a trim body. Next to him is a long brown station wagon, its front end smashed in like Ricky has seen in cartoons, all around it broken glass glittering like the stars.

His father is cradling the head of a boy, singing to it. Brown hair like Ricky's, dark eyes like Ricky's, a ring of blood where the neck has been severed. He knows, somehow he knows, that the boy is five years old like him. But the boy is not dead—the head turns and the boy's brown eyes open and look into Ricky's and the boy smiles. He smiles at Ricky as if Ricky is his friend.

For a long time, the dream confuses Ricky. He'll remember it even thirty years from now and tell it to a room of corrections officers. At five he thinks on it and he thinks on it, and then one afternoon when he wakes up from a nap, he asks Bessie who the boy is. The boy with the brown hair, like him.

———

When I was growing up, my mother kept a white filing cabinet in the long playroom my siblings and I shared. The rest of the room was ours, unmistakably the domain of children, its floor serpentined with mazes we'd built from blocks. Bits of Play-Doh crusted between the floorboards lent the air a faintly salty smell. In one corner sat a piano my parents had purchased in the hope that at least one of the four of us might turn out to be as musical as they were not; it was always going out of tune because we banged on it so hard. High up on one wall hung two laminated maps: one of the continents and the other a close-up of the United States. Whenever we returned from a family trip, we children would gather beneath these maps and tilt our small, satisfied faces up to watch as our father traced where we'd been in black grease pencil, plotting our ventures into the wider world.

The playroom was conquered land, ours and ours alone. Yet I knew without ever having been told so that the white metal filing cabinet was not. It belonged to my mother, to some other home and some other life, a life before the fact of us. The cabinet was a steely, shiny white, cold to the touch and stubborn, with a single drawer that had to be braced and then jerked. I watched my mother perform that move with the palm of one hand. What she put in never came out. Copies of our medical records, report cards, copies of our birth certificates, and, most commonly, the photographs we'd smiled for just days before were all shoved in, to be swallowed by the cabinet. My father often told us stories of his childhood, but my mother rarely did, and I felt about the cabinet as I felt about my mother's past. It was a thing guarded from me, and held both the allure of anything forbidden and a kind of silence as solid as stone.

So when, one rare afternoon that I was alone in the room, I mimicked my mother's flat-palmed lift and was rewarded with a hospital chart that I slowly realized wasn't referencing me or my sisters, but another girl, I didn't tell anyone. I hadn't been looking for the chart. I hadn't known it existed to be looked for. But there it was: proof of a baby, proof of the sister now gone.

Bessie braces her hand against the door frame and leans hard against her crutch. The rooms are small but clean, the wallpaper new. She's been making up the beds in Darlene and Ricky's room, and the effort, the balancing, has winded her. The baby Jamie is down for his afternoon nap. The girls and Ricky are home from school. Ricky has fallen asleep on the couch in front of the television and when he wakes up he runs to her and pulls at the corner of her housedress. She knows the look on his face, spooked. He must have had the dream again. "Mama," he says, "who's the boy?"

She's just about to tell him that the dream isn't real, just a dream, and the boy's not real either. Neither she nor Alcide has spoken to the children about the crash. But when she speaks, different words come out. "Follow me, sweetie." Who knows why the past comes through in the moments it does; who knows why a secret suddenly becomes too much to keep? She's never talked to the children about Oscar. The afternoon stretches dangerously before her, all those yawning hours to fill. Maybe time lets it in. Or maybe she's always planned to tell them. Maybe she's planned so privately she's kept the plan a secret even from herself.

Francis, Darlene, Judy, and Ricky follow her into her bedroom. Darlene's nine and I imagine her as overly responsible, a little grown-up, the one who'll shape the family's story. Slightly plump for her age, she takes after Bessie. Judy is eight and so stubborn she sleeps in the living room rather than share with her sister. For Judy I see both my sister's tomboy gait and my own scowl—in the way forty years from now she'll keep her answers curt on the stand at the trial. Francis is eleven and she trails behind, already one foot out of the door.

Then there's Ricky.

Bessie gestures into the closet. "Darlene, why don't you see if you can pull on that handle there?"

Darlene's awed. She's seen the trunk her mother gestures toward, but only by peeking through her mother's hung-up dresses while

Bessie gets ready in the mornings. It's always been a shadow in the dark recesses of the closet. She kneels down in front of the trunk and tugs and tugs but can't move it. Judy kneels beside her and together the sisters wedge and wheedle the trunk forward as Bessie watches. When they have it almost to the door of the closet, Bessie says, "Well, that's all right then," and the children let go the metal brackets and step back, watching.

Bessie settles herself to the floor. It's a complicated procedure but a familiar one. First Darlene takes the crutch from Bessie, holding it in front of her as if a guardsman with a rifle, her face turned away and nose wrinkled up, trying to avoid the smell of the washcloth that's been rolled and rubber-banded to the top to cushion Bessie's armpit. Francis stands on the other side of Bessie, and as Bessie starts to bend her knees Francis positions herself so her mother can balance herself on Judy's shoulder. Then it's a turn and a catch from Francis, with Judy helping, and Bessie is lowered to the floor. The girls settle beside her. Ricky, always a little shy, sinks to the carpet a ways back.

The catch on the trunk is rusted but lifts easily in Bessie's palm. The children watch, transfixed. They know their mama goes into the trunk. They know it the way children know what goes on behind closed doors. But they've never been permitted to watch.

Inside the trunk is a jam of paper. Photographs, dozens of them, black and white and sienna and even a few of the new Polaroids. Some in cellophane envelopes. Who are these strange faces, the children must wonder, these faces in black and white and with the funny dark clothes?

Darlene pops her thumb in her mouth and sucks, an old habit. Francis is sitting on one of her knees, the other leg splayed in front of her, and she shifts now, trying to get a clearer view. No one speaks. There is something about Bessie's quiet right now, her methodical movements, that sparks an undercurrent in the children. They are waiting, even if they don't know what for.

Bessie's hands know where to go. She slides her right hand along the far edge of the trunk, toward the back corner by the hinge, and withdraws two photographs. Then she settles back and lays them right-side up on her lap.

The children cluster closer. One photograph is of a baby in a white christening bonnet on a layette. The photograph is in black and white, but the baby's cheeks and lips have been tinted pink. It looks like a doll.

"That's your sister, Vicky."

The other photograph is of a little boy with a brown bowl cut grinning at the camera, his front tooth missing.

Ricky recognizes him immediately. "That's me!" he says, delighted, and pops off the floor to pluck the photograph from Bessie's hand.

She doesn't give it. "No, baby," she says. "That's your brother Oscar Lee."

Brother. The word must bloom dizzyingly around Ricky, this lonely boy, this boy whose only brother is a baby too young to play with and who spends day after day with Bessie and the girls. This boy who will always be hungry. Brother. "Where is he?" Ricky asks, but as soon as he says those words, he knows. He recognizes him. The brown hair, the eyes, the smile. He's the boy in the dream.

"He died, baby. He and Vicky both did. Before you were born."

There must be a flicker in Francis's mind, in Darlene's and in Judy's. They were four, three, and two that day in the car. The tires' screech as Alcide awoke into the moment, the sun's slant through the windows, then the bright hot slam. Pain. No one has spoken of Oscar since he died. Or the baby. But the memory must be there, living inside Darlene: her hands under the baby's armpits, holding her upright, the baby's ribcage as tiny as a fledging bird's. Darlene's knees pressed against Francis's as they bounced Vicky between them, coaxing her to laugh. Then the car flew forward. The jolt. She let go.

Three decades from now, when Darlene's an adult on the witness stand at Ricky's trial, she'll tell about the afternoon with the trunk simply this way: "That's when Mama told us about the crash."

Ricky returns to the trunk again and again to study the photo of the little boy. At five Ricky is still small for his age, bucktoothed and scrawny. He stutters and he wets his pants when he gets nervous. He has no friends. Oscar becomes his friend. One day Ricky steals the photo, and from then on it's his. When he plays in the woods, he props it up against the roots of a tree and has long conversations with it. He carries it in his pocket to school, patting it with jelly-crusted fingers when there is no one else to eat lunch with. Sometimes one of his sisters hears him talking in a room that otherwise looks empty, and when they ask him whom he's talking to he answers, "Oscar." Sometimes Darlene asks him to close the window next to his bed—she's cold—and he says he can't. Doesn't she see Oscar sitting there in the trees? He doesn't want Oscar to be lonely. The family decides Oscar is harmless, an imaginary friend for the boy who doesn't have any friends.

Then the crying starts. Bessie finds Ricky sitting on the carpet in front of the television set. They keep a framed picture of praying hands on top of the set, but he's knocked it facedown, as though to keep the image away. Ricky's rocking on his knees, clawing at his head. "Make him stop!" he says. "Make Oscar not see me!" When she tells him there's nobody there, he only cries harder.

STATEMENTS BY REPORTERS AND LAW
ENFORCEMENT OFFICERS, 2003
Ricky said he had been visited in a dream by a ghost who took him to the scene of the car accident. After this dream, he began asking questions and found out about the car accident and his brother. He claimed that his brother was his "tormentor/best friend." He said the brother would torment Ricky about taking his place in the family.

The brother died in a car crash before Ricky was born. He said his brother was a thorn in his side and Ricky wanted to get rid of him.

He said he had to get Oscar Lee out of his life.

Then, one afternoon when Ricky is in sixth grade, Bessie answers the phone, and it's his teacher. "Ma'am, who's Oscar Lee?" she asks. When Bessie, shaken, asks why, the woman tells her. Ricky walked to the chalkboard at the front of the classroom and, in front of the whole class, wrote I AM OSCAR LEE LANGLEY. Adult Ricky, looking back, will say this is when he began to molest children younger than himself. He did it starting at the age of nine or ten, he will say. It was easy; the adults were always sending the children off to play together. Luann took in kids as if they were stray cats. There were always plenty around.

Darlene will tell it differently. Ricky was so skinny with those big, thick glasses and jug ears, jittery and uneasy in his skin. Friendless. That everything was fine—that Ricky *wasn't* weird—was something the family colluded in to protect him. "He was just our Ricky, you know," she'll say on the stand when the defense attorney asks her if Ricky seemed sick and maybe she wants to say, *Well, he wasn't normal, but*—. Yes it's true that Bessie drank, and yes it's true that Bessie's cousin showed up some days while the kids were at school with a bottle of whiskey in her purse for Bessie because Bessie couldn't walk well enough to go get it herself, and yes it's true that sometimes when the kids got home Bessie would already be drunk and Alcide already angry. But who could blame her? That leg would be infected again and again before the doctors finally amputated it. They did their best with what they had. Luann and Lyle meant that Ricky had four parents. Not two. The children were looked after, Darlene will say. They were happy.

But the chalkboard writing—so public—demands their attention. Alcide doesn't believe in therapists, thinks the only thing wrong with Ricky is that he's weird and probably "queer," he says, and definitely not right in the head, but while Bessie follows him on most things, she insists here. Picture Ricky, a small boy sitting on a couch, confused why they're at the doctor but there's no ex-amination table and the doctor isn't wearing a white coat. The doc-tor explains to Ricky that Oscar is dead. "So your talking about him is hurting your mama, son. You're going to be a good boy now, right? You're going to give your mama a break?"

Maybe Ricky understands him. Or maybe he just gets the mes-sage that if he wants to be thought normal he should stop talking about Oscar. Either way, the doctor's words work, and Ricky doesn't mention Oscar again. The family thinks it's over.

It's not over. Just not spoken. At eighteen, Ricky is out drink-ing one night with two other boys: Three friends in a borrowed pickup truck, getting buzzed on the single bottle of peppermint schnapps they pooled their money to buy and now pass back and forth in the cab of that truck. The Louisiana night is thick with cicadas, with stars, with a silencing of the man-made that can make possibility stretch out before you. The cab of the truck's the kind of closed-in space that's made Ricky feel safe his whole life. His friends are beside him. He has friends. When the bottle comes back to him, when he feels the sticky sweetness on his lips, he gets brave. He doesn't know his friends will have the same problem with children he does. He can't articulate the mark that draws them together, what hidden knowledge. He has to let the booze do its work.

He says, "I been thinking thoughts I don't want to think." He says, "I think I might need some help."

A night-shift counselor at the mental health center answers the receptionist's page. Picture what he sees. Standing in the linoleum-tiled corridor, under the fluorescent lights, is a buzzed-up teenage boy, the cowlick of his hair sticking up, his glasses thick as jelly, undersized and twisty in his body, with a face half-cocked in a pro-tective sneer. Ricky must look like he's mocking when he says, "I'm here for help." Behind him, through the plate-glass doors, the counselor can see a rusted-up pickup with two more boys inside, the windows down, the headlights cutting recklessly through the dark, country music coming out loud. This is somebody's idea of a joyride. The teenagers' pranking. It's sick what these boys think is funny. The counselor boots Ricky out of there faster than the time it took Ricky to say those words.

When these boys have grown into men, one of them will testify at Ricky's trial. Ricky was serious that night, he'll say. Ricky wanted help.

But the prosecutor, assistant district attorney Wayne Frey, will point out that the friend's word is hardly good—he's a convicted pedophile himself, convicted by Frey. "So what was this y'all were having?" Frey will sneer. "Just a little molesting society here or what?"

At eighteen, in the cab of the truck, Ricky's not talking about Oscar anymore. The same way no one's talking about Bessie's alcoholism or Alcide's silence. But something's wormed its way inside of him. Something's lying in wait.

Fourteen

New Jersey, 1990–1994

A lonely child, I grow into a lonely teen. The summer before I enter seventh grade, we again rent a house on Nantucket, and there ticks infested with Lyme disease bite me and my sisters—but we don't know it yet. Nicola and Elize both develop chest infections that summer, and the antibiotics they're given wipe out the Lyme, before it's even discovered. I am healthy all that summer, in love with long walks around the center of town, holding a book in front of me to read while I walk. I spend hours curled in the back booth of the ice cream and coffee shop, watching the Irish boys who work there. Trying out the idea of having crushes on them.

Only when we're back in the gray Victorian house and school has started does it become clear something's wrong. I've been playing sports for a few years now, joining Nicola on the town basketball team, binding my hair back for soccer. Nicola's a natural, but I've never been the fastest on the team, that's never been my kind of energy. Now when I try to run my knees fold in on themselves, as if to force my body to conserve what little energy I do have. I am tired and my body aches from a place deep within. Lying in my bed each night in the yellow light of the doll lamp, I am alone but feel my grandfather's hands crawl over me. So it seems right that my body hurts. There's no way to escape the memories, not when they're coming from inside me.

The sleep I tumble into is deep and unrelenting. When my mother comes to wake me for school I turn my mouth to breathe in the starchy cotton of the pillow. I fight not to wake up, to hold on to the darkness. I miss a day, then a week, then a month. Test after test for mono comes back negative, to my relief—in school, the kids call that the "kissing disease," and I know I haven't kissed anyone, except the times I don't want to think about—but I'm not curious about what's causing my sleeping. I want only to rest.

Eventually my parents find a specialist and, in a rare move, take me to see him together. The doctor's face is stern over his white coat, his hand cold as it grips my calf and bends and unbends my knee. He peers at my kneecap, then prods it, then prods my hip. He gestures to my parents to step outside the room with him.

When they come back, my mother stands beside the examination table and slips my right hand into hers. Her hand is warm; my hands are always cold and her hands will always feel warm to me. I look up at her, but she turns away. She gives my hand a squeeze.

Lyme disease is new then, barely known. The doctor hasn't tested me for it. We can see only what we have a name for. Now he crouches in front of the table. His eyes are ice blue, too bright. "There is nothing wrong with you," he says, and his voice is artificially high, like he is talking to a child. "Not physically. Sometimes, when a person's very sad . . ."

Something inside me rings. I hate him. I hate him instantly.

Outside, in the parking lot, my parents walk brusquely ahead. I am aswirl with rage and grief, trying not to cry. What did he see when he looked at me? "My knees hurt!" I say. "That's not in my head!" My eyes are hot and stinging by the time we reach the car. I fight to keep the tears from escaping. "You don't believe him, do you?"

My father starts the car up, eases the wheel. It falls to my mother to answer me. For a minute there's only silence and my father's driving. Then my mother twists back in the seat. She still won't look me in the eyes. "Sweetie," she says, "we can't rule anything out."

To try to remember that year now is to slip from image to image, all with the faraway quality of a dream. The bustling sounds of my siblings' leaving for school in the morning, my mother's lips on my forehead kissing me goodbye, the hours of sleep with the sun warm through the window. Dragging the pink wool afghan my grandmother crocheted at my birth down to the living room couch, where I spend my day with its scratchy itchiness spread over me. The glass stein I fill with cinnamon tea I brew strong, so I can sip in the warmth. On that gray couch I slip-slide between wakefulness and sleep, between a blissful kind of nothingness and the cold bone boredom that I am still in this house, that time is not moving quickly enough. Even when I sleep it away.

My parents find a new specialist, who diagnoses the Lyme and prescribes intravenous antibiotics. Now, in the afternoon after school lets out, there's almost always a visitor on the doorstep, a classmate the school has sent with a thick manila envelope stuffed with mimeographed assignments from my classes. The front door my parents have put on the house is thick oak with stained glass lilies at its center, and my first glimpse of one of these girls always comes through the lily, its leaves fragmenting her face like a Picasso. I open the door. She's in tights, her skirt from school, her hair pulled back into a neat brush-gleaming ponytail. She smiles and thrusts the envelope at me. "These are for you," she says.

I glimpse myself as if from the outside. The dark sweatpants and oversize sweatshirt I live in, once kept for cool summer nights on the beach in Nantucket, but now what I want to disappear into. The hair I haven't washed for days, which sticks out from my head in fins of frizz. Plastic lines from my home IV crawl from the veins in my hand and coil taped around my arm. Do I see the awkwardness in her eyes, the way even a child can sense who's sick and has stopped fighting? I feel it. I feel exposed.

But strangely, I am all right. The world I belong to now is the one in the books I read. When I am awake, I am reading. My English textbook has an early Fitzgerald story in it, and I read that and then his others and only then *Gatsby*, tracing the development of Fitzgerald's spun-out dream. My mother, I know, loved Zelda, and the books let me imagine my mother as a younger woman in her studio apartment in New York, the sparkling brunch parties she's told me of. On my father's shelf I find Michener, and in those thousands of pages the wider world of exploration he hungered for. Both my parents I come to know better and differently through their books. In the books I find the thrum of everything unsayable. The characters weep the way I want to, love the way I want to, cry, die, beat their breasts, and bray with life. My days are webbed and sticky with the cotton of sleep.

When summer comes again, my father decides he's sick of going only to Nantucket. They've taken us to France—an idyllic month spent in a stone cottage on a mountain road just down from the cottage that still bears my maternal grandmother's maiden name over the door, ZANNE—but we have not seen, my father declares, America. He is in love again, with the West again, and Garth Brooks is back on our speakers and my father's jeans flare out over his boots again. For months, he spreads atlases across the Formica kitchen table and gathers the two-and-a-half-by-four-inch perforated cards that for my entire childhood he keeps in his shirt pocket with a fountain pen for notes, cards that will never run out and I'll never see him buy and I won't know to miss until suddenly, when he is an old man and his shirt style changes, they are gone.

On these cards, he sketches his plans. We will fly west and rent an RV. We will pick up my cousins in Arizona, drive to the Grand Canyon and up through Utah, then the edge of California, to see the national parks. My mother and he compromise: one night in a hotel, the night at the Grand Canyon. Otherwise, yes, the RV. Night after night, my father plans.

The trip is beautiful, and the trip is a disaster. Looking back now, imagining him in the high pilot-seat window of the cab, the woman he loves beside him and the four children they have made together in the back, I can feel the rush that summer must have been to him. What a triumph that this world was his. That he, who had no father, whose mother struggled always, had America to give us. He'll show us the brilliant rust colors of Bryce Canyon, the way the sun hits the high red rock at midday, the shadows cast by the cliffs and overhangs. He'll show us how vast the Grand Canyon is, and the Native trails etched into the rock at its bottom. His wife born of French and Italian immigrants, his own family Polish and Russian, this is his to claim. America. His enthusiasm is boundless.

But as a child I am curled in the back on a thin mattress on the metal frame of the RV, and I watch the country pass by through a dim foot-square window. I am up over twenty aspirin a day now, doctor's orders, to try to cut the swelling in my joints. The pain that sets in from the air-conditioning starts as a kind of burn in my knees and fingers and spreads into a prickling, nauseating ache. My father keeps the air-conditioning up high, and though I complain to him and to my mother, he either won't listen or can't believe me. And what he says makes sense: He is hot and I am hurting, but why should I think that my hurting should outweigh his hot?

This is the logic I will never find an answer to, the way in my family a hurt will always be your hurt or my hurt, one to be set against the other and weighed, never the family's hurt. Is what happens in a family the problem of the family, or the problem of the one most harmed by it? There is a cost to this kind of adversarial individualism.

But then, I'm the one who'll grow up to wear cowboy boots and a big belt buckle, even though I live in Massachusetts. I'll chase after this love he tried to show me.

Eighth grade begins. Not going to school seems more normal now than going. I spend my days in the slow haunt of the staircase, the room where we played as children, my bedroom. Every week my father drives to Queens and ferries my grandparents back over the bridge to see us. Each Saturday, my sister Nicola plays checkers with my grandfather on the porch like I used to. I can't anymore. I can't even watch them play. I'm too aware that I watched him touch her in our bedroom. Too aware that he touched me. The knowledge crawls across my skin. I can't even use the bathroom without thinking of his hands around himself there, the motion I didn't understand. But I know I'm not allowed to say that, just like I'm not allowed to tell my friends at school what happened. My mother has said that I will hurt my father's political career if I do so. My father has said that I will hurt my mother. Both of them forbid me from telling my grandmother, because it would hurt her, and my brother. He's close to my grandfather and, as the only boy in a house of girls, needs him.

So the hurt feels like it's just mine to carry. Every Halloween, when ghosts and witches start to appear in decorations around town, I become jumpy and sleepless, as though my subconscious believes what my grandfather used to tell me—that he's a witch, that someday he'll get me.

I start to hide. I dye my hair fire-engine red, sometimes purple, once green, and adopt a style of long, loose skirts of bright, clashing colors and oxblood Doc Martens so oversize that when I start high school the other kids call them "clown shoes." It's how I can disappear now: by giving people something else to look at, the clothing I wear instead of me. I cut class, missing so many days the high school won't give me grades. My friends have noticed that I can't be easily touched. If someone surprises me with a hug my body bucks and they get a swift, automatic elbow to the stomach— or else I am suddenly vacant, my body rigid. On my grandmother's birthday my family goes to a restaurant in New York and there— my grandmother seated to my left, my grandfather's hot breath on my right—what is inside me and cannot come out finally becomes unbearable. I go to the bathroom and make myself vomit. To feel empty is delicious relief, and from that day on, I have another secret. My parents must see the empty food wrappers in the kitchen, the mess I sometimes leave in the bathroom. They must see the way their daughter has gone sullen and silent. But we don't talk about it. The same way we don't talk about the slash my brother carries on his stomach, the missing sister, the way the phone is turned off sometimes and when it's on creditors call day and night, nipping at this life my parents have built like the pasts they've both run from, now that my father's rages have gotten so bad even the law firm is in trouble. If we acknowledge only the happy things, maybe that's all there will be.

One night, my parents call us to a family meeting around the Formica kitchen table. The room is still wallpapered in bright slashes meant to look like crayon marks that my mother chose when we were children. The clock overhead is made of wooden crayons. Over the table hang three cone lights on pull cords: one red, one blue, and one yellow, the colors bright and friendly. Each cone casts a circumscribed spotlight, like in an interrogation scene.

"Grandma and Grandpa are moving to Tenafly," my mother announces. "We'll be able to see them so much more this way." Writing the memory, I find myself searching for her face, frustrated with the shadows—but she sits outside the cone of light, and the memory is sealed tight. My grandparents move to downtown Tenafly, to the apartment building marked by a magnolia tree that is on the one main road into town and the one main road out. Weeks after the move, my grandmother slips in the bathroom. Recovering in the hospital, she suffers a stroke. Three days later, she dies. He is left, sitting alone in that apartment.

"Why don't you ever visit Grandpa?" my brother Andy asks me. We're sixteen, standing in the hall outside our bedrooms. My younger sister Nicola and I have moved out of the bedroom we shared in the back of the house. Now she's in the hallway space my baby sister, Elize, was in, and I've taken what used to be my parents' room at the top of the wooden staircase. I've gotten rid of my bed—a mattress on the floor seems closer to the dream I have of a New York City loft apartment—and put the stereo on the floor, too. Two big green Papasan chairs for curling up and reading, incense I buy in thick packets even though the smell gives me headaches. On one wall I have a mural going of images I've cut from magazines: the splayed limbs of a pinup girl, heavy black text, roses. With a can of black paint I brush whole poems on the other walls. Marianne Moore: *your thorns are the best part of you.* E. E. Cummings: *pity this busy monster, manunkind, not.* Richard Eberhart's "Rumination"— *death has done this, and he will do this to me, and blow his breath to fire my clay when I am still*—I paint on the ceiling over my bed so it's the last thing I see at night and the first thing I see in the morning. I like roses and images of guns and guitars. I like the Steve Miller Band and Johnny Cougar tapes from the days before he became John Mellencamp and I don't much care about television or movies. I make friends who go to the *Rocky Horror* show and once I go on-stage and pluck a cherry Life Saver out of a guy's mouth because it seems like what teenagers like me, in our fishnet stockings and Doc Martens, are supposed to do. Inside, I'm so shy I have trouble speaking sometimes, so shy I feel like someone has sewn tiny fishing weights around my lips, piercing the skin in two neat little rows, and moving my mouth is slow and heavy and painful. Across the hall, my brother's room is wallpapered in movie posters, the same bright style since he was eight. Every month he tacks up new ones, not removing the old, so that in places the posters bow out from the walls, six and seven and eight years of movies beneath them. He'll keep doing this until after he's in college, and by then the room will actually seem smaller, a couple of inches trimmed off on each side by the weight of all the posters.

Now we stand opposite each other in the hallway, he outside his door, I outside mine. He's still the entertainer, still as skinny as when he was a kid. His hair curls out in puffs from beneath his ball cap. The jean jacket he wears is covered almost entirely in souvenir patches from trips to Disney, whales from Nantucket, a breast-plate patch from my father's uncle's time in the Army. That man became a famous boxer after he came home, and at least once when my brother meets a ballplayer who's his idol the player will recognize the name on my brother's patch and grin, and he and my brother will start talking about the boxer's glory days. Who knows how those in a family find their roles, whether a role is assigned or chosen, whether it's a function of the way that even siblings— even twins—grow up in different families? Have different pasts. But while I am flinging myself around to escape the past, my brother is papering himself in it. He will grow up to be the family's keeper, the one who remembers birthdays and anniversaries and organizes the Christmas card list every year, the one who'll spend hours organizing family photos I can't look at into albums he has printed into photo books.

"Why don't you ever visit him?" he asks again. That's where he's going. I study his face for a minute, expecting to see accusation. Or curiosity. But in his brown eyes—a brown inherited from my mother and my grandfather, the brown that links them in the family—there's neither, only the rote expectation that he will ask this question of me, the one whose role in the family is separation. The one who, confused and swirling and angry, already wants to get away. Are we already who we will always be?

For an instant, maybe there's a different possibility. A chance. A world in which I tell him everything now and yes there would be fireworks but after the fireworks we would all talk about it. My parents would learn what I'm carrying. My brother would learn what has turned us into strangers, and why I seem so angry at the same family he holds so close.

I look at his face a long moment. Then I turn and click my bedroom door closed behind me.

Fifteen

The Louisiana mental health clinic intake worker's notes—notes that will later be entered into the court record—describe the nineteen-year-old, brown-haired man before him as depressed, submissive, "overly compliant." Ricky Langley is eager to please, the caseworker writes, but he seems to sense that Ricky may not know how. Behind the thick glasses Ricky wears, his brown eyes stay too steady, constant in a way that suggests a fundamental disconnect with life, a fundamental hopelessness. He doesn't get excited and he doesn't get mad, he just is. The caseworker gives him a mimeographed sheet listing problems Ricky could be experiencing and asks him to circle which ones he is, right now, experiencing. He circles: *nervousness, depression, guilt, unhappiness, worthlessness, restlessness, my thoughts*. He does not circle: *education, anger, friends, self-control, fears, children*. He begins to circle *stress* but stops. The pen leaves an arc on the page. He begins to circle *sexual problems*, then stops and crosses that arc out—but then he is rebuked by his mind, by the better part of his knowing, and makes the acknowledging circle. The page becomes evidence of the struggle. The circle around *want to hurt someone* he draws so tightly that it nearly touches all the letters, so tightly it strangles the idea even as it admits it, as if it wants to be its own undoing.

A year has passed since that tipsy, star-filled night he wanted help. Now he's been ordered into it. No, he checks on the intake form, he is not a veteran. No, he has no income. He gets no aid.

How long has it been since he worked? Two years. Sometimes, he tells the caseworker, he steals down to the bank of the Calcasieu River to sleep. The trees' boughs shelter him; the creek bubbles and his mind calms there. When he wakes he hunts and fishes to feed himself and pursues what he calls his hobby: "archeological digs." He looks closely then at the silt of the bank, searching for an arrowhead or a shard of glass, some scrap of the past. The past pulls at him. It can feel more real than the ephemeral present, just as Oscar once did. His head hurts, he tells the caseworker, "all the time." Only the river settles it, or going into the graveyard to sleep. The dead are peaceful the way the river is.

Drinking settles it, too. Yes, he checks, he often drinks or gets high to deal with stress. But no, not before going out or social situations. He can leave the question about parties blank. No, he hasn't lost time at work or school because of drugs or drink, because he doesn't have work or school. His drinking doesn't cause conflicts with friends, because he doesn't have friends. How many times does he have to say it? He prefers being alone. What about siblings? the form asks. "To tell you the truth, I ain't close to nobody."

I often drink or get high by myself. That, he checks.

"Who raised you, Ricky?" the caseworker asks. Ricky has just written on the forms that he lives alone. The caseworker was the one to correct it: He lives with Bessie and Alcide and Jamie, the four of them in one tight trailer. Medical bills cost Bessie and Alcide the land they built on and the house they built on it, too. I picture the caseworker as a young woman, just out of school in Baton Rouge, her hair pulled back in a ponytail and a photograph of her boyfriend in a plastic silver frame on the desk. She wants to go outside for a smoke; it's past time. She wants her boyfriend to take her out to dinner this Friday night and she wants a job anywhere but here.

He doesn't answer.

She sighs. "Ricky, who raised you?"

"Luann and Lyle."

This excising of Bessie and Alcide. It's easy to read a young man's anger between the lines. From appointment to appointment, his responses to questions grow shorter and shorter. Easy to imagine his hand cocked into a fist in his lap, his head ducked low, as though if she can't see his eyes she won't see him. He won't have to answer. He tried to molest a seven-year-old boy in Allen Parish. "Attempted molestation," the charge says. When the boy resisted, Ricky told him he'd shoot him. The boy's father reported Ricky to the police. That's why he's here now.

Just more proof that everyone thinks there's something wrong with him. He doesn't know what burns more badly, the shame or the anger. Sometimes he can't even tell the two apart, just knows what it feels like when his ears prick red and his heart thuds hard in his chest, whooshing inside him. He can't hear can't see can't think. That feeling—not wanting that feeling—is why he doesn't have a high school degree. There was a misunderstanding over a school car when he was in ninth grade. He'd been told he could use the car to run an errand for the school—Ricky swears it, but there's no need to take his word, the auto repair teacher backed him up—but someone forgot to tell the school officials, who reported it missing. Ricky was arrested. Grand theft auto. Everything was cleared up before charges were pressed—a mistake, everyone agreed—but it made Ricky burn so badly he never went back.

Because here's what he realized: They thought he would steal a car. You can bet if one of his sisters had taken the car, they'd have believed his sister.

He dropped out. When the other kids were in school, he'd be down by the river, fishing. He'd never had many friends, but dropping out was the last snip in that thread. It's like they all went in two different directions after that. Everybody else in one direction. Then him.

The caseworker drums her fingers against the desk. "So you didn't earn your degree, Ricky. Lots of people don't. But do you have a job?"

"I done gave up on jobs."

In these forms from the Lake Charles Mental Health Center in the mid-1980s, Ricky denies ever having been physically abused. He denies ever having been sexually abused. But ten years after these sessions, a social worker will put together a report that is heavily relied on at trial. The report will say his sister Judy said that Lyle and Alcide both beat Ricky. Ricky gave up on Alcide but, either unable or unwilling to give up on his family entirely, kept running back to Lyle. Once, Judy said, when Ricky showed up at Lyle's door, Lyle beat him so badly she had to pull a gun on him to make him stop. Judy told the social worker, who wrote it down for the defense, who gave it to the expert, who described it at trial, and the court reporter wrote it down—this is a game of telephone I am playing with the past.

Ricky is scheduled for five appointments in July and comes to every one. Last month, after his arrest, he says, he took forty over-the-counter aspirin and waited to die. The only way to get the bad feelings out was to kill himself. But the pills just gave him a stomachache and made his ears ring. So he's here. Angry but trying. Sometimes he carves long slashes into his arms and watches himself bleed. He drinks household cleaners and walks into traffic, daring the cars to hit him. Now he tells the caseworker he wants to be hospitalized so he can't molest anyone. "It seems like the harder I try not to do it, the more I do it."

But they won't hospitalize him. He is clean and kempt, the caseworker checks off. He acts appropriately. He is not that sick. Rather than being hospitalized, he is assigned to outpatient therapy.

So Ricky runs away. He's not going to keep sitting in a chair and talking about this; they're not listening to him. He'll hurt somebody. He needs to be locked up, but they won't even take him seriously for that. Twitchy in his body, unable to sit still, a failure at holding a job and a failure when he tries to kill himself and a failure at getting treatment, he flees. He hitchhikes his way across the Louisiana swamplands, through the piney woods of Texas and into the dry Arizona desert, where vistas of red rock burn more like the sun than any rock he has seen before. His skin burns crisp red, but he does not care. The blaze of color is beautiful, the dry air light in his lungs. He keeps going west. It is like he needs to find the beginning.

When he reaches California, he will stop. California is where the happy photographs come from, the photographs his mother kept hidden in the heavy trunk when he was a boy. From before what makes Bessie drink, before what makes Alcide angry. He'll live with his uncle in California. He'll make for himself a better life.

These notes from the caseworkers are some of the first I ever read of Ricky. The Christmas after I read them, I went back to my parents' house. I drove there thinking of him, of his desire to get away and of his hope.

Usually I see my family in neutral settings: hotels and restaurants. But at Christmas, I like going back to the gray house. My father and Andy tack lights up all over the gingerbread trim. Each year my family has lived in the house, they have added at least one lit plastic figurine, and now the front yard is a battalion of Santa Clauses and gingerbread men, toy soldiers and snowmen. Time has otherwise dragged the house into a shambles, the repairs Greg made so many years ago now failing, but the lights transform it into something both new and familiar.

They were having a Christmas party and the whole neighborhood was invited. That night I was walking down the staircase, a glass of wine in one hand and the other gripping the banister. Around me, mingling with carols from the speakers, rose the voices of people I've known my whole life. And above them, holding court, a single voice: my father's. I heard him tell a group of people that I was writing a book about something that happened in the past. "But if you ever hear about it, don't worry," he said, his words a little slurred by drink. "Alexandria's the only one who remembers it."

On the stairs, I froze. My family had always been silent about the abuse. But no one had ever implied that it hadn't happened.

My father kept talking. This moment that had changed everything inside me had changed nothing for him.

Go home, Ricky's uncle tells him. There will be no new life. He can't stay in California. The uncle buys him a bus ticket, undoing the whole journey he's just made. When Ricky gets to Louisiana, he calls his parole officer. The officer says, "Next time you're going to leave, tell me first."

The thoughts start again. When he sleeps he sees a child. The child is naked, and he touches the young, unmarked skin, and not until afterward, after the touching, does he wake, the sheets twisted, his panting guilty. Which means he's done it again, if only in the dream. When he tells the caseworker about these thoughts, he describes them as nightmares—not wishes, not fantasies. But once a week he masturbates. He can masturbate only by thinking about young children, he says. Ricky has never been on a date. He is a virgin. His only friend now is a sixteen-year-old girl and he says the friendship is platonic. Sometimes, he tells the caseworker, he's made young children, boys and girls both, take off their clothing and perform fellatio on him. Then he's removed his own clothing. He's performed it on them. Last time the boy refused and he told the boy he'd shoot him. "I don't know what I wanted to do that for."

But all of that is in the past, Ricky says; all of that is over. He is done with that life. (He must be. He is only nineteen. If he is not done, what will his life hold?) He would have a job now if he'd stayed in California, he tells the caseworker, he tells his mother, he tells anyone who will listen. "Long as I got something to do, I'm all right."

He begins a correspondence course in small-engine repair. He wants to acquire a trade, he says. He wants to move out of his parents' trailer and live alone. It's not right that a grown man should live with his parents and baby brother. His brother Jamie is sixteen years old and Jamie is normal. Ricky must know this the way he knows that he himself is not. Years from now, after the trials, when the state penitentiary prints a list of the nine names he has requested be allowed to visit him, Bessie, Alcide, Darlene, Judy, Francis, and even the sisters' husbands will be on the list, but Jamie's name won't be. Nine is an odd number, short of the round numbers the prison system tends to prefer. Likely Ricky could have asked for more. But his brother's name won't be on the list.

A month passes before his next appointment at the clinic. He has just turned twenty. He reports that he finally did take a job. It was at an auto dealership but then he quit it two weeks later. He tells the caseworker he doesn't know why he quit; he just felt like quitting. The caseworker asks again, why. This time he tells her: Each day he walked to the job, he passed schoolchildren playing, then passed them again on his way home. He'd see the children and he'd want. He'd *want*. Ricky wants to stop wanting. He quit the job just to never walk by those children. Long as he's got something to do, he's all right—but now he does not have something to do. He is not all right.

Bessie comes with him to the next appointment. I imagine she has on her good housedress, but, self-conscious, she's wearing a coat open over it despite the heat. She's glad her son's home again, she tells the caseworker, but it's draining to have him there. "I feel like if I leave him alone for a minute, he's gonna go off and molest somebody." She has forbidden him from running off to live by the river, but he's an adult. What can she do? Alcide's no help.

Picture Ricky, as he sits next to Bessie. They're in two hard metal chairs, the caseworker on an office chair turned catty-corner to them. It must be humiliating to sit here with his mama, she with the one leg and still carrying that old crutch 'cause they can't afford anything better. It should be him accompanying her to the doctor, not the other way around. A person can be angry and still feel shame. A person can burn with hate at his mama and still love her enough to want to be something that will make her proud. A person can feel overwhelmed by all he wants to be and see no way to get there. "I been thinking about dying or getting someone else to kill me," he blurts out now. He's drinking more these days, living with Bessie and Alcide. Whole bottles of peppermint schnapps. Last week he drank fifty dollars' worth. "I warned him that drinking might impair his judgment," the caseworker writes.

There is one last sheet in the file, titled "No Suicide No Homicide Contract." *I, the undersigned, do hereby voluntarily agree that I will not intentionally attempt to harm myself or anyone else during my therapy (treatment) at this center.* Ricky signs. The agreement is standard—likely given to every patient—but looking at it now it is hard not to notice the word "during." The last therapy session Ricky attends is October 1, 1985. On February 24, 1986, his case is recommended for closure. On May 16, 1986, it's closed. Ricky leaves home again, for Georgia.

Sixteen

New Jersey, 1994–1996

When I am sixteen, the boy I like is named Luke. He is twenty-two and lives in a Colorado suburb that, in the photographs he sends me, is lined with split-level ranch houses and pockmarked with churches. Across the Internet, in the AOL chat rooms that I have joined because I am still not going to school regularly, he writes to me that he loves his ex-girlfriend, Crystal, but that she wants nothing to do with him and that he needs to move on. He appears to be moving on with me. He is taking classes at a community college, trying to finish his degree. On my father's shelves I have found Robert Heinlein books that spin out utopian, sci-fi worlds, and he knows those books and likes them, too. He wants to know me, he says. He wants me to know him. He sends me packets of photographs taken every few hours, each photograph numbered in pencil on the back, so that I will see the sequence of his days. The parking lot of the McDonald's he manages, gray and boring in the afternoon sun. His grin as he holds the camera out in front of him. On his head perches a paper hat that reminds me of origami boats I made as a child.

The next photo is his college parking lot—his Colorado, I am starting to understand, has a lot of asphalt. Then the ugly paisley couch in his parents' living room. The black terrier mutt he grew up with, its mouth open, with a small pink tongue hanging out. There is a picture of Crystal. This I study. She is petite, with thin straight hair angled down her face in a mall haircut, a tiny gold cross at her neck. I permit myself the realization that she looks ordinary, and not much older than I am. Then, that night, pictures of his bedroom, of his stereo, of the Pink Floyd posters on his wall. He must be living with his parents, I realize, and though he is six years older this makes him seem not so different from me. I have finally told my parents about my eating disorder, and they've found me a therapy program where I spend part of my days. I'm too uneasy in the program to make friends there, and I haven't been in touch with anyone from school. Luke and I talk on the phone long-distance for eight-, nine-, ten-hour stretches, all night and into the day. Sometimes I fall asleep with the phone on the pillow next to me, listening to him breathe. His voice is low and dusky, and because it is all I know of him it seems to expand to encompass him, as though he is as steady and kind as his voice.

The phone bills are monstrous, $700 one month. My father yells, but he pays them.

Luke flies out to meet me. My parents have agreed that he will sleep at a friend's house, but the first night he stays in my bedroom, and then that's where he stays for the rest of the week. I don't know if they're just not paying attention or if they figure it's too late to protect me, as I sometimes do. In person, Luke is shorter than I, with a spray of acne across his chin. To cover for this, perhaps, he says, "You're lucky I don't mind how tall you are. Some guys would mind, but not me." When he says this we are standing under a streetlight at the center of my town. The ploy, the insecurity he is trying to cover, is so obvious that even at sixteen I can see it highlighted in the yellow from the lamp, and yet I also can't object. I want him to love me. I want it like a prize and because it is what I am supposed to want and because it will save me. In the parking lot of the town duck pond he gives me my first kiss, and when his lips hit mine I can't breathe. It's not my first kiss at all. Before him, wet in my mouth, is the taste of my grandfather.

When I am seventeen, the boy I like is named William. He's in college in the Bronx on a football scholarship, flunking his classes now that he's discovered Bob Marley and pot. He's big and mellow, with a blond round Charlie Brown head—but sometimes the mornings after our dates I have bruises on my arms where he's held me too tightly and sometimes when I see him my breath catches with a fear I can't name. It's as though I'm swimming through something I can't see; I can't even remember the hours when I'm living them.

The boys' attention frees me to feel loved. The boys are a threat. I don't know how to recognize when love and hurt are mingled. It's all I've known them to be. I can't tell who's safe and who's not, can't tell what safety even is. I only know I need someone to be.

Then, when I am eighteen, I find someone who really is safe. Dima is a cellist from the Ukraine. His family moved to New York from Kiev so he could apply to Juilliard. But when the time came, he bombed the audition. Now, at twenty-three, he's a student at a community college in the city. His hands are pockmarked with angry red splotches where I know he's put out cigarettes, his pale forearms snaked with carved white scars, but with me he's nothing but gentle. At night, when we lie on his bed and kiss, he puts his hand low on my belly and before I understand what is happening he is not Dima anymore and I am panicked, gulping at his touch, I am breathless and shaking, the tears run out of me until my chest heaves and my eyes burn. I go beneath the crust of silence then, somewhere down beneath where I spend my days. I dissolve.

He keeps his hand perfectly still on my body. He waits. His hand is warm, and below it I feel my body slowly settle. "Breathe," he says then, and I do, and as I breathe my body comes back to me. Night by night, we move his hand lower on my body. Night by night, I tunnel my way up through the layers of memory, until I emerge and he is there. We sleep at the small apartment in Bay Ridge, Brooklyn, where he lives with his parents and younger brother. His bedroom walls are lined with cassette holders tacked up like wallpaper, the work of every musician he loves alphabetized. In the living room, there's a big glass tank with carved mahogany braces that holds a single carp his father smuggled out of the Ukraine in a plastic bag full of water, hiding the fish through Romania, through Italy, across oceans and into the States. For the fish, and for Dima, his father has that kind of love. While Dima and I hide in his bedroom, and he plays me Alpha all the way to Yes, and all the time his hand goes lower and I gulp and breathe and am finally calm again, the carp swims lazy circles in its grand tank. I take Dima's story as proof, blazing bright as a bonfire: He failed at what his family wanted, but they love him anyway.

The week of our high school graduation, my parents throw my brother and me a party on the back deck they're building. The pilings are only half-constructed, the beams still unsecured and uneven, and this gives the night a slanted feel.

It's an epic party, strung with white lights and loud music and a dance floor set up in the backyard. My brother is rangy-thin but healthy. While I've been trying to hide on the sidelines he's found a home in the high school theater department and takes the center of any crowd he walks into, with his big gestures and his stage-lit laugh. He's buzzed tonight and his friends are, too.

So Dima and I hide away in the kitchen, talking our way around things. He's got something he can't say to me: that he wants me to stay close to home, to stay with him, to go to college in New York. I've got something I can't say to him: that the reason I am smiling tonight, the reason the world seems to have lightened for me, is that I am alive with the knowledge that I finally, truly, get to leave.

"Come here," I tell him, and back myself up against the refrigerator.

"Everyone's outside," he says.

"I don't care," I say, and I don't. For once, when his lips find mine, it's like they're blotting out the past, blotting out the memory of my grandfather's slime-smack, and if I concentrate on the dark wet feeling of his tongue in my mouth I can make everything else go away. It's like dancing, the way I wrangle the past that night—first the feeling of Dima, then the past, then I turn in his arms and it's him again. Every me I've ever been is in the kitchen, pressed up against the cold hard smooth white surface of the fridge. The girl I was at six who would come down to the kitchen at night and talk to her father, knowing she couldn't say the only thing she really needed to. Then the girl I am at nine, when I come to the kitchen to refill my grandmother's glass of water. I take a plastic ice cube with a bug resined in it from the freezer—it's a trick we're playing, my siblings and I, in love with whoopee cushions and handshake buzzers and a squirting plastic flower pin that never fools anyone—and plop it into my grandmother's glass. Suddenly my grandfather is behind me, his heavy breath, and I whirl around, not wanting him to see the glass and ruin the joke. But it's not the glass he's looking at but my body, staring frankly. Through the window, gliding over Dima and me as we move to the floor, come the voices of people I've known my whole life. For a moment I feel on a precipice between now and some future when this will all be over, when this house is no longer my world, when I create something new and unknown for myself and—I will, finally, I will—get away.

The sex we have on the kitchen floor is exaltation. I should stop us, I know; I should care whether someone walks in and sees us there on the linoleum of my childhood, my dress hiked up around my waist, my teeth on Dima's shoulder. But I am watching us as from above, the way our limbs splay against the floor as if we're swimming, and I know, somehow know, that nothing will hurt us tonight. Not when so much has. This is me getting away, finally. This is me throwing off the past.

Give me normalcy, that's what I want. Anything else can burn.

Seventeen

Indiana, 1986

Ruth's phone rings just past eleven at night, when she's already out of bed but still in her pajamas, not yet changed into her white nursing assistant uniform, and hasn't yet started the coffeemaker. She must consider, briefly, not picking it up. No one calls casually this late. No one calls with good news. But the phone's rattling away in the kitchen, and she crosses the tile floor and makes her way to the receiver.

"Yes?"

"Aunt Ruth?"

She doesn't recognize Ricky's voice at first. She and Bessie aren't close. She's barely met Bessie's children. On the stand eight years from now, at his first trial, she'll say she met Ricky only once before that night in 1986 he showed up by surprise, and then have to correct herself and say, why, yes, she guesses she must've met him when he was growing up, the few times she went to visit Bessie over the years. He must have been one of the children hanging around in the yard. But you have to understand, there were so many, with Luann always taking in kids. And Ruth was never one to notice children. Her sister Bessie was the one who wanted that life: a husband, kids. Ruth back then was just fine with living alone. Money was beyond tight, working midnight shifts at the hospital and moonlighting days when she could pick up a shift as a home health aide, but she made enough for her rent and the electric and even a car. She was good at working. She loved the feeling of supporting herself, only herself to look out for.

"Yes?"

"Aunt Ruth, it's Ricky. Bessie's son. I'm—" he sounds like he's gulping, trying not to cry. "I'm in Indianapolis. At a filling station, downtown." The boy—she can't remember how old he'd be now, maybe twenty? My God, are she and Bessie old enough for that? "Could you come pick me up?"

She's so surprised the words just fly out of her mouth. "I'm due at work, Ricky." She winces. She hadn't meant to sound harsh.

"Please."

So she does it. Dresses in a hurry, pulling on her white tights in the pitch dark. Skips the coffee. Gets in her car and turns on the headlights and drives half an hour through vacant streets to the filling station he's described, wondering the whole way how he's turned up here and whether her sister knows. Last she telephoned with Bessie, Ricky was in Georgia visiting his sister Francis. The buses don't leave off at the filling station. Did he hitchhike all the way here? But she must remind herself not to wonder too hard. Wondering is how you get mixed up in other people's troubles. When she reaches him, I see him huddled under the station overhang, his gray hooded sweatshirt dripping wet from the rain, carrying only a single small duffel bag. He opens the car door and starts to get in.

"Wait," she says.

He pauses.

"You got a towel?"

He doesn't, so she makes him take a T-shirt from his bag and spread it across the seat first. They don't kiss hello, they don't embrace. She doesn't ask what he's doing here. She stops in front of her apartment and gives him the key. "I'll be back at eight," she says. If she hurries, she'll still be on time for work.

He stays with her for a couple of months. She and Bessie may not be close, but that doesn't mean she can turn family away. At first, he's just sitting in the house, staring at the television and running up her electric, but then he finds a gig at the racetrack for the Indy 500. It's temporary—three weeks, tops—but soon it's all he can talk about, the race cars and the guys at the track. He's so proud of his polo shirt and assigned cap you'd think it was a military uniform. Maybe she starts getting up a few extra minutes early to iron the shirt for him, just to see the delight on his face. He can be like a child, so proud and excited so easily. Like her, he's a night owl, doesn't seem to sleep, so he's still up sometimes when she gets in from her shift. He makes her a cup of coffee, sits with her, and they chat about the coming day.

She likes him. That's what surprises her most, maybe. How much she likes having him around.

Which is why she gets so nervous when, after he's been there only a few weeks, one afternoon he hands her an envelope addressed to Bessie. At first she doesn't think anything of it, just says, "Sure, I'll mail this," and slides it into her purse. It's a good reminder to pay her rent, and she fishes her checkbook out of her dresser drawer, makes out a check at the kitchen table, and stamps it. Today the old lady she'll be looking after lives on the other side of town.

She's in her car, driving on the highway, when the letter starts to bother her from inside her purse. Something about the way he looked, his eyes darting away as he handed it to her. She's tried to ask him before what he's doing here, and he's been vague—he just needed a change, something new. Now she realizes he's never really answered. And then the simple fact that he's never given her a letter for Bessie before. It's not so unusual that he wouldn't mail an envelope himself. He's holding down a job, but things like the laundry, bills, basic planning he still seems to need someone to take care of. She minds less than she'd have imagined she would. It's nice to be needed.

But the letter. Something's wrong; she just knows it is.

She pulls over into a gas station, telling herself it's nothing, telling herself she's being silly. The letter in her hands, the engine still idling in park, she pauses. She doesn't read other people's mail. Never. She's not a nosy person. And she needs to get to work.

She slits the letter open with her forefinger. She can tape it up before she mails it to Bessie, and Bessie will never know Ricky wasn't the one to tape it. Inside is a single sheet of loose-leaf with Ricky's cramped handwriting that she recognizes from the grocery notes he leaves her. *I'm sorry, I know this will hurt you and Dad but I just couldn't do it anymore.*

The drive back to her apartment is half an hour but she does it in twenty, never mind the speed limit. At every red light she prays under her breath and her head fills with awful pictures of what she'll come home to.

But when she opens the door, her heart thudding with what she might find, he's still alive. He's still alive. Standing at the kitchen counter, clutching the telephone with one hand, the other holding her butcher knife to his wrist.

"I didn't want to tell you," he says later. This is after she's made him hang up the phone and after she's taken the knife, all the knives, into her bedroom and after she's made him get in the car and come to work with her at the old lady's house; she didn't trust him to be alone. I see him as he sits in the lady's easy chair, flipping through her *Sewing Circle* magazines, her Bible. I see Ruth as she watches him peer at the Bible, his finger pressed to the page and his mouth hanging open as he sounds the words. Every time Ruth goes from the lady's bedroom into the kitchen to refill a glass of water, or get her dinner, or carry the sheets into the laundry room after the lady has soiled herself, Ruth must find herself checking up on him. Just checking that he's still there, really. That he's all right. Now they're back at the kitchen table, two cups of coffee he's made growing cold in front of them, Ricky staring down at the table hangdog-style instead of looking at her. "I like little boys," he says. "I try hard not to, but—sexually."

She swallows. Her feeling in this moment must be peculiar. Like a vacuum opens up in the air around her, like someone's hit a pause button deep inside. What he's saying isn't possible.

"I didn't want you to know," he continues.

It's not that she recovers herself, and not only that she doesn't know what to say. She can do nothing with his words but take them in. She must make the decision even before she realizes she's making one: she isn't going to ask him if he's done anything. She isn't. She doesn't want to know.

Instead, she gets up and crosses around the table. She leans over him and gathers his bony shoulders in her arms, hugging him awkwardly. "Shh, it's all right, Ricky." It's the first time they've touched.

The next morning, she wakes before the alarm, her mind racing. He needs help. He should talk to someone. She knows without asking that he doesn't have health insurance. And she doesn't have money to spare. But there are charity hospitals, and if she calls enough times, she'll get him an appointment. She'll get him help.

TRIAL TRANSCRIPT, 1994

Prosecutor: Now, you took him down to the hospital. And were you with him when he was speaking to the therapist?

Witness: No.

Prosecutor: So you wouldn't have known that he told the therapist that he called the police himself that morning [he held the knife], to let them know where he was. Or that he told the therapist he'd planned to pull a knife on them.

Defense attorney: Your Honor, we need to approach the bench.

[Conference]

Defense attorney: She doesn't know about this. So I don't know how she could respond to it.

Prosecutor: You see, that's one of the problems with letting all this hearsay testimony in.

Obviously he's given a different story to somebody else. And if I'm not allowed to bring
that out, then the jury gets the wrong impression about what was going on there that day.
I mean, she's given her opinion that she
believed he was going to commit suicide in
her kitchen.

For the next month or so—later she won't be able to say exactly how long—she drives him to the charity hospital once a week
for therapy. They don't talk about why he's going. She just takes
him.

And then one day, when she's been at a funeral for a cousin she
grew up with, and her eyes and her head are blurry from crying,
she comes home and the house is empty. He's not on the couch.
He's not in the kitchen. Instead, on the table, there's a scrap of
paper torn from a grocery bag, the note on it scrawled in his hasty
writing: The police came and arrested him at her house to take
him back to Georgia. He's being charged there. All the stress of
the past few weeks, all the stress of what she's known and not allowed herself to know, all the stress of worrying after him and not
wanting to have to and worrying all the same, comes to her like a
deep sickening and she's suddenly so tired. She doesn't make any
calls. She doesn't try to find anything more out. She just accepts
that he's slipped from her life just as suddenly as he came into it. I
see her wet a paper towel into a cold compress. She takes it to bed
and she sleeps the dawn away, and when she wakes the next day,
the sun blaring in through the windows and her head heavy and
her heart heavy with the memory of her cousin's funeral the day
before, it must be almost like she's wakened into her old life, the
life before him. She must expect the loneliness so much she doesn't
even notice it. Not for weeks does she have the energy to call Bessie and ask what happened. He had been arrested for touching a
young girl in Georgia—his second molestation arrest, after the boy
in Louisiana he threatened to shoot—and for grand theft auto.

When she'd picked him up at the filling station, he was on the run from the girl's house. He'd just ditched her mother's Chevy.

When she walks into the courtroom in Baton Rouge in 1994, her eyes must go first to the back of the head of the man in the defense seat. All these years later, and something inside her still flies out to him. Grown-up Ricky. Dark brown hair cut jailhouse-short, glasses hooked over the backs of his ears. She prepares herself to meet his eyes, but he doesn't turn around. Instead, a woman with a round face and brown bangs waves to her from the left—his sister Darlene, full-grown, she realizes with a start—so she takes the seat next to Darlene and, to her surprise, finds herself reaching for Darlene's hand. She squeezes it.

Then she notices the photographs of the little blond boy blown up poster-size in front of the jury. Ricky is accused of killing him. She must remember the hush of Ricky's voice at the table, those awful words he said. "I like little boys." She must remember her choice in that moment, not to ask. As she sits in the courtroom, the bench beneath her sturdy as a pew, I see her close her eyes for a moment. Then she makes herself open them. She looks at the eyes of the boy in the photograph. What happened to him?

But even as she wonders, it must be Ricky's eyes that come back to her. She sped home the whole way that afternoon. She opened the kitchen door so frightened. First the cold shine of the knife in his hand, then above the knife his eyes as big and round as a raccoon's. Wide like he was trapped, like he couldn't quite believe what he was about to do. He needed her to save him from it.

She loved him then, she understands that now. The years have taught her that. Living with him, taking care of him, changed her. When she remembers his eyes, yes, she remembers the fear and the guilt in them—but how can she explain that what has stayed with her, what has opened her heart and what breaks her heart still, was that she saw relief? His relief at having been found by her. At having been saved by her. Relief that someone might finally make him stay.

"The defense calls Ruth McClary." She rises and smooths her

skirt over her hips. From the witness stand, she answers the attorney's questions. Yes, Ricky came to live with her. No, at the time she didn't know why. But he was polite and helpful, a hard worker. "I love Ricky," she hears herself say. "He's a very fine boy." Her body turned to the jury; she speaks into the transcript microphone for the court reporter; her presence here today is for everyone else. But inside herself it must be him she watches. Her words are for him. With his head bent down she can see the spot where the hair at the top of his head grows in a whorl, like a boy's. His hands are pressed together so tightly that his shoulders threaten to shake. She says, softly, "I got very attached to him. Like he was my own son."

When, in 1986, the police take Ricky back to Conyers, Georgia, there's no trial. Instead he pleads guilty to committing an unspecified sexual offense with a minor—now the second sexual offense on his record—and, at twenty years old, is sent to the Georgia Youthful Defendant Correctional Institution.

In Georgia, by all accounts, Ricky is a model prisoner. He's learned something living with Ruth and learned something working at the racetrack those few weeks. There's something satisfying about being told what to do and meeting those demands. It gives him pride. In May 1987, at the age of twenty-two, he earns his GED. "Ricky Langley was an excellent student and I would like to have him as my aide," the teacher writes in his postclass evaluation. "I really need one." One year later, he becomes eligible for parole.

The morning of his hearing, he must neaten down his hair with water and he must wipe his glasses clean and straighten his prison-issue shirt so that it hangs unwrinkled on his skinny torso. He wants parole. He's been dreaming of it. Dreaming of getting back to the Calcasieu River, back to spending his afternoons fishing and his nights sleeping next to the bubbling sound of water over the creek bed. He didn't know what prison would be like. And it turns out he likes it here all right, but it's still prison. It's too loud, all the yelling and the moans and the guys who have no other way to make themselves heard so they bang on the bars night and day. Sometimes it's like the noise in the prison mixes up with the noise in his head and it all becomes one vast incomprehensible yelling, the inside of him and the outside, and then it's like he blows apart in the noise. Being confined makes it impossible to get away from himself, from the self that's always too loud inside.

And besides, that pride he has? He wants others to see it. He doesn't want to be a prisoner anymore. He wants to be thought of as free.

But the board denies his parole.

Ricky's furious. At first his fury is just anger. Then it curdles into indignation. Since they arrested him, he's done everything right. What more should he have to do? "He feels," a counselor records in his file, "that his past should not have anything to do with his parole." Ricky complains and he complains and finally one of the other inmates, sick of hearing him complain, says, "Don't matter if you'd gotten out, you'd be back in here within a year."

At first Ricky reacts to the guy the way he always does, quick-twitch anger. But he likes the guy, even maybe trusts him a little, and the words make him curious. He'd expect shit like that from the guards. But from another inmate? A guy who should be on his side?

So he reacts in a new way. He says, "Why?"

The inmate explains to Ricky that that's what pedophiles are known for. That Ricky isn't the only one who's struggled his whole life. Pedophilia is known to be something you can't just quit.

Maybe Ricky asks for more therapy, maybe the system recognizes his need for it finally, but for the next two years in Georgia, as Ricky is shuttled among three different jails, the doctors give him something he's never had before: a way to understand who he is. In his therapy sessions, he learns about pedophilia. He learns that what he has is considered a disorder, and he learns, again, that abusing children harms them. At night, he dreams. Not the dreams of before, not dreams in which the children's skin glowed like alabaster moonlight and when he awoke he was panting and sweaty and knew he'd touched them. Now in his dreams he walks to a clearing in the woods. Sunlight suffuses the air around him, the smell of green so thick it clots his throat. A carpet of dried pine needles cushions his footsteps. When he reaches the center of the clearing he stands and waits. A child appears. He recognizes the child and his heart beats faster. One by one, the children he's molested enter the clearing. They walk hesitantly at first, their eyes widening when they see him, but then they see the other children and are suddenly confident. Each child takes the hand of the one before him until they are all holding hands, they are linked in a circle, every boy and every girl, and at the center of the circle is him. He turns and he turns—but he is surrounded.

Why, one child asks. *Why? Why did you do it?* Then another. *Why to me? Why to us?* He opens his mouth to answer them, but in his mouth there is only air. He doesn't know how to tell them why. He doesn't know how to tell himself why. They ask until the sound drums in his ears like the blood thrums in his veins. He trembles.

Then he bolts. He tears a boy by the hand from the circle and runs, pulling the boy behind him deeper into the woods, until they are alone and no one can see them. There is only one way to stop his trembling. He palms the back of the boy's head, feels the cool brush of the boy's hair. He unzips his pants. He pushes the boy's head to him.

When he wakes, he is sweaty and sick and shaking, but he writes down the dream in a notebook. He brings the notebook to his therapy sessions and hands it to the therapist. "Don't let me out of here," he says.

"If you want your life to be something different, Ricky," she says, "you have to make it something different."

His GED teacher is a lay minister, and now Ricky joins his evening Bible study class. He is shy at first, quiet. Sometimes, the teacher notes, he arrives in class with his clothing askew, his hair rumpled and deep bags under his eyes. Ricky, the teacher will later remember, seems like a man wrestling with something. But over time he starts speaking up in class. When Ricky is transferred to another jail, he writes letters to the minister, asking him questions about spiritual matters that vex him. Mostly they have to do with the problem of guilt. The minister takes his questions seriously, even researches them, spending two or three weeks on each letter and composing lengthy replies that Ricky pores over in his new cell. The questions are general and the answers are doctrinal, but both Ricky and the minister know they are talking about Ricky's soul.

He asks to be placed in the sexual offender treatment program at the adult prison in Valdosta. Two and a half years after receiving his GED, he earns a diploma from the success-skills course offered there. A month later, he earns a certificate from the appliance repair program, attesting that he's completed 863 hours of training and can now install household appliances as an electrical appliance apprentice. On his inmate evaluation sheet, relationship to coworkers is marked "above average." For the first time in Ricky's life, every category is marked above average.

In September 1990, Ricky Langley, the reformed prisoner, receives parole.

When the defense experts look back on this time, they're impressed by how much he learned during his Georgia prison term. When the prosecutors do, they sneer at it. One year and five months after being released from Georgia, he murdered Jeremy. So how much can you say he learned? An inmate in Georgia, after all, recalls him saying that his mistake there was leaving the girl alive. Next time, he would make sure she was dead. But that's not fair, the defense experts point out. Surely the inmate has his own reasons for saying this. And besides, child molesters are targeted in prison. Ricky may have had to try to appear threatening to be safe.

Like so much else, these years before the murder come down

to what it always comes down to with Ricky: What do you see in him? Do you believe that he's trying? Is his the story of a man who tries over and over again to get treatment, trying to change and take his changed self back into the world and live a new life, who tries and tries but is ultimately undone by the bulwark fact of who he is? Or is his the story of a man who leaves treatment over and over again, who never really tries but always runs? In the trial transcripts, the prosecutors and the defense psychiatric witnesses battle over this:

> Prosecutor: So while he was on probation [in 1984] and ordered to Lake Charles Mental Health, he leaves the state and stops his health treatment, is that right?
>
> Defense psychiatrist: That's correct.
>
> Q: He chose to do that, didn't he?
>
> A: Yes, he did that.
>
> Q: He chose to do that, didn't he?
>
> A: As much as it was his choice, yes, he chose to do that.
>
> Q: Are you trying to say he didn't have the ability to choose?

And:

> Prosecutor: So he didn't go to Indianapolis and [try to] see anybody [himself]?
>
> Defense psychiatrist: No.
>
> Q: Georgia?
>
> A: He did not see anyone.
>
> Q: He did not seek any kind of treatment whatsoever?
>
> A: No.
>
> Q: But he knew and had an insight into his behavior, that's what you said.

A: He had some insight into his behavior, yes.

Q: He understood that he was supposed to do it, didn't he, Doctor?

A: I believe he understood that.

Q: And he chose not to?

A: That's correct.

Q: Was he seeing anybody during the week before Jeremy Guillory's death?

A: No.

Q: So he knows enough to go to the doctor when he has bronchitis, but when he starts struggling with his sexual feelings towards Jeremy, it doesn't clue him in that maybe he needs help?

A: I think he knew he needed help. I think there's a real different situation, between going for bronchitis and going for your mental health. I'm sorry, I wish it wasn't, but it is.

Q: Why? Why is that different?

The man at the center of this trial, endlessly discussed and debated, endlessly documented and dissected in what will turn out to be nearly thirty thousand pages of documents, will remain an enigma in this way. What you see in Ricky may depend more on who you are than on who he is.

But released from prison in Georgia in 1990, clear and free except for needing to check in with his parole officer, his whole life suddenly seemingly opening up before him, Ricky faces a choice. He's been dreaming of the Calcasieu River, yes. But all these years of therapy have made Ricky interested in his past, and in the history of his family. In the questions of where he came from and how he became who he is. There's no record from these years of his saying that his dead brother, Oscar, has visited him or that he has heard Oscar's voice; it's not like that. It's more, now, the historian's interest, the genealogist's interest, and a personal interest.

Through his prison stays he's carried copies of Oscar's and Vicky Lynn's birth certificates, secreted out of Bessie's truck in Hecker. While he was imprisoned at Valdosta, he wrote to the coroner in Red Rock, Arizona, the site of the crash that led to Bessie's hospitalization and his birth. His letter received no response the first time—not even a note telling him whether he'd addressed his request correctly—but in prison he had nothing but time, so he went to the prison library and he looked up addresses and forms and he tried again. Eventually, copies of Oscar's and Vicky Lynn's death certificates arrived by mail. Over the years to come, he'll amass others this way: those of his parents' parents and their parents, census records and news articles and death certificates. He'll become so thoroughly the historian of his family that twenty-five years later, when I am digging into this story at the genealogical society just a few miles from where Ricky was born and a few miles from where Jeremy Guillory died, I'll happen upon a book about the history of the Langley family, self-published by a Louisiana hobbyist. In the book's acknowledgments section will be this: *A very special thank you to Ricky Langley, who was instrumental in obtaining and providing the majority of obituaries used in this book. To Ricky I wish all the best.*

In 1990, Ricky, carrying sheaves of the photocopied past around with him, makes a decision. He'll go back to California. California is still where the happy stories come from, the stories Bessie told him when he was a boy. That June, he hitchhikes there, searching for the past he never knew.

Eighteen

Chicago, 1996

For college, I invent a new life. I'll pretend the past never happened. Chicago feels far away from the gray house, far enough to
be free. The tall Gothic buildings of the University of Chicago look
like my dreams of a college quadrangle: Ivy twists up the sides of
stone archways and turrets, while at the buildings' center is a clearing girdled by the gnarled roots of trees, perfect for lying back and
reading on, and sheltered by a canopy of leaves. Campus legend
has it that because ivy doesn't grow naturally in Chicago, the
Rockefeller family endowed a separate fund to keep it growing.
Now, with the city of Chicago sparkling across the wide blue waters
of Lake Michigan, and the green ivy climbing through the wind
that rustles the tree leaves, the quad seems testament that you can
be whoever you want to. Walking across it each day, I embrace
my new role as diligent student. I never cut class. I sign up for the
maximum number of classes allowed and I go to the sessions prepared, not because I have to but because I am in love with the ideas
coming at me and I do the homework so soon after each class session that I do it over again before the next one. My grandfather
dies in my first weeks there, and when my parents tell me I hang
up the phone and don't tell a soul. That life is gone. I don't even
look like the old me anymore, the girl in her loose, ripped clothing and Crayola hair. I have bought a wardrobe of tight skirts and
tight sweaters and dyed my hair back to brown, going for something between a retro, safe can-do Mary Tyler Moore look and,

with one pair of black vinyl pants, Uma Thurman's character in *Pulp Fiction*, minus the syringe through the heart. What I am really going for is happy.

And somebody notices. In the dining hall one day a boy approaches. He's on the football team, he says. His brown hair falls over one eye, and now he looks at me from under it. His frat house is having a party. Do I want to be his date?

He actually says that word, *date*. It is like a movie, a movie I have dreamt for myself, and when Friday comes I queue up a funk CD and dress while singing along. The theme is seventies, and I choose a low-waisted pair of tight flare pants and a turtleneck that skims my curves. I blow-dry my hair straight, then fit a plaid woolen newsboy cap onto it, turning the cap around so that it looks, I imagine, a little jauntily unexpected.

The party is at one of the stone-and-brick frat houses on South University Avenue, houses I've walked by but never thought I'd go into. I don't drink. It's a point of pride with me. I don't want to be like my father. And what else does a person do at frat parties? In the house, couples make out against door frames. People in bell-bottoms and long hippie wigs sprawl across the living room couches and on the floor. Something silver gleams from the corner—a keg, I recognize, and only then do I realize that all this time when classmates have talked about kegs of beer, I've pictured them lugging around a wooden barrel.

The boy has shown up wearing a ball cap and a flannel shirt open over a white T-shirt. Now he fills a red plastic cup, tilting it to cut down on the foam, then holds it out to me.

"No, thanks." I'm happy to be here but I'm still not going to drink.

His face falls. He doesn't look just disappointed, but confused, and I know instantly I've done the wrong thing. This is not what the movie teenager would do. He takes the cup in one long swallow, then fills another and downs that, and then he wanders off and when he comes back to check on me later I'm pretty sure he's drunk and he can definitely tell I'm not and there doesn't seem to

be anything else to do but leave. "I'm not feeling so well," I say. I
have spent the hour sitting primly on a couch, trying to avoid other
people's elbows. "Maybe I'll just go home."

"I'll walk you."

This is as far as my memory gets, except for the memory of
the trees, which stab out of the dark grass sea of the Esplanade
and pierce the black sky. There is no light in my memory. There are
no stars and there are no people. There is barely him, and the knowledge of later—of another boy's hand on my arm, pulling me up, and
his voice asking, "Are you OK? Are you OK?"

The football player has held me down. Getting up off the grass,
shaking the earth-damp blades off my clothes and out of my hair,
I understand that. He has not raped me; I understand that, too. I am
still wearing my clothes. I was in peril but I don't quite know how
much. Though I am sober, my body has gone over to fright. I
remember nothing.

"Everyone knows his reputation," the boy says. "But no one was
sure how to tell you. You seemed so excited. So I thought I'd come
along, just to make sure you were all right."

From that point on I am instead with the boy who came along,
Ben. Ben is six feet six inches and at least in my memory does
not slouch like so many of the overly tall, but wears his gallantry
straight-backed. He has a rare condition known as Marfan syndrome. It has left him gangly, almost painfully thin. His thumb
joints grow out from his palms at right angles, like those of Abra-
ham Lincoln, who also had the syndrome. Lincoln, Ben tells me
on one of the early nights when we are lying on his dorm bed or
mine fully clothed, would have died within months even if he
hadn't been shot on that fateful day at Ford's Theatre. The syndrome had attacked the musculature of his heart. I am struck immediately by this idea, that the future was seeded secretly into the
present, the present seeded secretly into the past.

Ben's heart is safe—if I know anything about Ben I will always know this, that his heart is safe and big and beating—but the
syndrome has made his sternum protrude into a point and he is

self-conscious about it. Long before the Chicago weather turns so famously cold, he wears thick sweaters. It reminds me of how, even in summer, I have to lie under a blanket to be able to sleep. His skin is so elastic he can pinch his neck between two fingers and pull the skin there several inches away. It feels slightly waxy to the touch, like what I imagine the figures on display at Madame Tussauds to be. His height, his skin, the unusual prominence of his bones—all these put Ben always on display. It is not a costume or a disguise, the way my dyed hair and torn clothing was, the way my new streamlined clothing is, but for him it is an identity thrust upon him. Whereas I once kept trying to find a way to make the pain I feel inside show up on my skin so someone would notice, and now I pretend I don't feel it at all, Ben has no choice but to wear openly that he doesn't belong.

That, I realize, has made him kind. He is quick to laugh, quicker even to make others laugh, and dating him I am suddenly at the center of dorm life. When our dorm organizes a fund-raiser, Ben comes up with the idea of selling milk shakes in the lobby at midnight to the students, who are so famous for studying long hours that rumor has it that's why the cafeteria closes one night a week, to make the students go out. I, so in love with coffee that I briefly brew mine with caffeinated water, add the idea of using coffee ice cream and mixing in instant coffee granules. What we dream up is a tan sludge so gritty that drinking it is like drinking wet, sweetened sand, but when sales day comes around, the line of students in the lobby is long. At a school where students compete to say how little time studying leaves them for sleeping, and a good decade before Red Bull will become popular, drinkable highly caffeinated sludge is an undeniable hit. We use the first round of proceeds to buy more instant coffee, and advertise the next round of milk shakes as even stronger. That they're gross only adds to the hard-core appeal.

And I understand that. I will prove myself by drinking the gross thing, doing the hard thing. It will be years before I understand the value of softness. My body still hurts from the Lyme disease, and I am completely unprepared for the Chicago winter. Ben picks me up and carries me when my knees don't work. When I am well enough to stand and turn, he takes me dancing. He turns out to be an excellent dancer, able to spin and dip and lift me. I live in a dream, a dream of being loved.

But we are kids, me eighteen and him nineteen, and we are slow to realize what a threat looks like. Though I feel happy, I swear I do, since the night on the Esplanade I have somehow stopped eating. Before, in high school, I ate to hurt from the inside and then vomited for the relief of getting rid of what filled me. But now to have anything in my stomach is suddenly, inexplicably, scary. Only apples, nonfat yogurt, veggie burgers without the bun, and lettuce are safe. I haven't told anyone in Chicago about what happened with my grandfather, and I am determined not to. That belongs to the New Jersey house. That belongs to the past. My grandfather is dead and I am in college and free. At night, Ben and I lie on his bed, and with a single fingertip he traces the emerging bone-curve of my hip over my jeans and up the knobs of my back to my neck, which seems longer now that my body is more sparing. Pleased with my new thinness, I am wearing a lot of black, I am trying to be the New Yorker I long to be. I seem sophisticated to this boy from Kansas. We have sex only once or twice across the months, but he doesn't seem to mind. Neither of us knows yet that we are both gay. Neither of us knows yet how much we are a refuge for each other. He likes my turtlenecks and my fine-boned face and even my silence. "You're like a ballerina," he says.

But I don't stop there. I skate past ballerina, into danger. When I go back to Tenafly for Thanksgiving, I don't show the mark of the freshman fifteen like the other kids. I've lost thirty pounds since school started at the end of August. In the photograph my siblings and I pose for in front of the fireplace that will later become the Christmas card, I wear a smooth black mock turtleneck with short sleeves. My upper arms are the size of a wrist, my wrist the size of a child's. My parents send me to my old pediatrician. In my memory he tells me I really must eat, but that I don't have a serious problem.

That seems curious now, even impossible. Who would tell an anorexic teenager that she didn't have a serious problem? Looking back I imagine my parents standing at the side of a highway, their eyes wide and their mouths agape, watching a car wreck. My father still drinks too much. He is still depressed. My mother has found a voice in the courtroom, but she is still quieter at home. They still have two daughters to raise and a reputation in town to uphold and a law firm to run. And above all we are prisoners of the story we tell about ourselves, the story of the parents descended from poor immigrants who made it good and now have the Cadillacs and the beautiful, successful children and the most porch lights at Christmas. We are so determinedly fine it must be overwhelming for them to have a daughter who has suddenly shown up with the marks of all that is not fine so visibly on her. And a relief for all of us when I go back to school.

A month or so before spring break, my dorm adviser knocks on my door and hands me a typewritten piece of paper sheathed in a white envelope. I have lost still more weight, and the college is demanding that I see a nutritionist. I have already gone begrudgingly to a few sessions with a therapist, though I do not think a therapist will do me much good. I think a nutritionist will do me even less. The problem isn't that I don't understand that I need nutrients. The problem isn't even, not anymore, that I think I look good. I have stopped taking off my clothes in front of Ben. Only alone in my dorm room do I strip naked in front of the mirror. I have always had prominent hip bones, but now they are bladed, so clearly only a thin layer of skin over bone that they nauseate me. My backside seems to have deflated. When I was in fifth grade I was asked to draw a portrait of myself in art class one day. The other kids crayoned golden loops for their hair, scribbled in the red of their shirts. I remember my amazement when I looked at their portraits. They all seemed to know what they looked like so easily. I had drawn the only thing I could: a black swirl that emanated from the center of the construction paper like one of the swirls that obscure the screen in the Hitchcock movie *Vertigo*. Caught in the swirl

I'd drawn a gun, the electric chair, and hands that were reaching out for me, the stuff of my nightmares. That was the portrait of me I could imagine: what I thought and feared. What consumed me. My body was an unimaginable artifact swaddled in dark sweat clothes, something I tried hard to forget.

But in college, standing alone in front of the mirror, I find it strangely easy to look at myself. I repulse myself, with my bones and the knobs up my back and the bruises that, if I sit on a hard chair for too long, spread across the bag of skin that used to be my ass. That repulsion is comforting. I don't feel attractive, but I do feel safe.

The room in the college health clinic where I meet with the nutritionist is small and windowless and determinedly beige. "People have noticed," she says, that I seem to lose more weight after I go visit my family. She doesn't specify who "people" are. She sits on a white vinyl chair with arms of washed blond wood, her manner as carefully uninflected as her surroundings. The week before, at the Chinese dry cleaner's, the clerk had stopped me just as I'd reached to take my clothing off the rack. "Do you," he'd said, and then smiled. I'd smiled back. We always exchanged wordless smiles whenever I came in, but now he looked nervous. "Do you," he started again, "have the AIDS?" The next day in the cafeteria, I'd unfolded a note passed to me. *I know you think you look good but . . .* When I'd talked about signing up for a blood drive, a friend in the dorm had said, "You have to be a hundred pounds to give blood." I'd bit back the automatic words that I was five feet nine, of course I weighed a hundred pounds. But that night, I'd stepped on a scale and found I didn't. "Perhaps," the nutritionist says, "there is somewhere else you could go for the upcoming break?"

That's how I find myself seated in the cab of an old Ford pickup, Ben beside me and his older brother behind the wheel. The Kansas sunrise is like nothing I've ever seen, a dappled spew of lavender and pink that reaches to the heavens and seemingly beyond, exploding the earth into an almost obscene show of beauty. I am nearly dumbstruck by it and by the thought that the people in the buildings we are speeding past have this beauty before them every day. How many different kinds of lives there are. The buildings, too, surprise me. None is taller than two stories, three at the most, and though they look run-down with their neon-lettered signs turned off for daylight, there is nothing to compete with the gorgeously alive sky. "Beautiful, isn't it?" Ben's brother asks. I nod mutely.

For a week, we stay with his family. Ben's father is legendarily difficult, outspoken with strong opinions. But he is tall and thin and holds no opinion as strongly as he does his hatred of fat people— so he likes me. Ben's mother seems always to be watching me, and she treats me with such delicacy I could be made of spun glass. His brother is friendly. His brother's wife is just a few years older than Ben and me, and I learn that her first name is Roberta, but no one ever calls her that. They just call her his brother's "bride," even though the wedding was two years ago.

It's Roberta who finally gets through to me. Not something she says, but who she is. She seems lovely, kind and always smiling, content to live in this tiny town and not work and be referred to by the name of the guy she married.

But though the thought makes me feel small and mean, I know I wouldn't be happy with a similar life. I am sick, I realize, and if I do not find a way to make myself better, I am going to end up married younger than I want to be and living somewhere I do not want to because the truth is right now I *do* need someone to take care of me. How would Ben or anyone else know that this isn't my real life, that I'm still waiting for that to begin? How would he or anyone else know that in my real life, I don't need anyone to save me?

That summer, I break up with Ben, taking the cowardly phone call route. "But, but," he says, and I can hear his bewilderment turn to indignation like a newborn calf finding its legs, "I'm the one who should have broken up with *you*."

I flinch, but his words are true. In them I hear the conversations I'd never considered, the conversations he must have had with his friends.

I set about getting better with a single-minded devotion to the problem: If the problem is that I wasn't eating, I will eat. My body gets bigger. It softens. Summer passes, and when I come back to school, everyone can't stop telling me how good I look.

But I can't stand it. I can't stand how visible I feel. How unsafe.

I drop out.

I have wanted so badly to empathize with Ricky in Indianapolis, as he stands in the pouring rain in front of Ruth's car door, his hoodie pulled over his head, one hand shoved deep into his pockets and the other holding his blue duffel, his head ducked forward to keep the rain out of his eyes. In that moment, his life had spun off the rails of what he imagined for himself. He was trying to find something to save him, to make him normal. I understand that wish. In Ricky's files, there's a therapy intake sheet from the years after the Calcasieu Center days. On it, Ricky says he is no longer a virgin. He had a girlfriend once, he says. I came across this mention and that the Georgia girl—whom he touched when he was twenty—was fourteen.

And I thought of Colorado Luke.

Luke, who at twenty-two must have had his own reasons for having courted a sixteen-year-old on the Internet. For having assembled for her careful packages of photographs and curated mixtapes, for having flown across the country to see her while she was still in high school, a life he'd left behind years ago—except that he hadn't really, still living in his childhood bedroom, still as lost as a teen. Luke, who, no matter where I am in the country, still finds me online every few years and sends me an e-mail telling me we had a special connection, one he hasn't found since, and can we please, please get in touch.

I never write back.

I was sixteen. I didn't know I was too young for him. I just thought his attention meant that I was worthy of love, could be loved, and that I wasn't broken. When a lifeline comes, you don't evaluate whether it's the right one. You just grab for it, and hold on.

So I wondered, when in the files I reached the story of the Georgia girl, if this was what had happened. If that was who the girl was. If, when he took her mother's '69 Chevy to escape to Indianapolis, it was possible that maybe she hadn't known. If, when he described her telling him that she liked when he touched his tongue to her and could he please, please do it again, maybe there could be some truth to that. If at least for this one moment in Ricky's life maybe the relationship had been inappropriate, ill-advised, ill-chosen, unwise—but something short of my grandfather. Something more like Luke.

I let myself think that, because it made it possible to read the files. It made it possible to spend this time with him. To try, as I must try, to understand.

Not until I got the transcript from Ricky's first trial, at which the Georgia girl testified, did I realize my mistake.

She was fourteen when she testified at the trial. In 1986, she was five.

Nineteen

California, 1990–1991

California greets Ricky with seemingly unbound potential. He's free out here, free from Georgia, free from Iowa, free to invent his own life. A life that's new but that also makes good on the unfulfilled promise of Bessie and Alcide's move so many years before, and of his own attempt to stay as a teenager. He likes the open landscape, likes the palm trees, likes that the long coastline's always nearby even if he's not technically living on it. The stories Bessie used to tell him about the wildflowers, and how the Hollywood sign up on a hill was there for anyone to see it, even her, come back to him now, and the city seems all possibility. The shiny new cars on the boulevards! Everywhere he looks, people making money! Los Angeles is a city of people from elsewhere, come to make their fortunes. Just like him.

He finds work as a handyman with a contractor named Mike. Mike's girlfriend's name is Ellen, and the three of them take to spending their free time together, sharing a few beers and a couple of jokes after the day's work is done. Mike seems familiar to Ricky—he's from a barely-hanging-on working-class background like Ricky—but Ellen's people have money, and Ricky must find himself watching her. Not because she's pretty, though she is, but to learn. When she calls him up and asks him if he'd like to join Mike and her at one of her parents' parties, he knows enough to ask her what he should wear.

"Just wear something appropriate," she says. "No need to get fancy."

"Like what?" he asks.

"Oh, you know, just something appropriate." She's distracted, he can hear it, and for an instant he thinks it must be Mike distracting her and he feels something approaching jealousy. He's too embarrassed to ask her again. He doesn't know what she means by "appropriate."

I see him standing under a grove of palm trees. Someone has strung a strand of white lights off the slatted leaves, and the rays bounce off Ricky's hair. He's slicked it back with a can of Dep gel from the dollar store. He's not smiling—he's too nervous—but in his eyes and the tightness of his fingertips as he checks and straightens and checks again the powder-blue polyester suit Ellen Smith will describe four years from now at his first trial, when everything has changed, you can see he's thrilled to be here. The lights glint and his hair gleams and the black dress shoes he bought at Payless ("It's a California shoe chain," Ellen Smith says helpfully, the chain not having yet reached Louisiana in 1994 when she's testifying at the first murder trial) glow where he polished them. Even the black leather vest he got from Goodwill and is wearing now, incongruously, under his powder-blue polyester suit—even that vest shines. He's polished it, too. He's too skinny, the suit too big for him, a kid playing dress-up. Underneath the suit he vibrates with nerves. He's twenty-six but he's never been to a party like this before: little round tables dotted over a spacious yard, crisp white tablecloths over them. Somebody has ironed the tablecloths, he can tell. Even the grass looks like someone manicured it, the bright green so even it shouldn't be real. Ellen's parents are smiling big, real, relaxed smiles and pinching long-stemmed wineglasses. They clutch their guests' hands to their chests heartily and say how good it is to see them, how good. When they said it to him he froze like a possum playing dead. So now he's hiding out under the grove, watching.

But Ellen's in her element. She flits among the guests, answering questions. No, she and Mike have no plans to get married. No, they're not ready to have children just yet. She loves that her parents will invite anyone to parties like this. Would invite anyone. She's sure of it. That's why she brought Ricky. She hasn't told them Ricky was convicted of a sex crime. That's all he's told her: a "sex crime"—and what, she privately thinks, could be so bad about sex? But even after he's accused of murder a few years from now, she'll swear on the witness stand that if her parents had known what he was guilty of, they'd still have wanted him there. They're that kind of people, California people. It doesn't matter what you've done, what the past is; it matters who you are now. And Rick—what Ellen calls Ricky, the name he's adopted since coming out here, loving the cool hardness of that *k* at the end, how it says he's finally grown up—Rick is a hard worker. Like her Mike.

Mike. At the party she must look for him, catch his eye, smile. He's standing off to the side, not talking to her parents' friends, a bottle of beer in his hand. Ricky's with him, a bottle in his. The two of them angled in under the tree, keeping themselves out of the way of her parents' friends. Like brothers, those two. She smiles again, then looks more appraisingly, noticing Ricky's clothes. Noticing them so carefully she'll be able to describe them years later. She must wonder about his life for a minute, about the life that has brought him to those clothes. What does she write in her head for him? What, in this instant, does she imagine and forgive?

Summer passes, then fall. One night, Ellen, Mike, and Ricky are sitting around a bar, and talk turns to what they'll be buying for Christmas. Ellen says she'll get her father a golf shirt. Mike will get his mother flowers.

"The *real* question," Ellen must say, lowering her eyes at Mike over her drink, "is what this one's getting me."

Mike winks at Ricky. "Now Rick, you're not going to tell her, are you? We've got our secrets."

"No fair!" says Ellen. "He already knows what I'm getting you. He knows too much, I think."

This moment here? Ricky would nail this moment up like a fishing trophy if he could, mount it on the wall where he could look at it every day. In this moment, he has friends.

"What are you going to buy, Rick?" Ellen asks.

He gulps his beer and the beer makes him brave. "I've been saving up money." He doesn't even think of everything they don't know about him. About where he's from. "My mama, they took off her leg fifteen years ago and she's still on crutches." He must think of Bessie slinging her body through the space of the trailer, trying not to catch the crutch against the couch or a table leg. Those crutches are bad enough at home. But to try to go anywhere else he knows she cringes inside. "I'm going," he says, and he likes the taste of the word *going* in his mouth, how definitive it feels, "I'm going to buy her a wheelchair." The words taste right. They taste true.

"All right, man!" Mike claps him on the back. "That's a good son your mama's got." He raises his beer. "To your mama. What's her name?"

"Bessie."

"To Rick's mama, Bessie," Mike says, "and her wheelchair." The three of them clink glasses.

For two weeks, this idea fuels him. When Friday payday comes, maybe he takes his check and cashes it and folds a couple of bills into a coffee can before he takes a bill to the liquor store and buys a smaller bottle than he did before. When he pushes the bills into the can, he feels proud. He can see the shiny chrome the wheelchair will have, the big easy wheels. The first week, he sees himself polishing the chrome before he presents Bessie with the chair. He'll make it gleam. He'll tie a big red ribbon around it into a bow, the way they do in the movies. By the second week, he's got an even better idea. Maybe he could put a payment down on a wheelchair with one of those joystick things. Make Bessie's life one of luxury, the first luxury she's had. He pictures being with her in Iowa when she first sees it. How tentatively she'll lower herself onto the seat.

He'll show her how to work the joystick and she'll try and mis-
judge and crash the wheelchair into the couch and oh, they'll
laugh and laugh.

But by Christmas, his dreams have dissolved. Maybe work with
Mike dries up, maybe he's just so used to leaving that he doesn't
know how not to, or maybe something happens and Ellen and
Mike don't want him around anymore. He leaves and the records
hold no reason why. Ellen, later, will not say why on the witness
stand, only describe how badly he wanted to get the wheelchair for
Bessie, and that he then left. He never sees Mike again. Sees Ellen
only at the trial. Bessie never does get her wheelchair. He moves
to a different part of California, but after a few months he's back on
the road. He returns to Georgia, to live with his sister Judy. There he
goes to see a psychiatrist privately, as ordered by the Georgia court—
but those records were never found, either because they were destroyed or because they never existed. In December 1991, he leaves
Georgia and moves back in with his parents in Iowa, Louisiana.

A few months from now, Ricky will murder Jeremy. And after he
does, his lawyers and the experts and Ricky himself will all talk
about how he's been good "for a year" now, that he has not molested anyone in a full year.

But he was released from the Georgia prison not a year ago, but
a year and a half. And before his release, he was in prison for four
years—where he presumably didn't have the chance to molest a
child. So the number could be *five* years, not one year. There's something unaccounted for here, something the law can't concern itself
with because there is no evidence, no record. Are Ricky and his
lawyers leaving something—someone—out? One year's when he
left Ellen and Mike's. One year's when he left California.

When Ricky moves in with Bessie and Alcide in Iowa one final
time he is twenty-six. Still scrawny, not much bigger than a preteen,

with the emotional maturity, the doctors say, of an eleven- or twelve-year-old—but enough grown-up smarts to understand how he's perceived by others and to hate it. He understands he's a pedophile now. At his exit interview for parole in Georgia, he satisfies the officer that yes, he can move to Louisiana and live with his parents. They'll be responsible for him. Bessie attends and I picture her in one of the pastel day dresses my grandmother used to wear, this one nicer than the housedresses—Bessie would be a little nervous—with knitted lace around the collar and maybe the cuffs. She sits in a folding chair opposite the parole officer, her crutch leaning on the wall behind her and the stump of her missing leg angled in, so that her ankles, if she had both, would be crossed demurely.

"Ma'am, I want to make sure that you and your husband know what you're getting into."

She just looks at him. Thinks, maybe, of Ricky when he was a boy, the call she got from sixth grade when he said he saw Oscar. Thinks of the family reunions where he always headed off so willingly to look after the children. There is one note—only one—in the files that Ricky once molested a family member. It doesn't say whom. She must know. Maybe she remembers telling the counselor at the Lake Charles Mental Health Center five years ago that looking after Ricky had become a burden, that she couldn't leave him alone for five minutes without worrying that he was gonna go off and "molest somebody." Now, five years later, after probation and a prison term for Ricky, she knows that to be even more true.

But Bessie believes in the crosses one bears in life, and Ricky is both her love and her cross. Would she take it back now, the decision not to end her pregnancy with him, now that he's molested three children she knows of and who knows how many she doesn't? You don't think that way. She doesn't think that way. Likely she can't feel those children's—those strangers'—hurt the way she feels Ricky's presence beside her. Her son. You take family in.

So she looks the officer in the eye. "Yes, sir. His father and me, we understand."

It's in this interview that Ricky says, "I got me a preference for blond boys. Maybe six years old," and he must be proud that he can describe it now, that he understands himself enough to know this. The officer records Ricky's words but doesn't write whether Bessie's in the room then. Does she hear what Ricky says? Do his words pass over her with a chill? Does the officer's pen pause on this harbinger, or does he not even notice, the appointment perfunctory? No one—not Bessie, not the parole officer, not even, by all accounts, Ricky—notes that just a few miles away from the trailer where Ricky will stay, a little blond boy lives. He is six years old, he loves his BB gun, and he stays with his mother in a house where they struggle to keep on the heat.

Twenty

Massachusetts, 2002

The night I'm accepted to law school, I break in.

Harvard Yard is a long, empty expanse of black now that it's nearly midnight. The glow from the streetlamps in the Square pinpricks through the trees. Standing on an empty wooden porch, I shiver. The night is colder than I thought it would be, windless and clear and silent, the kind of Boston night that will always remind me that the city is on the water and that water becomes ice.

At twenty-three, finally graduated from college after a second try, I live in New Jersey with my boyfriend, Adam, and the dog we've adopted whom we've named Professor. We share the first floor of a house that's tucked into the armpit of a highway exit ramp. The road from my parents' house—an hour and a half north of ours—to the one Adam and I share is a snarl of factories that light up shiny and gray as the slick of fur on a rat's back in the highway headlights, that Jersey Turnpike smell like it's always summer in the city and you're always standing over a sewer. Our house is pretty enough, with a slap of peach paint and even a picket fence that used to be white. But at night, lying on my back in bed while Adam sleeps next to me, l listen to the husband and wife next door yell at each other for hours. Their voices scare me. All that clabbered bitterness.

It's too close to how I feel, still living in New Jersey. Still circling my parents' house, around memories I don't want inside me and can't escape. After a year of being in their house I went back to college, this time in New York, at Columbia. I did well, making straight As, but before two years were up I'd moved back in with them to finish school, commuting over the bridge. Living in the gray house makes me depressed, but when I'm depressed, to live there feels right, like the walls are confirmation of the memories. After graduation I moved in with Adam, but that didn't help, either. Then, in a Hail Mary pass to the future, I applied to law school. The old route that had worked for my parents. The old love from my childhood. And it turned out that all those afternoons I'd spent lying on my stomach on my parents' office carpet as a kid, doing logic games in books from the newsstand downstairs, prepared me well for the LSAT: I got into Harvard.

Now, as we stand under the motion sensor light on the porch in Cambridge, there's a bag at Adam's feet that holds two matching sweatshirts from a newsstand in the Square, the only store that is open at this hour. The acceptance letter arrived this afternoon while Adam was at work. When he came home I was still sitting cross-legged on the carpet, staring at it in open-mouthed, catatonic disbelief. "Baby!" he said, and spun me around until my tears stopped and I laughed. "How do you want to celebrate?"

As soon as he asked, I knew. I wanted a sweatshirt. I wanted a school-colors maroon sweatshirt with HARVARD on it. When I was six years old, my father had called me to a conference at his bedside. He was propped up against pillows with his reading glasses on the covers beside him. He looked so serious that when I saw him I paused in the doorway. He motioned me in. I sat down on the edge of his bed and he reached over to the stack of news-papers that was next to his bedside all through my growing up— that is next to his bedside still—and withdrew an envelope. Then he put on his glasses, opened the envelope ceremoniously, and we discussed: Was my very first report card on track to go to Har-vard? My father was from a New Jersey immigrant community and had gone to state schools. To him Harvard would mean we'd made it. By seven I had a maroon sweatshirt I wore everywhere, but by seventeen I wouldn't have applied to Harvard even if there had been a chance that I, with all my cut classes and blank spots on my high school transcript, could have gotten in. For me *Harvard* means a time before things went wrong.

Adam drove us six hours up from Jersey right then. Now we stand at a building I'm pretty sure must be on the law school campus, though in the dark I can't find a sign. It just looks like what I want a law school building to look like: large red and tan stone bricks, wooden columns, turrets that carve out from its sides. He blows on his hands and watches me, waiting for my lead. "Do you want to go home?" he asks. In eight hours I'm due at the bookstore where I work. "Or"—he draws the consonant out and arches his eyebrow at me—"do you want to go in?"

"In." If we're caught, I'll pretend I'm a student. It will be true soon enough.

In the photograph of me Adam takes that night, I lie on my back on the maroon benches inside Austin Hall at Harvard Law School, my black wool coat still buttoned around my neck, the maroon turtleneck I'd worn without realizing peeking out of the coat's collar, my hair spread around me and my eyes half-closed. I look how I feel: peaceful, finally secure.

An idea strikes. "Be my lookout?" I say.

Adam grins. "Anytime."

I find a narrow staircase that looks like it goes up the full length of the building. The first floor is dark, but surely there's a security guard somewhere. One more flight, to be safe. I try the first door I come to after the landing—open.

The classroom is surprisingly small, cloistered with only a single, postage-stamp window and fewer than a dozen chairs arranged into neat little rows. And a green chalkboard. With chalk. Can I? Yes. "Thanks for letting me in!" I write.

I mean, thanks for letting me *in*. Not just to law school, but to the law.

Months later, when Adam has stayed behind in Jersey with our dog and I have moved to the city that grows so bone-chillingly cold,

I am thriving. All around me the books I borrowed from my father's bookcase have to come to life. My torts professor is a skinny woman, nervous as a rabbit, with a disconcerting habit of using her two toddlers as the examples in hypotheticals. "Now imagine," she says, "that my daughter Marguerite is crossing the street one day, and an hour before a gasoline truck has leaked all over the road. In the explosion, she loses her foot." In torts—which are really a measure of how you judge the harm a person does to another, how you assign fault, how you understand cause—someone is always catching fire, losing a limb, or being maimed. In my favorite case, *Palsgraf v. Long Island Railroad Co.*, a man leaps for a departing train, dropping a package onto the train tracks. The package contains fireworks. They explode. At the other end of the platform, a scale falls on a woman. It's a chain of events, and really a question of how to tell the story. A question of cause. The day we learn that Marguerite, the professor's daughter, really doesn't have a foot—that the limb she keeps losing in these stories is already gone—we sit in awkward shock. "It's OK to laugh!" the professor says. "It's funny!" Property class becomes not about rules to be memorized, but the question of what can be owned; constitutional law about the commitments we've made, what binds us together as a country.

My classmates and I love ideas. At night we argue over beers in our dorm rooms, or glasses of red wine in bars. Sometimes we tape sheets of white paper end to end and draw maps of our belief systems, trying to plot out our ideals as if they were logic trees. Consistency is what we prize, and coherency, and reason, and to be true to our ideals so that they fit together into the neat puzzle of us. I want to be driven only by my ideals. That's why I'm here. In my law school application I wrote about standing on the tarmac as a child and knowing instantly that I did not believe in the death penalty. Why wasn't taking a human life considered cruel and unusual? I wanted to come to law school, I wrote, to understand.

When it's time for me to apply for summer jobs, death penalty defense firms are where I apply. I find two firms that specialize only in death penalty cases and are looking for law students to work for them for the summer. One's in California, and while the summer that the lawyer from that firm describes to me sounds great—I'd love to live in San Francisco—the office has only one case. "You'll get to sit in on brainstorming meetings," he says on the phone.

The lawyer from the Louisiana firm sounds strapped and harried. "Let me ask you a question, try something out," he says. In Jefferson Parish, a parish formed by white flight out of New Orleans, prosecutors have begun showing up for the sentencing hearings of young black men facing the death penalty wearing ties printed with nooses. I'm shocked at the story—in 2003, nooses? I stammer out that it's got to be prejudicial but admit I don't know any rule that would cover it.

He laughs, the sound sharp as a bark. "Neither do we. I'll let you know what we come up with. But we've got more work than we can handle. We'll have plenty of work for you."

By the time the follow-up interview call comes around, two weeks later, I'm certain I want to work for the Louisiana firm. I take the call in my dorm room, a single room in a converted hotel where the back of the door still has checkout instructions, the heavy paisley drapes are foil-backed, and my bathroom has a rack meant for a flurry of small towels. I'd chosen to live in the dorms hoping to make friends, but the dorm I picked was a mistake—I accidentally chose the one for grade-gunners. My classmates don't cook in the communal kitchen or hang out in common areas. There's no friendly gossip or late-night study breaks. On move-in day I'd been wearing torn jeans and a sweatshirt, wrestling a giant cardboard box of clothing into the elevator, when a man had passed by me wheeling a clothing rack. His hair was parted to knifepoint precision, and he wore a blue oxford shirt and khakis that had clearly been freshly pressed. The bar contained five more identical pairs of khakis and twice as many identical blue oxford shirts. As I held the elevator door open, he wheeled in a pressing machine.

But I've made other friends here, idealists like me. They're the reason I worry about what I'll be asked during the job interview. Because after a year of law school and our late-night debate sessions, I am starting to understand that I really don't believe my opposition to the death penalty—or anyone's support of it—comes down to reason. It's still that simple, basic conviction I've always had: that everyone is a person, no matter what they've done, and taking a human life is wrong.

But on the phone, the lawyer never asks why I oppose it. "Tell me," she says, her voice low, at once formal and somehow intimate, a practiced tone designed to elicit confession, "how do you feel about defending the guilty?"

"I have no illusions that all my clients will be innocent," I say. My words sound awkward even to me, but I'm a little irked at the question. I want to talk about reasoning, not feelings. I'm glad to know that there will be female lawyers at the firm—unlike most other public interest law, the death penalty world is heavily male— but her words strike me as condescending. Does she really think I'm that naive?

"How about defending people accused of murder?"

"I believe everyone deserves a lawyer," I say. It's a death penalty firm. Of course some clients will be accused murderers.

"You may have to meet with them. You may have to sit with them."

I change tactics: "My father's a criminal defense attorney. I grew up around his clients." When I was a young teenager I spent one of my parents' office Christmas parties hovering around a tall, slim man whose teeth flashed whenever his face stretched into a wide smile. All evening I offered him cheese cubes from a tray, a fresh napkin to replace the one he was holding, anything to get him to shine that smile on me. Later I realized that he was a client my father had told me about, a hit man for the Korean mafia. After the party he entered the Witness Protection Program. My father has always defended the bad guys. He has told me more than once that his job is to be amoral, never to think about what the people he defends did—"if," he always adds, a defense attorney to his core, "they did it."

The lawyer continues. "Some of them may be charged with other crimes in addition to murder."

"I *understand*." I get up and pace around the room. How can I make her hear me? "Look, I believe in what your firm does. I've always opposed the death penalty. I'd like to help fight it."

"Our clients are not the most popular people." Her voice lowers. "We just finished a case, for example, in which we defended a man who'd previously been convicted of child molestation. Can you defend a child molester?"

My grandfather has been dead for eight years, but suddenly I see him and my body seizes. I see him alive, wearing one of his tweed newsboy caps, sucking on a hard violet candy, and me as the adult I am—sitting with him, a legal pad propped on my lap, trying to take notes but noticing only those hands that touched me, the body I know too well. In the vision I hold my knees very still, trying not to let them brush against his. Then suddenly I'm a child again, and there's his face after he's taken out his false teeth, grinning gummily, his breath wet and murky, tinted with a note of lavender. I am very small, small enough to be both fascinated and repelled by the black expanse suddenly inside his mouth. The doll lamp bathes his face in yellow as he grins at me. "I'm a witch," my grandfather says. "You remember what that means."

This job will be my test. If I really oppose the death penalty, I must oppose it for men like him.

"Yes," I say. "I can defend a child molester."

Twenty-One

Louisiana, 1991–2000

Early December 1991, and Ricky lasts a few scrub-brush weeks living with Bessie, Alcide, and his younger brother Jamie, but he hates it. Living with them is like going back in time. He works whatever odd jobs he can pick up and spends the rest of the hours smoking pot by the river, trying not to think about where Jamie's going in his life and where he so far has failed to go.

But then he catches a break. There's an opening at the local Fuel Stop, doing maintenance. Maybe one of the guys from the river gets him the gig; maybe Ricky stops in one day for a Coke and sees a handwritten HELP WANTED notice in the window. But he stops in. He can push a broom and he takes orders well, at least right now, now that he's trying to please. He's proud of the polo they give him. Maybe this one will be his for longer than a few weeks.

First payday, he cashes the check and rents a motel room to live in. He's not thinking straight—the room will burn up the checks faster than he can earn them, if he thought about it he'd know this can't last long—but back in the Georgia prison, when his counselor asked him to make a list of his goals, he wrote, "Get my own place," and he's got one now. It's so sweet to be living alone. The room isn't much, but it's his. Iowa is dotted with welfare motels, longer-stay rentals, and his room is made for a man down on his luck who's looking to invent a new kind. He's got a coffee-maker and a hot plate and bedsheets he pays a couple of bucks extra for and a small television he can play as loudly as he wants, and he can smoke in the room, too. He spends his evenings lying flat on his back on the bed, his head cocked up on the pillows, chain-smoking into a black ashtray on the nightstand with a plastic cup of peppermint schnapps next to his head. Doesn't seem lonely if it's the best kind of aloneness you ever had. Even the noise from the other rooms—there's a man a few doors down who smacks his wife and kids; there are people selling drugs and who knows what else every hour of the night—can't get to him. It's nothing like prison. It's not even anything like living with Alcide and Bessie and Jamie in the trailer, so much emotion and history and hurt piled atop one another. This room may not seem like much, but inside it, he's free.

Then, one evening, he goes to the parking lot to have a smoke under the stars.

Standing outside is a woman. Maybe she's leaning against the side of the building, one hand resting on the top of the trash can, her head thrown back as she exhales into the night sky. Tired skin and tight eyes, her hair falling out of a ponytail, but she's pretty in a closed-up kind of way. The kind of face that has lived, that holds secrets.

The woman brings her head back up. She stubs the cigarette out on the top of the trash can. She studies him a minute. "I know you from the Fuel Stop, don't I? You work outside?"

Ricky nods.

"My name's Pearl," she says. "I'm a cashier there." Maybe it's the late fall night that makes them talk with each other, that turns them reflective, the grace of cool dry air in a state that spends so much of the year so hot and muggy, the grace of the darkness to two people who right now in their lives want nothing so much as cover. Standing there in the motel parking lot, maybe rooting in her pack for another cigarette, perhaps knowing that when this one's empty it'll be a stretch to buy another but still needing that cigarette, trying not to hear the sounds of her children June and Joey as they play-tussle on the other side of the motel room door while Terry's got the television up too loud again, to drown out their chatter, Pearl is cash-strapped and kid-exhausted. She's smart enough to see that the motel is wearing her and Terry and the kids out, but there's no way to have anything different, not on her salary. Ricky feels free in his room. But she feels trapped.

That must be what she's thinking when she listens to Ricky talk under the night sky. Maybe he tells her how he wants a little bit of land down by the Calcasieu River where he can go and not bother nobody. He'll hunt and fish and earn a little money at the Fuel Stop, just enough to keep him in cigarettes and booze and pay off the land so it's truly *his*. When Ricky dreams, he doesn't dream friends. He dreams a place where he can be who he is and where there won't be anyone around to look that other damning thing, normal. Where it's just him and *he's* normal. True, a man living by the river, talking to no one, would be an object of fun or bogeyman stories among the neighborhood kids. But he kind of likes that idea. Because maybe there'll be some kid like he was who doesn't fit in, who just wants to get away, and he'll hear about Ricky and he'll know it's possible.

Pearl listens, then drops the second cigarette to the concrete and rubs it out with her foot. She chews her lip like she's thinking. Finally she says, "I want a house." That's her dream. She and Terry and the kids in a proper house, the kids with proper bedrooms, not whaling on each other like they do in the motel room, all up in each other's spaces. Some privacy and a good night's sleep. They've been talking about a house, but to afford it they'll both have to take on more hours and then who'll look after the kids? Maybe Ricky could rent a bedroom from them, in exchange for fifty bucks a week and help with the children.

Ricky says this is how it happened, the two of them talking under the stars. They became friends, and when he moved in with her and her husband and the kids he became better friends with Terry. Before he moved in he told them he was on parole for molesting a child. But they could see he was trying. They accepted him. They trusted him.

Pearl? She never mentions this night. Not the smoke, not the stars, not Ricky's talking about his dreams and not her admitting to hers. She says Ricky became friends with Terry, and that the two of them invited him to stay on account of that. She never says he told her he was a molester. Not after one of her son's friends goes missing, and she asks him to leave. Not after they find that boy dead in her house. Not even after her son and her husband die colliding with an Amtrak train, and it's only her and her daughter left and she flees to New Mexico, where for a long time not even the lawyers can find her.

But she never says she didn't know, either.

For a few weeks, Ricky has the life he wants. He and Pearl and Terry rent a big white two-story house on a street the landlord calls Watson Road. The street doesn't really have a name, the lane so far back it might as well be in the woods, and the house is run-down and strange-looking, with a staircase running out the back of the second floor, into the woods. But it's the only two-story house in the neighborhood, and this makes it special. Pearl and Terry pay to have the phone line turned on. The only phone in the neighborhood; this, too, makes the house special. Ricky goes to his job at the Fuel Stop and looks after June and Joey and takes good care of his khakis and polo, washing them nice and even ironing them sometimes, and when he gets a little extra money saved he buys himself a bottle of schnapps and goes out to the river to do some fishing and suddenly he isn't a loner out there, suddenly he isn't a weirdo, but a workingman who lives in a nice house, spending his day off enjoying some much-needed downtime.

Ricky is normal.

But nothing in this life can last. One afternoon, Joey's friend Jeremy comes over. Ricky draws a bath for Jeremy and Joey. He brings them soap, the files say. Maybe Joey calls to him that they need it. Or maybe Ricky, half knowing what he's doing, goes to the cabinet and gets a new bar. Takes it to the bathroom, where he sees Jeremy in the bath. Says, "Oh—I thought you needed soap."

That night, Ricky can't sleep. He keeps thinking about Jeremy. The next evening, he and Pearl are sitting on recliners in the living room, watching a crime television show, one of their favorites. Carefully, as casually as he can, he asks, "Whose kid was the blond boy from yesterday?"

"That was Lori's son," she answers.

He doesn't want to let on how curious he is, so he waits. On the screen, I imagine, the show has just shown the actress playing the victim. Next they will reenact the scene. Ricky watches. Then he asks, "Where do they live?"

"With Melissa, just down the street."

The actress is lying on the couch now, conspicuously not noticing the man at her window. "You think Joey will have him back over again soon?"

This time Pearl gives him a queer look. She doesn't answer.

When, the day after that, Ricky opens the door and Jeremy's standing on the threshold, Terry Lawson off fishing with June and Joey, and Pearl nowhere to be found, he thinks, *Oh, you'd better run, kid*. He has a flash of what's going to happen. There will be no turning back now.

He could shut the door. Instead he opens it wider. Jeremy steps across the threshold, into the house.

Where Ricky kills him.

Ricky will spend the rest of his life puzzling over this act. An hour after Lucky and Dixon arrest him, he confesses to the murder, but tells them he didn't molest Jeremy. An hour later, he confesses again, slightly different details, and says he did. On three videotapes and over several months in notepads hastily scribbled on by prison guards when Ricky says he has something to add, he gives different versions of the murder. He describes undressing Jeremy to molest him. (When Jeremy was found, he was clothed.) He says he killed Jeremy in an effort not to molest him. (Possible, but Ricky's semen was on Jeremy's shirt.) He says the crime wasn't sexual at all, but murder, and what he really wanted was to get a gun and go down to the elementary school, "do some shooting." (Maybe, but it's pedophilia that Ricky's struggled with for decades. Not violence.) He says he killed Jeremy because he was "overcome with a feeling" of not wanting Jeremy to become like him. Ten years later, he'll still be confessing, unable to stop telling this story different ways. He casts about for stories as if he's casting about for an identity, trying to figure out who he is and who this means he'll be.

When they take him locked up in handcuffs to the parish jail for his holding hearing, there's a news van waiting for the police cruiser. Lucky gets him out, and the reporter scurries over, zooming the news camera in close on Ricky's face. Ricky looks into the lens, grins wide, seems to realize he shouldn't, looks down. He's awkward in his body, shuffling along. It's as though half of him wants to be seen and the other half wants to hide away. The sun's clear and bright behind him, making the orange jumpsuit glow against the blue sky and the scrub grass and the trees. The jail's a squat building of red-brown brick and institutional beige. Along one side of the building slouches a group of corrections officers, smoking. When they see the reporter their heads bob up like apples and they stare at Ricky. Among them is Sergeant Larry Schroeder, thirty-two years old and working as a transport guard for the Louisiana Department of Corrections. For the past five years he's spent his days accompanying inmates all over the state. Today he's responsible for a man called Jackson and a couple others. But really Larry's a local. He lives in Lake Charles and he's raising his children here. So he recognizes Ricky immediately. Iowa's only eight miles away. Larry's "not one of them local-news watchers," he'll say later, he prefers CNN, but everyone knows who Ricky is. Ricky's mug shot was all over the state.

After they've all gone inside and the day's hearings have begun, Larry's sitting on a folding chair in the hallway outside the courtroom, waiting for Jackson's case to be called, when he hears banging. The sheriff's deputy in charge of the holding cell signals him to come over. It's Jackson, twitchy and agitated, hitting the door of the group cell. When he sees Larry he stops. His eyes are all bugged out. "Man, you got to get me out of here," Jackson says. "Move me or something."

"Calm down," Larry says. "Calm down or I'll have you put in lockdown when we're back."

"Get me out of—"

"Calm down," Larry says, and walks back to his chair. It's as if the inmates think that because he's not their regular guard they'll be able to get away with something. As if he were a substitute teacher. Larry's not having any of it.

But then the deputy asks Larry to watch the inmates for a minute. Larry walks back over and leans against the door of the holding cell. The first thing he notices is that the inmates are all in bench seats cramped on one side of the room. And on the other, in a chair by himself, is Ricky. Jackson's in the row closest to Ricky, and he's rocking in his seat, still agitated. "Man, leave me alone!" Jackson says. "Leave me alone."

Then Jackson spots Larry. "Sarge, you gotta listen to what this little dude has to say!" Later that's the phrase that will stick in Larry's mind. "Little dude." Because while Jackson, so much bigger than Ricky, can't seem not to comment on Ricky's size, what strikes Larry is his tone. Jackson's genuinely scared. Too scared not to show it, even if the other inmates will give him grief later.

Or maybe, Larry thinks, they won't. Look at the way they're all on the other side of the room.

To Ricky, Jackson says, "Tell Sarge what you just told me about killing that kid."

From his folding chair, leaning forward with his arms crossed and pitching his voice loud enough that everyone in the holding cell can hear, Ricky says that he enjoyed killing Jeremy. "Enjoyed killing the other ones, too," he says. "The cops will never find them all." He says that he molested Jeremy and that he was molested by his father, Alcide. "But I'm not angry at him, not at all. I know he enjoyed it. I did, too."

"That's sick, man!" yells Jackson. To Larry, he says, "You better not lock me up with this dude."

What are we watching, as the inmates separate themselves from Ricky just like the schoolkids used to? What are we watching, as he tells and retells the story of the murder? I have read every document I can find from Ricky's life. I have read psychologist reports and death row reports and even his commissary order forms from the Calcasieu Correctional Center, trying to discern who Ricky might be from the detritus of the record his life has created, and he is still a hard person for me to understand, to know whether to believe. This is the only time on record that he says Alcide molested him. One other time he says he was abused—doesn't say by whom—but every other, he says he wasn't. This is the only time he says he killed other children. When he was first arrested, he said, "I never even thought I could, I mean, that's the first time."

Still, he has his consistent themes. He likes to say he only chose kids who were hurting already. That he recognized something in their eyes that let him know they'd already been abused. He claims to have recognized that in Jeremy.

He's told the story in so many ways that it's hard to know what to do with the telling that's coming.

There is a grave in Louisiana that bears the body of Oscar Lee Langley, a body of a five-year-old boy decapitated along the side of a road in Arizona, a body his father accompanied home to Louisiana so the child could be interred next to the relatives he'd met only as a baby. That grave has held the dead child for sixty-three years.

But if you listen to Ricky Langley, he will tell you that on February 7, 1992, five-year-old Oscar Lee Langley appeared in an upstairs bedroom of the Lawson house to dance and skip around six-year-old Jeremy Guillory. Ricky will tell you that Oscar grinned a little boy's gap-toothed grin at him but that Oscar didn't want to play, he'd come to the house to taunt Ricky. Oscar told him that he was in charge now, the way he'd always been, and that he'd make Ricky molest Jeremy, molest him even though Ricky had been good for months. Ricky shouted and argued with him—and that, Ricky says, was what scared Jeremy and made the child start to run. Ricky grabbed Oscar by the throat—the throat that was Jeremy's. He wanted Oscar to stop talking, wanted to stop that voice he'd heard in his head since he was a child—and it was Jeremy whom he choked. Ricky grabbed Oscar by the throat so hard that he lifted Oscar off the ground—it was Jeremy's body that hung from Ricky's hands. Jeremy stopped breathing.

Only then, if you believe Ricky Langley, did he realize whom he'd killed.

The trial is quick. The jury convicts Ricky of molesting and murdering Jeremy and, with only three hours of deliberation, sentences him to die. When Ricky arrives on death row at Angola, the Louisiana State Penitentiary, roughly eighty men are housed in the cells, across tiers of a white octagonal building just yards from the entrance gates. Each tier holds fourteen cells. The cells are concrete, with a small opening on one side that has iron bars over it. All the openings face the same side; the men cannot see one another. What they see is the corridor and the passing guards, the same concrete day after day. They hear the same sounds: the yelling, the snoring, the toilets' endless flushing. Each man is confined in his six-by-nine cell for twenty-three hours a day. For the remaining hour Ricky is let into a small chained pen where he is permitted to stand and feel the sun on his face. He is permitted the blue sky. Then he is escorted back into his concrete cell, where the temperature in the summer is regularly as high as 120 degrees. The heat, the sameness, the noise—it is the men's shaving mirrors that save them. If they hold the mirrors out through the iron bars, angled just right, they can see one another. The space is tight and loud and suffocating, but though it is called death row, it is where men live.

In 1995, one man, Thomas Lee Ward, is executed. In 1996, another: Antonio G. James. In 1997, John Ashley Brown Jr. In 1999, Dobie Gillis Williams, who's widely believed to be innocent and about whom Sister Helen Prejean, who wrote the book *Dead Man Walking* and was played by Susan Sarandon in the film, will write *The Death of Innocents*. Then, in 2000, the guards come to Feltus Taylor's cell. Feltus is on Ricky's tier, and Ricky can hear the guards at Feltus's grate. Every man on the tier knows whose cell the guards have come to. Every man on the tier knows why the guards have come. It is Feltus's turn to die. Three years older than Ricky, with a shaved head and a Mr. T smile, Feltus is well liked by both guards and inmates. In the photograph taken of him when he arrived at Angola, a photograph that now hangs in the penitentiary museum alongside the photographs of every man executed there, he is a young man with tautly muscled arms and eyes that roll their whites to the camera's every shot, as though he will not, even now that he's caught, submit to the booking frame, to the height-measured wall. But Feltus now? Now Feltus is good-tempered and talkative, open about both his guilt in killing a coworker and also how sorry he is for it. Feltus is proof that people can change.

Then Feltus is dead. At 8:00 a.m. the next morning, the guards make their rounds of the tiers. Ricky—who has shrunken in his jumpsuit, losing weight on death row, his face gaunt and neck corded, his eyes too big in their sockets—will not move from his cot. "He is accepting the execution last night as well as can be expected," a guard writes.

But by 10:00 a.m. Ricky crackles with anger. The guards are jerking them around, he says. Them free men—on death row, that's what they call the guards, their defining characteristic not that they're guards but that they are free—love this shit. When Ricky mouths off like this, other inmates get nervous. On the tiers, unruly inmates are dealt with by piping in tear gas. And the gas doesn't stay in just one cell. John Thompson, the man in the cell next to Ricky, reaches out to rattle the bars between his cell and Ricky's to try to get his attention, but Ricky doesn't respond. "Ricky, please!" Thompson says. "Cool it down. Chill out."

Ricky won't listen to Thompson. The guards love execution days, he says. They love picking the inmates off, one by one. They'll be happy when every man there is dead. This is Feltus's joke, now said with bitterness: "You know, you might think I'm paranoid," he used to say, "but I think people are trying to kill me."

The next time a free man comes around, Ricky shouts, "You should've killed me instead." He's ready to go. He's sick of waiting; it should've been him. It's as though he's suddenly realized that they're being held there to die. The guard is disturbed enough at the change in Ricky to fill out a request for an evaluation. The phrase the doctors write on his chart, they will write for him again and again: "Mood appropriate to situation." Just as in Georgia, prison may be the place Ricky's thought the least strange.

While Ricky slides between fury and resignation, spending day after day in his concrete cell not knowing when he'll be assigned a date to die, on the outside a lawyer fights for him. Clive Stafford Smith is a gangly six feet six with a hawkish nose and blue eyes so piercing he makes sure to take his glasses off before a photo of him is taken, lest, he jokes, the magnification make his stare look insane. Born in 1959, he had just turned six when his own country, Britain, outlawed capital punishment in 1965—just old enough to notice what all the adults were talking of. That early horror at the thought of executions had never left him. He'd received his law degree in the States and devoted his career to fighting the death penalty in the American South. Now, at forty-three, he is an unusual sight in the courtrooms here, with his clipped accent and a manner so decorously proper it can twist past propriety and land on outlandishness. Challenged on a hearsay point by the prosecution, he cites the Roman Empire. Describing an attempted execution by the state, he says, "They were doing something unkind to one of my clients." Once—the tables turned at a hearing, him on the witness stand for a change—a lawyer asks him, "Now, where are you presently employed?" and Clive begins his answer with "Beside the abuse of the word presently . . ." until the lawyer has no choice but to cut him off to demonstrate he knows the right word. "Currently."

His record, too, will make him a rarity. In two decades in the South, and after more than three hundred death penalty cases, Clive will lose only six clients to execution. For his efforts, he has an Order of the British Empire from the queen herself—a medallion he keeps strung around the neck of a plaster cast of Zeus, mounted on the burgundy wall of the home he and his wife, Emily, have made not in the well-heeled Garden District of New Orleans but in the Lower Ninth Ward. It is still years before Hurricane Katrina will ravage the area. The Ninth Ward is no longer the more rural side of the river it began as, no longer the place of backyard farms. Crack cocaine has flooded in, and with it gangs. The streets of the Ninth still lack functioning streetlamps. In a city with a famously high murder rate, the Ninth has the highest. In choosing to live in a place many are left to live in by circumstance, Clive is a man not just dedicated to his work, but defined by it.

And he is determined to save Ricky's life. He begins to dig and learns that the jurors at the trial took a Bible into the jury room and prayed together before deciding to sentence Ricky to death. That's unconstitutional, but in Louisiana it'll be a tough sell for appeal. Instead he has Ricky's conviction and death sentence over-turned on grounds never before raised in the state: Though Ricky is white, he was entitled to have blacks on his jury, and there were none. The state supreme court justices who rule in his favor practi-cally hold their noses as they do so. *Fortunately, here, Langley will prob-ably not go free.* Ricky is taken off death row and eventually transferred back to the Calcasieu Correctional Center to await retrial.

Some years, the law firm Clive founds will represent half the men on death row in Louisiana. But even then, asked by reporters to speak about his career, it will be Ricky's story he returns to.

There is something unusual about this case for Clive, something that's just beginning. His father was mentally ill. When he looks at Ricky, he sees his father. Can Clive feel yet, in this moment, how far that vision will drive him?

Because of legal skirmishes, because of fights over motions and venues, because the swift wheels of justice are in fact creaky and slow and no one can identify whether they are justice at all, Ricky's case will take years to resolve.

Which gives me time to arrive in Louisiana.

Twenty-Two

Louisiana, 2003

There's no sign on the building when I arrive at the New Orleans address the lawyer gave me over the phone. Just a smoked-glass door, not even numbered, and windows with slat blinds pulled tight. Though the other buildings on the block are all gray, this one is Mardi Gras purple, and the color only accentuates how vacant the blocks feels, how evacuated, as if it were a night or a weekend. But it's Monday morning, 9:00 a.m., and still no one's here. Maybe this isn't the right building, but the address is all I've got. I press the bell.

A man answers the door. Behind him, the room is so dark it's like a pocket of night in the middle of the morning. He's wearing jeans and a short-sleeved, button-down shirt, no law firm suit, and now I'm really wondering if I've got the right place. Then there's the man's dark skin. When the lawyers talked about the noose ties on the phone, the way they talked made me realize that they were all white, most of their clients black. They wouldn't have a client answer the door, would they?

If the man can sense I'm startled, he doesn't show it. He smiles. "Come right on in. You're an intern, right? The others are upstairs."

This is John Thompson. The man who spent a year on death row next to Ricky, and fourteen years before he was exonerated. If he tells me his name now, if he sticks out his hand for a shake and introduces himself, the moment doesn't tack into my memory. His name doesn't mean anything to me yet. Instead my attention is on the office that is suddenly visible: how after the threshold the floor sinks and the two black fake-leather couches in the waiting room have seen better days; how the magazine covers are dated and dusty and the desk where the receptionist sits is behind a thick layer of plastic that looks like bulletproof glass. This isn't a reception area for actually receiving anyone. Not like my parents' firm, with its gleaming mahogany designed to impress. A dry-erase board on the wall lists an alarmingly long roster of names, its markings smeared. There's a column for "in" and a column for "out," magnets like poker chips meant to mark which lawyers are available. But only a few magnets are clearly in a particular column, the rest strewn haphazardly across the board. The board, like the reception area, looks like someone set it up long ago in a burst of optimism before succumbing to dust, time, and too much work.

"The library's right up this staircase," John Thompson says.

So the man who knew Ricky is the one who leads me to his story. One hand on the slim banister, I climb. The staircase is narrow and tight, the wooden ceiling so low I can just barely straighten my back. The room I leave and the room I walk toward are both dim. All summer this passage will strike me as strange to climb: to leave the overcooled office space and enter this pocket of hot darkness tucked to the side. Always it will seem at once illicit and stifling. Only years later, flipping through the photographs in Ricky's file, will I see another staircase that perfectly evokes the same feeling, and stop short. The staircase in the Lawson house that Lucky and Dixon climbed, following Ricky. The staircase Ricky climbed, following Jeremy. The way the evidence photograph was taken, angled up, is exactly how the memory of this staircase will feel.

Up top, the corridor opens into a cavernous space with a wide table at the center. The ceilings are impossibly high, leather-bound books climbing the walls as though trying to reach them. Case registers. These books hold the sources of the hypotheticals I love, the cases that are the foundation of the world I am entering.

Eight other young people sit around the table—law students, like me, here to spend their summer working for the firm. At the table's head stands a thin woman with a British accent, wearing a black suit. We make our pleasantries and our introductions. For the whole day we sit around that table. We learn the firm's history. We learn its methods for keeping track of files. We learn what to wear when visiting clients.

The next morning she again steps to the front of the room. Today, she says, we were supposed to meet her husband, Clive Stafford Smith, who founded this office. "But Clive is still in Texas, being the awake lawyer in the sleeping lawyer case."

We laugh, a little awed. That case is famous right now, one in which a condemned man has appealed for a new trial because during the original, when he was sentenced to death, his lawyer actually fell asleep during the proceedings. All of us at the table are from northern schools. All of us at the table are from the North. Until now, that case has had the feel of a story from far away. But we're actually here.

"Instead," she says, "we'll show you this." She holds up a videotape. "This is the taped confession of the man whose retrial we just finished, recorded in 1992. Nine years ago he was condemned to death, but this time the jury gave him life." She hadn't planned to show it to us; that much is clear. But we're here, the time needs filling, and what better way to preview the work ahead than to show us whom we're here to defend?

"Could you please," she says to another lawyer, "get the lights?"

On the screen a face flickers into view.

Thick, Coke-bottle glasses. Too-big ears, the legacy of Bessie's drinking. Brown eyes that were the last Jeremy saw.

He is talking about molesting children. "Sometimes I, you know, rub my penis on them," he says—and my grandfather's hands are at the hem of my white flannel nightgown with the little blue stars; he is tugging it up and he is tugging down my underwear and he is undoing his fly.

I came here to help save the man on the screen. I came to help save men like him. I came because my ideals and who I am exist separately from what happened in the past. They must. If they don't, what will my life hold?

But I look at the man on the screen, I feel my grandfather's hands on me, and I know. Despite what I've trained for, despite what I've come here to work for, despite what I believe.

I want Ricky to die.

Part Three: Trial

Twenty-Three

That day I stepped away from the conference table knowing exactly whose confession I'd seen. But an hour later, I no longer knew the man's name. I couldn't remember it. When I tried to, darkness licked at my field of vision and the name was suddenly gone. I never worked on the man's case, but I worked on many others, and afterward, too, I felt myself changed. Now it was the victims whose names I noticed in cases, the victims I suddenly wondered about.

I knew it was strange that I couldn't remember the man's name. Something was happening inside me. I would read his file again and again to try to make myself remember it, my glance skidding short on those letters—why couldn't I quite hold them? Always my vision would jolt just slightly, as though the focus on a camera had gone out. A high-alert flood washed over my body. Seconds later, I no longer remembered the name I'd just read. It was gone as neatly as if snipped from my consciousness, only the black mark of the excision left behind.

When summer ended, I returned to Boston. I finished law school. And then I left the law—how could I become a lawyer, after wanting the man to die? My opposition to the death penalty had helped drive me to law school. And I still opposed it—or thought I did. But how could I fight for what I believed when as soon as a crime was personal to me, my feelings changed? Every crime was personal to someone. I went back to school for writing instead. But still I thought often of the boy the man had killed,

Jeremy, and of that boy's mother, Lorilei. That she'd testified for his killer stirred complicated feelings in me: admiration but also anger. Yet I'd run from that complexity, I knew. I was a coward and I still couldn't remember the man's name.

Which is why, twelve years after that day in the law firm library, I am standing under a giant truck-stop sign. Because it is not possible to let the past remain a haunting. The sign says CASH MAGIC. There is no sun, so the sign gives no shade. It is August of 2015, ninety-five degrees with ninety-five percent humidity, and the sky looks like sludge poured from a contractor's bucket. Westward of Lake Pontchartrain, New Orleans's exuberant purples and yellows, its neon and its billboards, have given way to reed-choked swamp. Two hundred miles outside New Orleans, as I-10 snakes its way across the lower half of Louisiana toward the town of Iowa, the road and sky bleed together on the horizon, oozing into one vast blank gray expanse. I got part of the man's court record and read thousands of pages of files to get here. I read his name over and over, until the shaking subsided and I learned it.

Ricky Langley's case didn't end in 2003 with the retrial Clive fought for. It didn't end when Lorilei told the jury she could hear his cry for help. The verdict from that trial was thrown out, and in 2009 Ricky was tried again and sentenced to life again. That brought the trial count to three. In 1994, a death sentence. In 2003, life. In 2009, life. Before the 2009 trial, the appellate court had held that since he'd escaped a death sentence once, he couldn't be made to face another.

So it was the 2003 retrial—the one at which Lorilei had testified for Ricky, and that had concluded right before I arrived in Louisiana—that decided his fate. Why, then, had there been another trial after that, the third? He'd committed the murder. Who would have pushed for it? And how had Lorilei been able to fight for him when he'd killed her son—while I, despite my opposition to the death penalty, had been unable to? I hoped the court record would answer my questions. I hoped it would help me understand.

But reading it, I soon realized that what I needed was everything that hadn't made it into the words of the record I'd read. The emotions. The memories. The story. The past.

The past. Which had happened here, in the parking lot of the Cash Magic, once the Fuel Stop. In the heat, the lot is nearly empty. It looks as though it could accommodate at least sixty cars and a dozen trucking rigs, but there's only a dented burgundy four-by-four truck with a purple-and-gold LSU fleur-de-lis on the back and a muddy white sedan with rusted hubcaps. A lone black truck jackknifes across four spaces at the back of the lot. Nearby squat two Dumpsters, one green and one blue, both mottled orange with rust. The back door of the gas station has been blacked out and painted with white letters reading ADULTS ONLY. Later tonight the Cash Magic will become the local casino, and the locals will search for the jackpot to change their luck.

Sweat beads on my skin. My mouth feels like I've been sucking on a wet rag. I raise my camera and frame the green Cash Magic sign over the trees. There's a glossy black hat on it, from which a magician's gloved white hand extracts a rabbit. *Click.* The trees across the road seem to tremble in the heat, their branches snaking like arms, their tiny leaves like bejeweled fingers. *Click.* The leaves reach over the concrete, the land ready to reclaim itself. *Click.*

Through my camera I frame the red metal signs over the gas pumps. I frame the shiny silver pumps and the dark asphalt that stretches beneath them. Twenty-three years ago, this lot wasn't paved. Twenty-three years ago, a pale, skinny twenty-six-year-old man with jug ears and glasses that swallowed half his face sat perched on a tractor, spreading crushed shell across the ground I now stand on. If I squint, I can almost make out Lucky, as he steps out of the police cruiser and removes his hat.

It's all here. Just as it was twenty-three years ago. Just as it is in the files.

Then the feeling begins. The feeling that—as much as any of the rational reasons I tell myself—is still really why I've come back to Louisiana. Why I've had to. My skin flushes and grows tight and prickly, my heart pounds and the sound echoes in my head. I lower the camera from my eyes and without the shield of the view-finder the image in front of me seems to warp and blur. Everything suspended. Like being hurtled back in time.

Two nights before I came here, I was in bed with my girlfriend, Janna. After law school, I came out as gay. It was as though leaving the law—jettisoning the life I'd planned—forced me to accept the rest of who I was. For years I'd been afraid that if I came out, and anyone learned I'd been abused as a child, they would think that that was why I was gay. As if that had turned me gay. In my heart I knew that wasn't it. The first time I slept with a woman, my chest opened up. I hadn't known until that moment how closed it was. I'm gay because I love women, it's as simple as that. But for so long the possibility that anyone might even think otherwise kept me hidden.

Janna and I are opposites. I have my mother's narrow shoulders and broad hips, the olive skin and dark curly hair of my grand-father. Janna is broad-shouldered and muscled, her hips as narrow as a boy's and her blond hair as short, her Germanic skin so pale it's almost translucent. When I came out as gay, my eating disorder faded, as though my body had been waiting for me to accept who I am. Now I cook elaborate meals. Janna would live on protein bars and caffeinated gum if she could, whatever she can fit in a hiking backpack or on the back of a bike. Maybe our differences come down to that I am a writer and she is a scientist. But often the su-perficial differences seem to reflect something larger: the way we experience time. For me, always layered. For her, the moment. We haven't been together long—only a little more than half a year—but part of what we give each other is the chance to see differently.

That night we were lying on my bed kissing. My studio apart-ment in Cambridge is tiny, chosen because it's an affordable way to live within walking distance of Harvard, where I now teach writing. Stacks of books are everywhere—and at the room's center, there is the bed. We were lying on top of it, not quite gone to bed together but not quite denying what we were doing, either. I turned onto my elbows so I was above her and I leaned down and kissed her. I love kissing her. My whole body seems to dissolve into sensation, nothing of the past about it, only that moment and her mouth and my tongue. We kissed and we kissed, and soon my hands were at her shirt and I was tugging it off. She slid her hands up my back and fumbled with my bra's clasp. I yanked hard to pull the elastic band of hers over her head. Then I let my body fall forward into hers, closing my eyes to concentrate on the feeling of her skin meeting mine. I kissed her again and her tongue found my mouth. I reached down between her legs. She reached down to touch me and then we were moving together and it felt good and I moaned and it felt good again.

And then it didn't.

When this happens I know it only the way you realize that the water has suddenly gotten too hot in the shower, has crossed over some invisible threshold and is now burning. Though it would be smarter to just hop out of the shower entirely—damn the bathroom rug, so it gets wet, who cares?—you stand under the spray that is now scalding you and you grope and fumble for the shower knob.

"Oh, fuck," I said when I realized I was going under, into the memory. All I could say, before panic overwhelmed. "Oh, fuck."

My breath quickened. I gulped air. I fumbled for something to hold on to. She was there and so it was her, but in that moment I was so gone I only wanted something solid. "Hold me," I gasped, and I felt her arms go taut around me. I gripped her arms. I clung.

Where does the mind go in these moments, while the body trembles? For me it is a white-hot slipstream blank-out, the nothingness of no time and nowhere and no one. It used to be a feeling, a single concentrated excruciating feeling: the smooth hot texture of my grandfather's penis against my hand, for example, or the specific purple-pink color his penis had, a color that still makes me uncomfortable no matter where I see it, though the discomfort is vague now, the signal no longer traced back to its origin, with only the effect felt. But as the years have blotted the origin out (I am grateful), they have blotted the sensations, too, as though the film reel of the memory has been played so many times it has gone torn and blotched. Now I have only to ride the panicked blankness. "Oh, fuck," I say when the wave of sensation starts to break over me, inside me, and then I breathe to keep up with the panicked race swell of my body, the heartbeat and the breath. The wave builds and builds, it crests and breaks.

(It sounds as though I am describing something else, doesn't it? But this isn't an orgasm. It is terror.)

When it breaks, I cry. The wave flows out of me. My breath slows, and I can feel the tears on my cheeks, hot, though I am not aware of them leaving me or even of any feeling of sadness. I am a sack into which the wave has broken, and now it must come leaking out of me. I have been a vessel; I am now only a throughway. Who I am outside this feeling becomes as irrelevant as time.

I meant to book a motel room a comfortable distance from Iowa. I intended to stay in Lake Charles, where, yes, the trial had happened, but where none of the sensitive events of the murder had. I had in mind that I would sleep somewhere safe and distant and would dip my toe into the past each day as comfortably as testing bathwater from the solid stance of a tiled floor. I did not book the cheapest room. I read reviews. I studied addresses. I wanted something clean and safe, a refuge I could grant myself at the start and end of each day.

I flew into Baton Rouge, not New Orleans, intent on giving myself the shortest trip possible. Two hours from the airport, I had only a third of a mile left to drive, my phone's navigation told me, when I noticed the CASH MAGIC sign ahead. There it was, high in the ashen sky. My breath raced. My chest grew cold.

I drove past the sign as if in a dream. I'd looked at the motel's address. How had I made this mistake? Wanting to book away from the murder, how had I instead booked into its heart? There on my right was the counter where Pearl had worked, the pumps Lanelle had turned on for the drivers, and the window through which she had watched Ricky one long day and wondered whether he was the kind of strange that could kill a child. There on my right was the asphalt that had been laid down where crushed shell used to be.

My motel was one block away and across the street. From its entrance I could still see the green CASH MAGIC sign. At the front desk I gave the clerk my name, I must have, and my credit card and I made the kind of small talk one makes and then I took my room key and went to my room. I fell onto the bed. I fell into thirteen hours of blank dark memory-sleep.

I am pulled to this story by absences. Strange blacknesses, strange forgettings, that overtake me at times. They reveal what is still unresolved inside me. They plunge me toward what I most want to avoid.

Ricky brought me to this story. He's the one I keep thinking about and chasing after, trying to understand. But being here, and what happened the other night in bed with Janna in Massachusetts, makes me realize I have to start with Jeremy. He's who carried Ricky's crime in his body.

I hear the birds first. Where I live, they are drowned out by passing cars, by pedestrians on cell phones, by scraps of music that float through car windows and the beep of horns and the artificial chirp of street signs indicating it's safe to walk, by the chatter of my own thoughts as I go through my day. City noise. To reach Consolata Cemetery, where Jeremy is buried, I have driven fifteen minutes west from the Cash Magic, hooking south of the high buildings of Lake Charles and south of the lake. Now, on the western outskirts of the city, what is man-made struggles while the natural world gasps: run-down farm-equipment-repair shops and Laundromat signs, the grass on both sides of the road crushed by rusted trailers. Birdsong bursts through, like the way the line of a melody flits over the undertones below, counterpoint and lightness.

The trees must draw so many birds. Consolata Cemetery appears through the concrete like an oasis of arranged beauty, wide oaks with bright fluttering leaves and steady brown boughs. An artificial calm. No upright gravestones here like I'm used to from the Northeast—less than fifty miles from the Gulf of Mexico and surrounded by lakes, the water table would topple them—and without them there's little to disrupt the land's flatness. One stone bench stands vacant under a lone oak tree, waiting.

I step to the grass. From this angle, I can see what the sun and my angle of vision obscured: dark metal plaques dot the lawn, flush against it. The dead. That their markers are so low and unobtrusive reinforces the quiet. Yet the birds keep chirping. In them, at least, Jeremy has company.

"Can I help you?" a man calls out to me from behind the spoked wheel of a golf cart.

"Thanks." I walk toward him. "I'm looking for a grave."

"What's the lot number?"

The question catches me off guard. "I don't know." I've carried his story with me for so long that part of me expected intuition would lead me there, that I would just walk around until I recognized his name. But the plaques are so flat there's no way to read them until you're hovering right over the dead. "His name was Jeremy Guillory."

The man's face registers nothing.

What did I think—that while I had been driven here by this mystery, he, too, would have the name of a boy dead two decades on his tongue?

"I'll call it in," he says. The location crackles back over the speaker and he starts the motor and motions for me to get in. "When did he die?"

"Ninety-two."

"An old man?" This must be cemetery small talk. To our left, an expanse of graves appears, rows and rows of little black plaques dotting the earth. The cemetery is larger than I realized, and for a minute its size stills my chest. I've come here in search of one person. One story. But there are so many buried around us.

"No," I say. "A child."

"That's a shame."

We drive along in silence. The sky has become a more concentrated gray, the birdsong become more urgent, spiked with shrieks, and I wonder whether the birds are heralding something. Graves keep coming at us, rows and rows of metal plaques, rows and rows of unseen names and the buried bodies beneath them. Suddenly I want the man to know a little more of the story. To know whom he's keeping watch over. "Jeremy was murdered."

He whistles low. "What year did you say?"

"Ninety-two."

"That's a shame," he says again. "A real shame. Around here?"

"Iowa."

He shakes his head. "I wouldn't remember it, then." The cart stops. "This row, down on the left. Want me to show you?"

"Thanks, but I've got it."

He drives off.

Which leaves me and Jeremy alone. The silence comes shockingly strong once the engine is gone. It's the birds, I realize. They've fallen quiet. The spot the worker pointed to lies against a curb, in the first row of this section of the cemetery. Beneath my feet, the grass is damp and spongy. The concrete curb juts up against the grass and picks up again across the street, a paved lot over which a big red gas station sign announces the mundane world of the living. The entrance to the cemetery was lush and green, but with the concrete all around, this patch of grass feels tucked away.

JEREMY JAMES GUILLORY. He's a plaque like all the others, set into the grass. I step closer. In the left corner, a child engraved into the metal reaches his hand up. From the top, two larger hands reach down. THE LORD REACHED DOWN FOR JEREMY'S HAND. Then that date: FEBRUARY 7, 1992.

No words for everything that date ended. No words for everything that date began. I stand here, where Lorilei once did in her blue blouse, and it starts to rain.

Twenty-Four

The day Lorilei buries her son, it rains. The rain begins in the early morning, when the Hixon Funeral Home in Lake Charles is open only to the family. The rain sops the wide lawn into a marsh; it slicks the white railing and the white columns and darkens the red brick of the building; it jewels the leaves of the tall trees. The rain is still falling as the reporters arrive, and they pop their wide black umbrellas open. Assistants hold tarps over the cameras while the on-air talent crouch to freshen their lipstick and straighten their ties. A week has passed since Jeremy's body was found. The community is still in shock. One of their own, taken. For the cameras, the reporters pull their faces into solemn masks and intone that one hundred people have shown up, that the mother is here. Later the newspapers will raise the number to 250. The day has the feel of a quiet conclusion. They've been reporting on the missing boy every night for two weeks now.

Lorilei steps out to acknowledge the reporters. In the rain her heels sink into the sponge of the grass and the blue blouse that the newspapers note dampens, even through the coat her brother, Richard, must have hung over her shoulders. He stands beside her with an umbrella. All day Richard will use his body to shield her, any trouble between them forgotten.

She looks up at the reporters. Her glasses must fog a little. "I knew it was gonna rain," she tells them. "But I'm kind of glad, because it's like the angels in heaven are crying."

The funeral parlor is thronged with people she doesn't know, people she hasn't seen in years, people she sees every day. Their arms come at her, their cheeks, she must feel herself wrapped into their hugs and held nervously at a distance between their palms. She is surrounded by a buzzing, like she's wandered into a colony of bees.

She folds her arms around herself. "I couldn't bury him in a suit," she tells her neighbor. She says it again to Jeremy's classmate's mother. Then to a reporter. "I just couldn't. It wouldn't look right. He likes his jeans and his sneakers." All of them keep saying how sorry they are. She keeps talking. If she stops talking, she'll have to take in what they're sorry for.

At the head of the room sits a small white casket, its lid propped open. In the casket lies her son. The mortician has folded Jeremy's hands across his chest and nested a small bouquet of red carnations between his palms. He is wearing his favorite jeans and a burgundy sweater, and part of her—the part that can still forget—must be glad for the sweater. He'll be warm against the February damp. Tucked at his sides are a toy Batman and a Batmobile, Christmas gifts from his cousin Bubba. "He should have his BB gun," Lorilei says. "He loves that thing. But the sheriff's got it as evidence."

Richard appears and pulls her to his shoulder. The service is about to begin.

People crowd the aisles, the back of the room, its sides. The benches are all packed. Two preachers will speak, the first an old friend of Lorilei's from her wilder days. The years have changed them both. "Life is but a passing episode," he says. Jeremy called him Grandpa. "Jeremy's was awful short. The wicked one took him from us."

The revival preacher is younger, with more energy, more bluster. I see him with wavy hair and a wiry build, a crackle of energy running through his body like the smiting hand of God. Though they are sad, he entreats them, they should rejoice. "In the Bible, when David saw that God had taken his child, he took a bath and he cleaned up and he called for something to eat. Then he said,

'That child can't come back to me, but I can go back to him.' He knew that the only way to see his son again was to make of his life something the Lord would approve of." The preacher stares intently out at the crowd, his eyes ablaze. "We can meet Jeremy again if we can only be as humble as he was."

Lorilei's father slowly reaches his hand toward the ceiling and waves back and forth to his grandson. The reporters scribble it down.

After the service, people come to put their hands on the coffin. They cross themselves as they stand over Jeremy. Some lean down to kiss the boy's forehead. His face is as bloodless as porcelain, no marks. But under the sweater, bruises from Ricky's forearm cover his chest. Two days ago, the coroner held a ruler to the dark ligature marks on his neck and photographed them. Four times the flash-bulb went off, four times capturing the deep bruised score around his neck, from four different angles. The bulb captured the red pin-pricks that bloomed across his neck from capillaries that burst from pressure, where he'd bled into his skin. The spots are called pete-chiae. Later, after the developing fluid works on the film and the images mist into view, the photographs will be marked as evidence. In the years ahead they will be photocopied and then photocopied again for the case files. Twenty years into the future, when the three trials mean that even the photocopies have been copied yet again and again, the wounds on Jeremy's neck will have blurred into the dark undifferentiated blotch of time.

But now, with the sweater collar pulled up over his neck, you could almost believe he was sleeping. If he weren't quite so pale. If he weren't quite so still. If the dead stink of flowers wasn't quite so heavy in the air.

Outside, on the steps, a boy weeps freely, his small shoulders shuddering under the jacket his mother must have made him wear. A woman wraps her arms around him. "Shh, baby. I know, I know." She rocks him, cooing into his hair—"Shh, baby, Shh"—but the boy only sobs harder. "Y'all had some good times together." A few feet away, a reporter writes down her words.

Six miles away, Ricky Langley sits in an isolation cell at the Calcasieu Correctional Center. He yells out to the guard, "Won't anybody come talk to me?".

The coffin is so light that the five pallbearers must each just barely feel it. Richard stands at the front. He is a big man with a bushy beard and a stomach that swells top to bottom. He is a hunter and a fisherman who poses in camouflage for snapshots with his trophies. He is a man used to the death of animals—but nothing has readied him for this. I see him there, his hand hooked under the casket, and I try to fill in the black-and-white news photo that ran of this moment with the color of real time. The red that flushes up his cheeks. The red that lines the rims of his eyes. For Richard the coffin must be as light as carrying a baby. Light as the first time he picked up his son, the first time he held his daughter. Light as the first time he held the newborn Jeremy, and marveled at this familiar stranger his sister had produced. When my sisters gave birth to their children, each time it seemed a miracle that some-one I had known for so many years had made something so new, so a part of them and at once so different. We'd grown up together but we'd had such different lives, such different troubles. The differences had long driven us apart, the way it had once been for Richard and Lorilei. But there, in each new baby, was a chance at a new beginning.

At the grave site, with the wide oak trees in the distance, the red gleam of the gas station across the gray concrete corner, and the sharp song of the birds above, Lorilei stands over the hole in the ground that is her son's and reads a poem written by Jeremy's kindergarten classmates, copied out in the kindergarten teacher's careful cursive. "It's so hard to say goodbye." The tears start before she can finish. She allows Richard to pull her back from the grave.

Then she watches as her father and Richard throw in handfuls of dirt. She waits, I imagine, until almost everyone is gone. Until she's almost alone with her baby.

The grave digger gives his signal, and the coffin is lowered gently into the earth.

Lorilei is four months pregnant with Jeremy's half brother. The nausea must have woken her this morning. She must have felt the dull twinges of the pregnancy in her stomach, the twinges that meant the baby was alive.

But as she watches the coffin bump to a gentle stop in the earth, I can only imagine she feels hollow, the pain a scythe that's carved her out. She'll wake from this week soon. She will. She'll wake and Jeremy will be tugging at the blanket at the foot of her bed, telling her to get up now, come on, come play. She'll see him and the fog of this horrible dream will lift.

The day they buried Jeremy, the rain cleared after the funeral. The rain bookends the news reports: first Lorilei's saying that the angels were crying, then the way the angels stopped when the boy had been laid to rest in the earth. In the time I've been standing at Jeremy's grave, the rain has only started to come down harder. I look at his name on the plaque and I try to make myself understand that he's below me. His autopsy report is in the file I read before coming here. I have held in my hand the grim weighing out of each of his organs. The rest of the records from this case are in the court archive. Somewhere in the court archive are the pictures of his body. Once he wasn't only a name in the files, a school picture flashed on the evening news, a cautionary tale. Once he was a boy.

The week after the funeral, twenty-five people gather to march from the local state senator's office to the Lake Charles Civic Center in protest. They should have been warned about Ricky. "He was around children all day," says a neighbor. Perhaps she was one of the searchers gathered on the porch of the Lawson house, comparing their routes and trying to cheer each other up in the long stretches of finding nothing, and perhaps she is remembering Ricky's bringing them out Styrofoam cups of coffee. She took that coffee from Ricky's hands, they all did, and she thanked him. Perhaps now she is remembering sending her children up to his bedroom to play with the others. She feels the horror of having trusted. "People got a right to know if Jeffrey Dahmer's moving into their neighborhood," she says. Before Jeremy's disappearance, the Dahmer trial consumed the media for weeks. The people of Iowa and Lake Charles saw updates on the front pages of their newspapers and in clips on the evening news. The week Dahmer was sentenced to life, Ricky killed Jeremy. No longer does it seem just a spectacle.

Lorilei stands at the head of the march, her leather motorcycle jacket open over her T-shirt and jeans. The marchers carry signs all with the same black-markered handwriting, the same white poster board. The sign lettered for her says: SAVE YOUR CHILD FROM BEING A VICTIM. "I believe this is what my baby's death was meant for," she tells a reporter. "This is what my baby was born for."

Everybody's watching her in this moment. Thrusting their microphones in her face. Flashing their camera bulbs. The sheriff made her go through two lie detector tests before Ricky confessed. Soon the defense attorney will have things to say about her mothering. Soon the prosecutors will, too. Here, at the head of the march, she is a symbol of loss. The woman no one wants to be.

When the marchers reach the state senator's office, he comes to the door and listens to their chanting. Then he joins them. The senator knows a movement when he sees one. They'll get their law, he promises the group. "I don't want to see another Jeremy Guillory case ever happen again."

As the marchers raise their signs—as they chant, as they demand what they believe will keep them safe—I understand their need. It is the way I feel when I look at the forms Ricky filled out in the mid-1980s at the Lake Charles Mental Health Center, when he said he was afraid he'd molest a child again and asked to be locked up, or when I read that Lanelle turned away when Ricky blocked her on the stairs. Why didn't she force her way upstairs? Why didn't she go tell a cop what had happened?

But even if there *had* been such a law when Jeremy knocked on the Lawson house door—or before that, when Lorilei first went to stay with Melissa, or before that, when she couldn't keep the heat on and she realized that she and Jeremy would have to find somewhere else to sleep—that law likely wouldn't have saved Jeremy. No one in law enforcement knew where Ricky was; the last place they'd kept track of him was his parents' house. There were at least ten known sex offenders living around Iowa, ten whose names I will find in the records. Ten whose names the Louisiana parole officer actually gave Lucky and Dixon *before* she gave them Ricky's name. It wasn't as neat as the story was told. Of course it wasn't. One of the ten actually showed up to help search for Jeremy. The cops turned him away—and meanwhile Ricky served coffee to the searchers and watched the children play in his bedroom, shooing them away from the closet door.

The marchers, they get their law. But six months later the newspaper runs an editorial pointing out that it just hasn't worked. Thanks to the law, eighteen sex offenders have been identified in the area—but for only three of them has community notification happened.

All across the nation it is like this. Laws passed in blusters of well-meaning. Laws failing, because so rarely do the notifications work and so much of the burden falls on already burdened parents. You could make yourself sick worrying about who was on the registry and who'd moved into your town, you could drum those people out of your town or under a highway overpass, and half the time you'd be worrying about someone who had gay sex a few years before it was legalized in an area, or someone who slept with his underage girlfriend when he was barely of age himself, or someone who did something awful thirty years ago and had been all right since. In some places even prepubescent children will end up on the registries, gone too far in schoolyard games of doctor. And even then you'd only be worrying about the people you knew to worry about. About those someone had called the law on. Not the coach, the best friend, the babysitter, the stepfather, the uncle. The grandfather.

Twenty years after these laws begin, sexual abuse rates won't have dropped at all.

But in 1994, in Louisiana, the marchers get their law. Every news article about its passage refers to an unnamed "Iowa boy"— Jeremy, now turned into a symbol. By the time of the trial, Lorilei's drinking again. She's using drugs again. She's suicidal. Her son's killer is convicted and sentenced to die and when her brother Richard tells her the news she thinks, *Good riddance*. She gives birth again and names this son Cole. Jeremy's father is long gone, never once mentioned in the files, but this baby will have his father's last name.

Then, a few months later, she and Cole's father split up. Lorilei's alone with her son again. So she tries to give Cole another new beginning. She says goodbye to Jeremy where he lies in the earth, and she moves to South Carolina. She'll raise Cole far away from this place.

After I leave Jeremy's grave, I drive into downtown Lake Charles. It could be any small southern city, the road wider than the roads of the Northeast, the buildings lower, with more space between them—but the lake sets it apart. All roads draw to the lake— including the road the funeral parlor was on, which now curves around it and settles at the court-records archives division. Lorilei said goodbye to Jeremy—and his story came here.

When I called ahead from Cambridge, I was told that fifteen file boxes were waiting for me. But I'm still caught off guard when the clerk appears, pushing a dolly loaded with four banker's boxes. Each box is about three feet long and two feet wide and high. I lift the lid of the box marked #1. A row of packed-in folders, each folder maybe three hundred pages thick. I calculate quickly, my heart sinking and soaring at once. Fifteen boxes—maybe thirty thousand pages? There is so much here. There is so much here.

I understood, of course, what I was told on the phone. Fifteen boxes. But I didn't understand at all.

"Let me know when you're ready for the next batch!" the clerk says.

Nothing to do but begin.

In the first box, I find the years after the 1994 trial: Ricky sentenced, Ricky on death row. In the second, his lawyer Clive files briefs to earn Ricky a new trial. Thousands of pages, all focusing on Ricky.

Then suddenly, eight years later, Lorilei appears.

Twenty-Five

June 7, 2002. A pretrial-hearing transcript. Clive and the prosecutor Wayne Frey argue about the white Fruit of the Loom T-shirt Jeremy wore when he died. For ten years it has sat yellowing in an evidence room at the archives division, behind two locked doors that require two separate keys. Will the jury see the T-shirt at the retrial? Clive and the prosecutor Cynthia Killingsworth argue over how much of the prosecution's evidence—such as the testing on that T-shirt—the defense is entitled to discover. Lucky takes the witness stand and describes finding Jeremy in that T-shirt. Then a technician from the evidence lab describes having cut small holes around stains in the T-shirt to test them for semen.

A man rises from the benches in the back of the courtroom. No one knows him. It's one thirty in the afternoon. Ricky was there for the beginning of the hearing, but is now back at the correctional center. The lawyers have been gathered in the windowless room since nine thirty, with only a break for lunch. Strangers are rare after ten years on this case. Even rarer are ones dressed as I imagine this man is, in jeans and a work shirt.

"May I address the court?" The man walks to the front and stands in front of Judge Alcide Gray, looking up at Gray in his black robe. The suited lawyers all stare at the man.

"Yeah," Gray says. He's bored with this hearing. He's been bored for hours.

"I'm—I'm King Alexander Jr., and I'm not attired for court today," he begins. "But I represent the—the—"

His voice falters. This request he's about to make? He knows it's unusual. "I represent the mother of the victim, of the crime in the Langley matter. And she wishes to address the court regarding matters that the district attorney has declined to respond to. It has to do with her feelings on the death penalty."

Frey, the assistant district attorney, must whip his head around long enough to recognize the blond woman seated in the back of the room. This woman he and his office have been forcibly ignoring, not returning her calls, not responding to letters. This seems to be the first anyone takes note of her. She is thirty-eight now. No one's seen her in eight years. People have been going in and out of the courtroom all morning: cops, detectives, technicians, court personnel. No one has noticed her.

"I thought we were finished with Langley for today, Judge," says Frey. They were ready to move on to the next case.

Gray cuts him off. "I'll hear from her."

Lorilei doesn't walk to the witness stand. Instead she walks up the center aisle between the benches until she's standing in front of Gray, looking up at him like a supplicant. He wasn't the judge on the first trial—that was a white man. Gray's black, a rare sight in the Louisiana judiciary. Lorilei has never met him before. But he holds her fate in his hands. "I am the mother of Jeremy Guillory," she says.

"I know who you are." Gray's voice is kind.

Lorilei is no longer the young woman in the news photographs: Shorten her hair, scrub off some of the eyeliner and the hairspray, remove the jean jacket she wore when Richard sat with her to talk to the press. The years have thickened her body, but she dressed carefully this morning in a skirt the lady from the Victims Assistance Fund helped her pick out. This plea has to work. "I am here today," she begins, but the strangeness of what she's about to say gets to her, too. Her throat goes dry. This will be the most directly Lorilei has ever asked anyone for anything on this case. When her boy went missing the cops did the searching and while they searched only rumors reached her. All she could do was wait. When they found her baby's body, she let Richard arrange the funeral. When they tried his killer, her name wasn't on the case. The state's was. *Louisiana v. Ricky Langley.* Like that was whom he'd harmed. At the trial the prosecutors told her where to sit, and she sat there. They practiced with her what to say, and she said it. Your own son dies and it becomes the community's tragedy, as though it's the system's tragedy. Public.

But ten years have passed since they told her that her boy was dead. And Lorilei could tell them all how private grief really is, how constant. She could tell them about the quiet. All the noise a six-year-old boy makes and then how loud the silence is when he's gone. She carried Cole inside her, and every kick she felt in her sternum, every flutter of new life against her heart, must have been an echo of what she'd felt with Jeremy. Her longing for him was sometimes a balm, sometimes an endless ache. Then the early weeks of Cole's infancy, being grateful for how bone-tired she was because having to just survive took the echo briefly away.

Now Cole's reaching ages Jeremy never did, and it's a new kind of pain, the endless accumulation of what-ifs. When she got pregnant a third time she named the baby Rowan and gave Rowan up for adoption. Then one morning two years ago when Jeremy had been gone for eight years, another morning when she'd shaken one child awake for the school bus instead of two, and she was standing in the kitchen packing one school lunch instead of two, her phone rang. On the line was an assistant from Clive's office, telling her that there would be another trial. Telling her she'd have to relive her son's loss again.

Now she's desperate. The lawyers have been talking for hours as if what matters is only whether they kill Ricky. They don't understand what loss is. Her boy's gone. Killing his killer won't change that.

"I am here today, Your Honor, to ask your mercy for Ricky Langley's life."

Maybe there's an intake of breath. Maybe the room is as quiet as a tomb.

"Your Honor," she continues, "I beg you to please put this to rest."

The clock on the wall ticks forward. Judge Gray looks at her. He takes in, he must, how carefully she's dressed, the bags that must be under her eyes, how dignified she is holding herself erect in the small room. Maybe he considers that word she's said, "mercy." It must sound so strange, so lofty, in this room. They have been talking about hearing dates. They have been talking about filing deadlines. The procedural bureaucracies of the law. Not mercy. Gently, Gray says, "Believe me, ma'am, I take no pleasure in trying this case."

For a minute the only sound is the tap of the court reporter's fingers on her keyboard. The words must sound hollow even to Gray. The room waits. He tries again. "I can tell you, on the record, it doesn't matter to me if the DA knows it, if everybody knows it—I don't believe in the death penalty. I take no pleasure in five or six years from now, or ten years from now, looking at the television and Mr. Langley is placed in the chair and being executed and I know I signed the death warrant. I don't know how I'd react to that, if that happens. Fortunately for me it hasn't happened yet. But I know it happened to one judge in the court a couple of weeks ago and he caught—I mean he feels it. He feels it. It's something."

Oh, Gray should be careful. He should watch what he says. Patricia Hicks, the court reporter, is sitting to his right and she is touch-typing her way through every word that he utters, recording it in shorthand she will transcribe later. When it has been transcribed it will become a document, and that document, years from now, when Clive is trying again to get yet another trial for Ricky, will be excerpted and entered into evidence. Gray shouldn't, as he soon will, tell the jurors that he doesn't believe in the death penalty. A judge is supposed to be neutral. A judge is not supposed to influence the jury. He shouldn't tell the jury, as he will, that the trial is driving him to drink. That his wife is angry at him for coming home so worked up, from what he has to watch, from what he has to learn, from looking at Ricky day after day and knowing that they are voting on this young man's life but also that this young man strangled a boy. Gray is fifty-five years old. He used to be a lawyer. At least once, he was the defense attorney in a death penalty trial. He fought for a man's life.

Gray tried to get off this case. Ten years ago, he succeeded. But this time he lost the judicial lottery. It's his case now. His courtroom. He is the one who must preside over the evidence—but today, as Lorilei stands in front of him and makes her plea, something inside him begins to break. When the lawyers talk about Ricky's hands on Jeremy's neck, he will comment that this case is tormenting him. When the lawyers question prospective jurors about whether they'll be able to listen to testimony about pedophilia and keep an open mind, Gray will get up and leave. And then again, during closing arguments, as the lawyers talk about Ricky's semen on Jeremy's shirt, Gray will stand in his long black robe, lay the gavel carefully on its side, and walk out.

Later, some will speculate that his behavior is a sign of early dementia. His mother has Alzheimer's; maybe the disease is beginning in Gray. Maybe he just has no judgment—though he's had a long, distinguished career until now, a career that has required him to rise above what people expected of him, and there's never been an issue like this. Maybe it's just that growing up where he did, growing up black where he did, he has a deep respect for struggle. His father was in the Army and his mother was a maid and it took him nine years to finish college. He is on the bench now in a state that at this time has few black lawyers and fewer black judges, he knows what it's like to be discounted and dismissed the way Ricky has been, but the grief he feels when he considers Lorilei's son is real, and this case is killing him from the inside.

The humanity that leaks out of Gray and spills into words all over the transcripts—it will be the reason the verdict from this trial is overturned. Gray will be the reason Lorilei has to suffer not only through this trial but another. He'll die an early death just a few years from now, this trial the last major event in his judicial career. Before he does, he'll recuse himself from all death penalty cases.

People think the robe protects you. It doesn't protect you. Not from the stories.

"I can tell you you're not alone," Gray says to Lorilei now. "But I can't help you. It's the prosecutors' decision."

The way Lorilei looks at Frey right now, she is drowning.

"We will pursue our seeking of the death penalty in this case," Frey says.

In the file box, after the transcript, there's a contract. I stop short to see it, a contract amid the Miranda forms, search consents, subpoena receipts—documents you'd expect to see in a criminal court record. But the language is unmistakable: "Waiver & Agreement," signed by both Ricky and Lorilei. Ricky, through Clive, indicates his understanding that Lorilei would like him held not in a mental institution (as would happen with an insanity verdict) but in a prison, and states that, having caused her such pain, he "wishes to do as she wishes." He promises never to seek commutation or lessening of any life sentence—something an insanity verdict would allow—and never to seek release from confinement. In return, Lorilei promises to visit him in prison. The contract makes it sound as if Ricky, through Clive, is promising not to seek an insanity verdict.

But an insanity verdict is exactly what Clive will push for.

Lorilei, after the hearing, as she sits on the hard hallway bench of her future, can't know this yet. She has a chance to lay this story to rest. She signs. She met Ricky once when she came to the door of the Lawson house, when he let her in to use the phone. Her boy was upstairs dead and she never knew. According to at least one account, she met him again that night as the searchers combed the woods. He brought her a drink and she took it from his hands, never knowing what those hands had done. Now she'll meet him once more. And this time, she'll know.

But though Lorilei either doesn't remember or never realized, she and Ricky met long ago. Long before he killed her son.

Twenty-Six

My second morning in Louisiana I wake to the sound of the air conditioner's dull buzz. The motel room is stiflingly hot, the air trapped by the heavy drapes. My eyes still closed, I can feel sweat bead on my skin, the scratchy dampness of the sheets. In the parking lot below, a man and a woman call out to each other while cars pass on the highway. Some must be pulling into the old Fuel Stop, the drivers getting out to pump gas and buy their morning coffee. I can picture the blue sky above, with its clear blaze of light. It's morning; the world is fresh; I should get up and start my day.

But my body won't move.

All right, I think. I'll just stay here. I'll keep my eyes shut, and the world will stay black and there won't be anything to flee. I don't have to face the files. I can decide that coming here was a mistake, that I can live with both Ricky's story and my past staying unresolved inside me. I can live with the fear that flares through me too often when Janna touches me and the anger and grief I feel in my heart when I'm in my parents' house. I can live with anything; I can hold all of it. Just as long as it stays down.

Then what? Be just as stuck as before?

I sigh. I shove myself out of bed, kicking my body upright, and feel the rough slip of the sheets away from me. I yank open the drapes, and the weakest light steals in. The coffee I brew in the motel coffeemaker is tepid and weak, the faint taste of burn, but I suck down two cups of it. The past already has its hold on me. There's nothing to do but face it.

Downtown Iowa is one street: a public library tucked behind the broad face of a bank, the post office and the fire department, the quilting store and the hardware store. It looks like a movie set of small-town America, but on the drive here I passed welfare motels and payday-check-cashing outlets with blinking neon signs. I passed long fields that abutted straggled woods. Between the fields were a few houses, spaced like outposts, each with rusted car parts on their lawns and plastic chairs that had long ago turned from white to gray. A plastic Jesus was glued to a mailbox. Every pickup had a gun rack. Now, downtown, I am on the dividing line that separates the cluster of commerce from the miles and miles of pretty, rusted, run-down landscape that stretch across the horizon. Here is Iowa. But where Ricky lived, where he grew up, was out in that great flat in-between expanse. Where Lake Charles, Iowa, and LeBleu could all hear about a missing boy and all, at first, decide it was some other place's problem.

The library walls are plastered with colorful posters that exhort the value of reading. One corner of the one-room space has most of the posters and there the wooden chairs are miniature, their colors red and blue and yellow. The chairs are empty today—no children in sight—and I look at them hard for a moment. The newspaper photograph of Lorilei standing over two-year-old Jeremy as he was fitted for his first bike, her hands resting on his hard little shoulders, was taken in a parking lot near here. Did she read to him here? Did Jeremy ever sit in one of these chairs, or its precursor?

I've already been through the online archives of the main paper. That yielded scanned articles about the long-ago crash, Oscar and Vicky's burial, even an announcement of Bessie and Alcide's fiftieth wedding anniversary, with their children listed—Ricky's home given as "West Feliciana Parish," where the state penitentiary is. But the library has folders of old news clippings, so maybe there's more here. Inside the green cardboard folders are clips from yellowed newspaper, each hemmed in scissor lines from someone's long-ago careful hand. I read of bake sales, of car washes, of local citizens' good deeds. A lot about flowers. On one page the much younger face of District Attorney Rick Bryant grins out at me from before he was the DA, before he was the man who would push three times to get the death penalty for Ricky. Nothing mentions Jeremy or Ricky, not even in the folder marked CRIME, which is nearly empty of anything dated after the 1950s. A small town's history, curated by a small town. Nothing included that anyone wants to forget. The books in the local history section are a bust, too, Iowa so small that *local* really means the region.

"Do you have any yearbooks?" I ask the librarian.

"A few," she says, and leads me to a shelf. My first thought is disappointment—though the shelf holds a row of yellow-and-purple spines for the Iowa High School Yellowjackets, the years stamped on them are from the fifties and sixties. Next, the nineties. Bessie and Alcide didn't go to school here, only their children. These books won't help me.

Then I notice one—only one—tucked in the middle of those decades, 1981 on its spine.

My heart races: 1981. I pull the book off the shelf and thumb its pages rapidly, calculating. Ricky was born in 1965. He would have been a sophomore. The girls are fresh-faced young with their bangs teased and sprayed high, the boys' hair is hacked into mullets. Faces are splotched with acne and meet the camera in the broad grin beam of the confident, or look down in the sink of the resigned.

Ricky isn't among them.

Then I see him.

A freshman. At fifteen, he looks younger than his age. His face is small and his chin weak, his skin clear as a preteen's. The wave in his hair that will develop into a high cowlick is already there, his eyebrows already unruly. He doesn't wear glasses. He does not smile and he does not frown. His mouth hangs open. He looks straight into the camera, but he isn't staring. His eyes are vacant. This is the boy who grew into the man who killed Jeremy.

I sit down on the carpet and page through the yearbook. High schoolers sitting seriously for portraits, mugging in candids for the camera, goosing one another or busting into laughter as the shutter clicks. Their faces ripple across 140 pages, repeating. A small school. A small town. On the bright yellow inside cover, Ricky's class-mates have scribbled messages to the yearbook's original owner, a girl named Cindy. "You can get everything out of life that you put into it!" I flip through all the pages, but Ricky is only in this one place. One photo.

This, then, was Ricky at fifteen: scrawny and unwritten, the future seeming as blank as the expression on his face.

But no, his future is there. Ten pages away, captured together in this moment. Her name catches me off guard. I wasn't looking for her. Her brother went to school in Lake Charles and I thought she did, too. But she's here: Lorilei Guillory. A senior, her face un-mistakably the broad one that appears, older, in news clips; her light brown hair winged like Farrah Fawcett's; her eyeliner already heavy in the style she'll wear for years. A graduation cap on her head—she's done it, she's graduating. And she's there again in the photograph of the school newspaper staff, her arms crossed and one leg cocked over the other, with her jeans rolled up over hik-ing boots, a fleece sweatshirt. She's left her sunglasses on, and she stares at the camera through a mask of black. The thick, oversize clothing, the dark glasses—she looks like she's hiding, but not out of shyness. Out of armor.

The future is coming, eleven years ahead. It sends its long low warning signal over the pages of this story.

Behind me, the librarian coughs once, signaling politely. Some-how it is 5:00 p.m. The day has passed and the library is closing. I slide the book back onto the shelf and stand and stretch. "Thanks," I say.

Outside, in the parking lot, I sit in my rental car for a long time.

It's still clear and sunny out—beautiful, really—but I keep the windows up and the engine off, the key in my hand. The car is stiflingly hot, but my body is suddenly immovable, heavy as the air. I've found something. Evidence, as much as the files are. Of the boy, when he was still a boy and not the murderer. Of the girl, when she was still a girl and not the victim's mother. The future was waiting for them, unknown and unseen.

Twenty-Seven

I know almost nothing about my grandfather before he became my grandfather. When I was growing up, my mother didn't talk about his childhood—or about hers. My father was always telling us stories of the upside-down pineapple cake his mother baked for special occasions, or the floppy-eared Great Dane he had as a boy, who tugged the doghouse all the way to my father's schoolyard gate. Compared with his, my mother's life before us was a void—and so, too, was my grandfather. I know I played checkers with him often as a child, and that he was the one to teach me to draw, but those memories have been blotted mainly to black—by his hand as it draws the soft cloth of my nightgown away from my legs, by the cool brush of air against my stomach and the dread that crawled my thigh. By what came next.

When I first got Ricky's treatment records from Lake Charles Mental Health Center in the mid-1980s and I read about his struggling in the years before he killed Jeremy, he started to become a person to me. Which made me wonder about my grandfather. I wrote my mother a letter, the first and only letter I've written to her. *Please tell me about Grandpa. I have realized that all I know about him is what he did.* For months, the letter went unanswered. I asked her about it by telephone and she ignored the question. I e-mailed her and got no response. I asked again. I feel for my mother. With her determination not to talk about the past, I must sometimes seem to her a walking time bomb. A bomb made of time.

Then one morning, six months after I sent the letter, I woke to a long e-mail of stories. Each was just a sentence or two, dashed off and tentative in tone, but together they formed a trickle. The next day another e-mail arrived, lengthier. Then another, and another.

My grandfather, Vincent Jimmy Marzano, was one of nine children born to an Italian immigrant couple. He and my grandmother Emily were childhood sweethearts who met when both families moved to Queens. In the summers, the siblings all went to Coney Island together, and soon Emily's older sister married my grandfather's older brother. After the second grade, my grandfather left school to help support his younger siblings by working as a newsboy. He taught himself to read by studying the papers he hawked, calling out their headlines on street corners. That he could read helped him find work as a film cutter. When he and Emily married, my grandfather was working for Paramount Pictures.

He worked nights and my grandmother worked days as a telephone operator, so he took care of my mother and her two older brothers when they came home from school. (Here I think of Ricky looking after June and Joey, and of the neighborhood parents sending their children up to play in his bedroom while they searched.) *He was always the fun parent*, my mother wrote. He liked to arrange little surprises. He would unwind a roll of toilet paper, hide a dollar bill in it, then roll it up again for one of his unsuspecting children to find. Each night he would cook them dinner (I remember my grandfather's red sauce bubbling on the stove in the Queens house when I was a child, needling into my nose, making my belly growl), and when evening arrived he would turn off the stove and cover the food, so that it would keep for my grandmother to feed them later. Then he would bundle the children for the walk to the bus stop. So that the children would not complain of the length of the walk, or of the cold in winter, he would hide small toys and candies in his pocket that he doled out along the way: a piece of Chiclets gum for my uncle from a two-cent pack he'd bought at the subway station; the wooden spool from a skein of thread that he'd had the shoemaker hammer four nails into, so my mother could knit on it. At the bus station, he would hand the children off to my grandmother and continue on to the night shift at Paramount. There he'd spend hours wearing jeweler's glasses, hunched over strips of film. I can see him as he presses his blade to the images: the way he touches his tongue to his lips in concentration, the bushy eyebrows I remember so well furrowing. My grandfather is a surgeon of stories. He splices them together to make something new.

And no, to the obvious question, no, my mother wrote—though I hadn't dared to ask her directly. She had no memory of his ever having abused her or her brothers.

Five e-mails came. Then, as suddenly as they began, the e-mails stopped.

That's all. That's all I have. Only those e-mails, my memories like a filmstrip burned black at the center, and her silence. No archive from a trial I can search, no thousands of pages to pore over, and no answers. Because in addition to whatever else is true about my grandfather, there is also this: He got away with it.

The walls in the prison visiting room where Lorilei meets with Ricky must be gray paint—nothing that would show dirt as easily as white—over large bricks and shine-rimmed with the faint stink of bleach. I see an old soda machine sitting in the far corner, its light emitting a barely audible hum. The chairs are plastic molded primary colors, red and blue and yellow, somebody's idea of cheer but a little too small. She comes in the morning, but inside the room's cast of gray it could as easily be night. The guard shows her to a small round table where she sits and folds her hands in her lap, so she can't fidget too much. The door in the corner has a small rectangle of glass. Every few minutes she glances up at it, checking.

The next time she tries to make herself wait longer. But then she checks again.

She recognizes the back of his head first. Brush-bristled hair cut short, the orange rim of a jumpsuit at his neck. It should just look like the back of any prisoner's head, she shouldn't be able to recognize him, but she does.

He turns, and yes, it's him. Those eyes. The thick glasses. The door opens and he shuffles through it without looking at her. He puts his hands out and the guard unlocks his cuffs.

She stands. She's not thinking now; she's gone blank, her whole body watching his, and her hands find their way to her hair and smooth it. Ten years have passed since she last saw him. Entering his late thirties, he's no longer young, and his hair has started to pepper with Bessie's gray. Off death row, his body has slackened and settled. He was in prison here before the first trial and has been here again for several months now. This is where he lives.

He reaches the table, and she realizes she has no idea what to say. For a minute she just looks at him.

"Do you want a soda?" The lawyers told her she could offer this. They gave her a few bills to bring.

He nods, so quickly it's as if he needs the motion to be over as soon as he starts it. "Coke."

She must be grateful for the few steps to the machine, the chance to look away. She doesn't let herself think. She just holds herself, like she holds the dollar, and when the machine spits the soda out she cups the cold can in her hand, faintly wet with condensation. The wetness is like a reminder of the world beyond this place. Of water, of the way the water crawls through the bushes of Henderson Swamp and how it will stretch beneath the overpass on her way back to her motel. When she reaches him she holds the can out without saying anything.

"Thanks," he says.

Such small talk they make with each other first. Lorilei does all the asking. How's it to be back here? All right. You must be glad to be off death row. Yeah. He's shy with her. He looks down a lot.

His shyness makes her bold. She's in charge here, as if Ricky's one of ten-year-old Cole's friends after he's nicked a piece of candy from her cupboard, a guilty schoolboy mumbling into his hands who can't look her in the eye. She coaxes him. "You must have a lot of time to think."

"You know my mama was in that crash," he begins, and his voice trails off.

"Yes," she says, encouraging, and waits. She must feel the idea settle inside her. Ricky as a boy. Ricky as a small boy, confused, not knowing what haunts his parents, only seeing Bessie's pain. Lorilei chooses her words carefully. "That must have been so hard."

This is a mother who lost the son she mothered. And this is a man who has two mothers, but one, the defense attorneys say, was sick or drunk his whole childhood and the other, the social workers say, was so harsh with discipline that none of the children under her care ever bonded. (Not true, Darlene and Francis say on the stand. They were loved. They were happy.)

Neither Bessie nor Luann testified for Ricky at any of his three trials. They don't even seem to have attended the trials. The prosecutor brought this up pointedly when the defense presented evidence of Bessie's pregnancy in the cast. "This case isn't about Bessie Langley," he said. "I don't know Bessie Langley. I've never met Bessie Langley. I've never seen Bessie Langley." So did the defense. "If you were sitting where Ricky was, wouldn't someone be there for you? Your mother?" (But in the files, Bessie often sits beside him in counseling appointments. So who is telling the story correctly?) Almost every counselor who comes into contact with Ricky notes that he seems much younger than his actual age. He seems twelve, they say: right on the cusp of puberty, not yet grown into his own skin. Twelve not intellectually—Ricky's IQ tests as normal, and in prison in Georgia he took some college classes—but emotionally. If Ricky as a child was shunned by his peers, Ricky as an adult seems to make at least some people want to take care of him. ("Would you remember me to Ricky?" one social worker said, interviewed by a defense investigator for the trial. "I was unusually fond of him. Of all of them, I remember him the most.") Ricky in his adult body sometimes seems like a child caught in a permanent game of dress-up. The child inside him needs looking after. And is it too much to say that, in this moment, Lorilei needs to be soft, needs to be tender toward someone? Is it too much to say that Ricky, in this moment, needs someone to be soft to him?

Lorilei must watch his face closely. The way his eyebrow twitches when he gets nervous. The way he looks down at his hands. Ricky is a killer. He killed her son. At times, he is boastful about this. At times, he is angry.

But right now he must seem, somehow, fragile.

She has one more question. "Ricky, did you molest my son?"

"No," he says.

Then she does something that must startle even herself. She reaches her hand across the table and takes his. The hand that killed her child.

His hand is skinny, light as a frightened animal. But she waits, and it settles. "Ricky," she says, "I'll fight for you."

Those words. That promise. Those are the words I had such trouble with when I learned about this case. He killed her son. He was a pedophile. He molested children. But she fought for him?

The defense lawyers and the news media told this story as a story of the power of a mother's forgiveness. But that's too simple. Lorilei herself has said she doesn't forgive him. Instead, she has said that she now believes that Ricky did not molest her child. When she visited him in prison, she asked him whether he molested Jeremy. He said no and she believes him. That was part of what made her feelings change between the first trial and the second.

But I've read what wasn't admitted at court. It isn't that simple, either. For that first trial, the jury saw some of the evidence of Ricky's past pedophilia. They saw his diary, in which the descriptions of molestation he gave were either recollections or fantasies; no one knows which, or how many, of those stories were true. The

Georgia girl who was five when he touched her took the stand at the trial, and, at age fourteen, described what he'd done. A Georgia inmate described hearing him say his big mistake was leaving the girl alive. A great deal of time was spent on the tests showing Ricky's semen on Jeremy's white Fruit of the Loom T-shirt.

And Ricky told investigators he'd hurt hundreds of children. I don't think that's true—I think he was inflating things. I think a pedophile was what he knew he was now, what he'd always be, and because that's who he was he wanted to make that identity bigger. He didn't have anything else to be. But I do think he must have molested more children than those for whom he was caught. I know my grandfather molested at least one child outside my immediate family, but only years after he died did it occur to me that there might have been more. That five years of molesting us was not a one-time thing, and perhaps, in its length, implied more. The silence my parents kept may have allowed more children to be hurt. Ricky struggled with pedophilia for decades. At Ricky's second trial, none of the evidence of Ricky's prior "bad acts" was admitted. The test results were barely mentioned. The prosecution implied many times that Ricky had molested Jeremy, even accused him of it—but they could present little of the circumstantial evidence that he might have. There are reasons for that, good ones. The trial was about the murder, not the whole story. But is an act ever really only about itself? Does any element of this story occur in isolation?

I can see why Lorilei shuts the door on the whole question behind her, opts to believe that her son was not molested and leave it at that. How can I fault her for wanting something easier to live with? How can I fault her for choosing a neater narrative?

But the determination to turn away from the past isn't benign. The morning after the Christmas party when I overheard my father telling people that I was writing about something that only I recalled, I confronted him. My sister Nicola backed me up, and told him that was nonsense. Of course she remembered the abuse. We all did. But two years later, she said to me, "I've decided to think of myself as someone who wasn't abused." This was brutally hard for me to hear. We'd shared a room. I'd watched my grandfather touch her. He'd pulled me from my bed and taken me to the bathroom where she stood, waiting. He unzipped his pants and made us put our hands on him. She can't just pretend none of that happened. She can't.

But of course—she can. I have changed my sister's name in this book, out of respect for her choice, and as much as possible I have changed my other family members' names and the names of some of the people in Ricky's life. But I can't bring myself to write a narrative that puts my experience alone in my family again. I won't do on the page what was done in life.

Twenty-Eight

I couldn't find any real information on the cemetery in Hecker where Bessie and Alcide are buried, near where the house Lyle and Alcide built once stood. When I called the cemetery caretaker, he told me to meet him at his house and he'd drive me out there. Nobody new would be able to find the cemetery alone.

"Who did you want to see, again?" the elderly caretaker asks, once I'm seated in his living room, his wife beside me on the couch and he sitting in an armchair across the room. Both the couch and the armchair are covered in hand-knit doilies.

"Desier Langley." Alcide's father, who's buried next to them. Oscar's at his feet. It feels too close, somehow, to say I want to see Oscar or Bessie. Then I remember that the caretaker corrected my pronunciation on the phone. "Dezzy-ch."

"You're not from Iowa," the caretaker's wife says. She peers at me.

"No," I admit. "I live in Massachusetts."

"Not kin, then."

"No. I'm not."

She waits, clearly wanting more of an answer. Her eyes are like pale blue marbles.

I feel myself let go of the pretense that I'm here to see Desier. I am thinking too much about my grandmother lying on the sofa bed at the foot of the stairs, and my father as he hoisted my grandfather into the car to bring him home to us. I am thinking too much about Bessie and what she knew about her son. About how much loss Bessie had to live with, and about Lorilei's walking away from her baby's grave, another baby inside her. About the missing birth certificate on my childhood wall and about all the silence in my family. The caretaker and his wife are being so kind, having me here in their living room. I owe them something. "You know about the crash?" I ask. "My parents lost a child. I think the death kind of—" I pause, searching for the word. "I think it haunted my parents."

The road into Hebert Cemetery is long and winding, made of packed dirt that cuts between tall leafy trees that blot out the sun. I follow the caretaker and his wife as they drive ahead in a white pickup truck. Around us, the woods thicken into a snarl. Nothing else could be out on this road, the cemetery's location even more desolate than I thought. Great dust clouds rise up behind their truck and soon the only things I can see ahead are the white bay of the truck, the high, twined trees on my sides, and the haze I am driving into.

Then, up ahead, there is suddenly sunshine. A clearing. The trees fall away and light floods in. At the center of the clearing is a waist-high wrought-iron fence, perhaps forty feet long on one edge, around a rectangle of cement graves. The caretaker sidles his pickup next to the fence and I pull in alongside him. The cemetery is so small, so tucked within the trees, that it strikes me immediately how many times he's pulled in here. How well he must know this drive. How intimate it must be to spend decades caring for just this patch of graves.

His wife stays by the truck while the caretaker and I walk to the fence. At the gate, he clears his throat. "So how did you get interested in the Langleys?" he asks. Something about the way he asks makes me realize they've been talking.

For a minute I let his question rest. The sun is brilliant and strong, the light stark white around me. To walk I have to place my feet carefully between the graves. Here, just a few miles from Lake Charles, the water table is different. The dead can't be buried beneath the ground. The dug grave would fill with water. The body might rise up. So they're entombed. In the famous New Orleans cemeteries I've visited, that means structures as ornate as tiny houses. But those were families that had money. In the woods, in this hidden clearing, the graves are burial vaults, half-submerged in the ground, so that the tops rise inches above the grass. They look like coffins. Their shape suggests bodies.

As a child I never thought about my sister's having had a body. I never wondered where she was buried. She wasn't a baby to me. She was absence. The absence of a birth announcement on my childhood bedroom wall, when Elize's and Nicola's announcements were framed over their beds. The absence of any stories from right after we were born. The absence of any explanation the day my mother ran barefoot sobbing and screaming across the lawn, or once when she had too much to drink on a family vacation and was suddenly the one flung facedown on my parents' hotel bed, swearing she was too sad to live.

When I was lonely as a child I would sometimes go to the small bathroom right off the kitchen. My two sisters were into dolls and sports and my brother loved movies and baseball and I loved books and quiet and there was never anyone it felt right to play with. That would get worse, later, when I was angry and the others either weren't or couldn't show it, while I was always, helplessly, loud as a spouting fountain with my feelings. But the bathroom was always peaceful. It was the size of a closet. The ceiling was wallpapered in a midnight sky with white stars and the walls in white with pastel stars, so that standing in the bathroom with the door closed was like being inside an impossible mash-up of the dark of night and the light of day while the infinite stars swirled around you.

I stood in front of the cabinet mirror and studied my brown curly hair. I studied my green eyes. I looked at myself, looking for her. Her eyes I knew, from the medical chart I'd found once in the white filing cabinet, were blue. But maybe they'd have darkened with age. And her hair was brown like mine. Andy and I weren't identical, obviously—though strangers, befuddlingly, sometimes asked, even if we were standing right in front of them—but wasn't it possible that she and I were? That somehow I had been robbed of a true twin? In my mind, I grew her up. I made her my age; I gave her my curls. I made her shy. I made her love books.

It never quite worked. I could never get hold of the idea of her. She was gone, unimaginably gone. I was alone in my family. I couldn't imagine myself being otherwise.

But in Ricky's story, I started to see her everywhere. In Cole's growing up in Jeremy's absence. In the trunk Bessie kept in her closet. In the photograph of Oscar that Ricky carried, making the boy into his imaginary friend.

Oscar wasn't imaginary. He has a grave.

The fact of a body. But where? I decided I had to ask. I'd gone to visit my parents on Nantucket, where they were staying for a month, as they did every year. I waited until the end of the weekend, until the house we were all staying in—my parents and my siblings and I—came to feel like a too-tight shirt over sunburned skin, scratchy and congested. The island had changed over the years, the backpackers playing guitar and the dogs roaming free on the beaches now replaced by men with sweaters knotted over their shoulders and women in Lilly Pulitzer dresses whose hair stayed perfectly blow-dried even in the humidity. The old five-and-dime was now an antiques shop. It was too much to hear all our voices piled on top of one another, all crammed into the same spaces we'd occupied as children. For how many more years could we gather this way? For how many more years would we be able to find a house that held us all? Would we never talk about everything that had happened? I waited until just before I had to leave or I would miss my ferry. Then I went through the house to find my mother. She was dressing in the bedroom, her hair curled onto hot rollers. She'd dabbed a strong floral perfume on her wrists, and though she hadn't brought pantyhose to the summer island there was the same half-closed bathrobe. The perfume filled my throat. Time buckled.

"Where was Jacqueline buried?" I said.

My mother froze, her mouth a little round O. She'd moved on to applying lipstick and now the top half of the O was a raisin brown, the bottom her bare lips. Her hand suddenly trembling, she finished painting her lips. Then she straightened her back, carefully screwed shut the tube, placed it down on the vanity, and walked out.

The next morning, when I was back in Boston, my cell phone rang. I saw it was my father. My father has called me perhaps twice in my life. This time when I answered he did not say hello. "I hear you've been asking your mother some questions."

I grabbed a pad off my desk, and a pen. I knew I wouldn't get another chance.

"Jacqueline's buried in a mass grave," my father said. "I don't know where. Somewhere by the hospital, probably. The Catholic Charities took care of it." When the three of us were five months old, and Andy and I were home and Jacqueline was still in the hospital, my father had taken my exhausted mother to Puerto Rico for a much-needed vacation. They'd landed at the airport, he said, and he'd heard his name over the public address system. Jacqueline had died. Standing with the emergency phone in his hand— I imagine the porters all around him, the vacationing families overburdened with colorful luggage, the honeymooners holding each other's hands and leaning into each other to steal kisses—he made an instant decision. "Could you bury her?" he asked.

They couldn't, they said. Only the Catholic Charities did that.

My parents are atheists. He told them to baptize her.

"It was simplest," he told me on the phone, his voice gruff against tears. My parents never asked where Jacqueline was buried. Later my aunt would tell me they asked never to be told. "It was the right thing. She only lived in the hospital. She belonged there." He sounded as though he was pleading. Not with me. With the past. We hung up, and never spoke about it again.

The caretaker has stopped walking and is watching me, waiting for me to answer his question. The grave to my left has a coffee cup cemented to its slab, the flowers in the cup crumbling and long dead. The cement at the bottom of the cup is unevenly applied, clearly a job done by a mourner rather than a professional. The mug says DADDY. I choose my words carefully. "I heard about the Langley family and I suppose their story just stayed with me. I had a sister, a triplet sister. She died when we were babies."

"But how did you hear about them?"

It's brutally hot in the clearing, the air stilled by the wall of the trees. The caretaker's wife is waiting at the gate. But the caretaker just looks at me. In the long silence I feel keenly just how strange it is that I know so much about this family. How strange it is that I've come here at all. I want to tell him something that will make it all make sense for him, but how can I explain that I am trying to chase down the origin of this story because I can't find the origin in my own life? That I need to understand how Bessie buried her children—because in her is Lorilei, and in her is my mother? That I need to understand the way that love warped what Bessie could see—because in her son is my grandfather, in Bessie is my grandmother, and in all of this is the click that Lorilei's heels make as she walks up the courtroom aisle to argue for Ricky's life and the strong grip of my father's hand as he hoists my grandfather into the car, to bring him over the bridge to us? We are standing in a graveyard. But the past isn't in the ground for me. The past is in my body. "I was doing some legal work and came across the story," I finally muster.

We walk a few steps farther in silence, the sun strong. Then I almost cry out, because I see what we've come to. LANGLEY.

Twenty-Nine

I've never been to my grandparents' grave. Not since my grandfather was laid to rest beside my grandmother. Before that—not since the stone went in, long before he died. The stone is rose-colored, engraved with a rose, and inlaid with their wedding portrait. My grandmother loved roses. So do I. I have the outline of a rose tattooed on the nape of my neck for the Marianne Moore poem "Roses Only" that I painted on my wall as a teenager. When my grandmother lay dying in the hospital, I sang "The Rose" to her. *Some say love, it is a river that drowns the tender reed. Some say love, it is a razor that leaves the heart to bleed.* I sang it to her, too, a few years before she died, when she came to stay with us alone while my grandfather was in the hospital. I had never seen her so restless, so plagued with fearful energy—I had, I realized, never seen her alone. The first night she stayed with us I went down the stairs to kiss her goodnight. My mother had made up the green pull-out sofa bed for her, but she wasn't lying in it. She was sitting on its edge. When I walked into the room, she looked up. "More than fifty years we've been married," she said. She had her mother's prayer card in her palm and was worrying its edges with her fingers. "I've never gone to sleep without your grandfather. Not one night since."

I was thirteen, maybe. I had never thought about the accumulation of all those nights. The way they added up to a life.

Who my grandfather was must have come to my grandmother like a pebble inside her: impossible to ignore one moment, impossible to admit the next. An awareness, then a vanishing. She must have willed herself not to feel him leave that bed at night. She knew who my grandfather was as a man. She couldn't let herself see who he was as a molester.

Driving away from the cemetery, I am thinking about the Langley graves. The concrete over Alcide had darkened; the concrete over Bessie, still light. She died just a year before my visit. Someone put in markers for their children, with Oscar's school portrait and Vicky's christening one, and their concrete was the same color as Alcide's. Bessie was probably alive when they were put in. The four graves together—the two big and the two little—looked unmistakably like what they were: a family. I am thinking about this, I am thinking about my grandmother lying in that bed, missing her husband, and the way she smelled of lavender when I leaned over her to kiss her papery cheek goodnight—when I see through the trees that the road ahead of me stops at an intersection. I see a yellow railroad crossing sign.

And then the name of the street I am coming to, which blows high and loud inside me like a whistle.

Packing House Road.

On the evening of May 27, 1992, eighty-two-year-old Della Thompson is sitting out on the patio at her house on Packing House Road, watching *Wheel of Fortune* through the patio door. The sun is setting over the wide flat grass of this part of Louisiana, the sky lit up in the fuschia bursts and golden streaks that are the gorgeous legacy of pollution in this part of the land, and out of the corner of her eye she notices a motorcycle going, she will later say, "real fast" down the road, so fast she cannot make out any passenger or driver. So fast she cannot make out Joey's small arms clutching his father's waist and Terry leaning forward to turn the throttle up faster, to make the motorcycle fly. Does Joey close his eyes against his father's back? In this last moment, is what he feels the wind?

A train whistle pierces the air, loud and long, long enough to startle Della. You could see the train coming before that. It didn't need the whistle. Then the train speeds past, the sunshine knifing off its silver body. After that, nothing. She goes back to watching her program.

But soon there's a rumble of a pickup truck coming up the road. Della likes to watch passing cars. There aren't many. So she watches the pickup stop near the crossing. She watches a woman get out and walk over to inspect something on the ground. She watches as the woman bends over and starts to pick it up.

Then Della hears screaming.

The woman runs toward Della's house, yelling for Della to call the police.

On the diagram submitted with the police report is a figure eight drawn flipped on its side in front of the tracks. It looks like an infinity symbol. Above it, on the tracks, is noted "gouge marks." This is where the train collided with the motorcycle, whose wheels form the loops of the symbol, and flipped it. Then the infinity symbol repeats again and again, tossing through the air before coming to rest. *Airborne.* The small outline of a body, marked "Victim #1," lies parallel to the tracks—fifty-eight feet and eight inches, the diagram notes, from the point of impact. Terry Lawson. Between his body and the tracks are two carefully labeled circles representing the motorcycle's gas tank and seat, and then the fender much farther away. The motorcycle blew apart in the impact. Closer in to the tracks lies the outline of a small body, apparently ejected much earlier than Terry. "Victim #2." Joey, his son.

The train didn't hit Terry. He hit it. He hit the second car, at such velocity that, the record notes, the train engineer never knew he'd hit anything at all and continued on toward Chicago. The re-

port I found in the files said "accident." The police never investi-
gated it as anything else.

In all the briefs the defense filed in this case, the briefs with the
unenforceable and strange requests, the brief that argued that
though Jeremy was found dead and wrapped in blankets it might
not have been murder, I found one in the boxes marked "Motion
for Exhumation." A hair sample was taken from Ricky Langley,
Clive noted. But all that the sample proved was that the pubic hair
found on Jeremy's lip had not come from Ricky. Given that, wouldn't
it make sense to test whom the hair might belong to? "There is
information that Mr. Lawson molested June Lawson, his daughter,"
Clive wrote.

The motion does not specify what this information was.

Terry satisfied all the criteria they were looking for in a suspect.
If not a suspect in the murder, then a suspect in—something. He
had access to the bedroom where Jeremy's body was found. He
had access to Jeremy. In the time since Ricky had moved in with him
and Pearl and the children, he had become a close friend of Ricky's,
and the two of them would go hunting together in the woods for
hours. Ricky, the motion argued, was an easily influenced guy, and
a very lonely one. A steady friendship would have been incredibly
important to him.

And—the motion went further—Ricky *wanted* to die. Ricky,
who had been suicidal for years, knew that if he was found to have
molested Jeremy Guillory he would be more likely to be executed.
He wrote notes to Lucky in jail. "I still think we should push for
the death penalty." He wrote notes to the newspaper. "Jeremy was
sacrificed for reasons you will never understand." But what if Jeremy had been molested—but it wasn't Ricky who'd done it, or
Ricky wasn't the only one? The semen on Jeremy's shirt was from
Ricky. The pubic hair on his lip was not. What if Ricky was covering for his friend, the father no one suspected?

Three months later, Terry drove himself and his son into the
second car of an Amtrak train. "Anyone who knows the railroad
crossing on Packing House Road will recognize that the presence

of an oncoming train would be obvious to anyone from a mile away," Clive wrote.

So rather than rushing to convict Ricky without understanding the whole story, wouldn't it make sense to exhume the body? Terry was dead. He didn't have a constitutional right against search and seizure. Your rights expire when you die. Clive was careful to note at the hearing that the presence of the pubic hair on Jeremy's lip didn't necessarily mean he'd been molested. There were other ways the hair could have gotten there, with the blankets piled on him. But the blankets were from Ricky's bed and, so many of them printed with cartoon characters, likely from the children's. And the pubic hair wasn't Ricky's. So—wouldn't it make sense?

The motion was filed December 3, 1993. Jeremy had been dead for a year and ten months. Terry and Joey, a year and six months. The motion struck people as ghoulish. There was briefly talk of filing a disciplinary complaint against Clive with the state bar association. The motion was denied. Pearl took the stand tight-lipped and no one ever asked her what happened after they found Jeremy's body in her house, or where her husband and son were now. The whole thing was wiped from the trial.

But there is still the problem of the body. The problem of Jeremy's dead body in the upstairs closet of the Lawson house for three days. The problem of Pearl and Terry living alongside it. Waking their children up in the morning. Tucking their children into bed at night. When I found the accident report in the files I called a friend of mine who runs a medical school cadaver lab in Boston and asked her how long a body would last before it started to stink. Could someone really not notice that there was a dead body in the house for three days?

"What was the weather?" she asked.

"Louisiana in winter. The house probably wasn't heated very well. The family had little money and there were all these blankets out."

She thought for a minute. "Borderline," she said.

"Borderline?" The word came out as a cry. How could I tell her how much I needed to understand what had happened in that house? "I need to figure this out."

"Borderline."

Thirty

When I was eighteen years old, I confronted my grandfather. It was June of 1996 and I was about to graduate from high school. August rose on the horizon, flooding my vision with the promise of escape. In Chicago, a dorm room waited for me. A bedroom I'd never once slept in, in which I'd never had a nightmare's visit. A whole campus—a whole city—full of buildings full of rooms in which not a day of the past had unfolded.

But I was starting to understand just how solid the silence was. That if I didn't say anything no one in my family ever would, and my grandfather would never have to answer for what he'd done. I wanted him to answer. I wanted him to hear me say the words for what he was. For those words to become as solid as the memories I carry in my body.

That morning the magnolia tree outside his apartment was in full white bloom. Inside, the hallways were the silent, functional beige of space that belongs to no one. As I neared his door my nose began to burn with the ammonia stink of old urine. His body was failing him; that thought made me strong. I wonder now how it is that I didn't pause, how I could have just kept going. But in my memory my stride is quick and unflinching. Through his door I could hear the television priest saying Mass, the long tones of the Latinate vowels. My grandfather watched this same program every Sunday morning he stayed over to babysit when I was a child. Every Saturday night, his hands. Every Sunday morning, a priest's voice.

He came to the door slowly. He was dressed in slacks and a tucked-in shirt, his glasses on straight. My grandfather was never like my grandmother, she in her housedresses. He was always prepared to meet the world. I'd never been to see him alone before, but when he opened the door and saw me he didn't seem surprised. He didn't fuss, or hug me, or ask why I'd come, or do whatever it is that grandfathers do when they see their granddaughters. He was silent. He watched me. He stood there, waiting.

I stepped past him. The smell of the room hit me first. Then the photos. Every surface was crowded with knickknacks from my grandparents' house: their wedding portrait in a silver frame; salt-and-pepper-shaker sets; tiny teacups and tinier thimbles. An orange clay bust my grandfather had sculpted of himself and that I used to like touching when I was a child, the hair looped into curls like mine. There were framed photographs of my mother and her brothers as children, then us as children. Across the shelves, I grew up. From the television came the priest's voice.

I turned to my grandfather. "You molested me," I said. Such simple words and they'd never been spoken. "I remember."

I told him what I remembered. That when I was three I stood in the musty dining room in the Astoria house, the house my mother grew up in, wearing a dress. The room was darkened, my parents off somewhere. My grandfather and I were alone. I was looking at a painting that hung on the opposite wall. The painting showed a young Italian peasant girl's face framed in a kerchief, her head turned to the side, a double cherry looped over her ear so that the bulbs of the fruit hung, glistening like earrings. Suddenly my grandfather's hand was over my mouth, stifling my startled cry, and another rough hand up my dress. He shoved his fingers under my tights and panties.

I told him about the doll lamp on my childhood dresser. About the doll's yellow gauze dress, and how it had tinted his face yellow in the light. How he'd pulled out his false teeth and grinned at me. "I'm a witch," he'd said, and scared me to silence. I stared into that yellow light as he pulled up my nightgown and pulled down my panties. He unzipped his pants. He pushed himself against me.

I couldn't tell him then what I didn't yet know. That years after this day—eighteen years after he died—there'd come an afternoon when I sat in my gynecologist's exam room and she said, "There's scarring inside you." I'd been told this before, but I'd always avoided it.

This time I didn't. "What could cause that?"

The doctor didn't answer. She looked at me.

"I was abused as a child," I said. I tried to keep my voice level. "By my grandfather. Could it be from that?"

She nodded.

My face was already wet from tears. During the exam she'd taken a biopsy. When the scalpel scraped inside me it had burned sharply and I'd begun to shake. I'd had no feelings—no fear or sadness or even consciousness of pain—just the shaking and a profound sense of absence, like the shaking was happening to someone who wasn't me. Then the shaking rose up from inside me and came out in gulping, ragged sobs.

I sobbed for a long time. The doctor rolled her little stool away from me, pulled the thin paper cover over my legs, and handed me a tissue.

"Are you all right?" she'd asked.

I nodded through my sobs. I tried to speak, but no words came out.

What I wanted to say was this: I recognized the feeling. My body recognized the feeling of pain inside me. My memories had always ended with my grandfather rubbing himself against me, then the nothing of black. I'd always thought that where the memory ended the fact of the past did, too.

But: the scarring. Is the scarring evidence of what happened after the pain, after the black? What happened after my memory ends? What fact does my body hold? I don't know. I will never know.

In my grandfather's apartment, I made no demands. I laid out my memories calmly. I still wanted to be a lawyer someday. This was my first case.

My grandfather listened. He didn't turn away, he didn't argue or dismiss me. He listened, his face impassive. Behind him, the priest droned.

When I was finished, it was his turn.

"What do you want?" The words had built up force inside him while he waited. Maybe through all the years. Now he spat them at me. "I know I did. But what do you want?"

A part of me may always be eighteen, standing in that room with him. The old-man, wet rot of his breath and the stench of urine, the face I loved and the face I feared. That question.

And the way he seized on this answer.

"Do you want me to kill myself?" he said. "I'll do it, if you want me to. I'll kill myself." He was taunting me now. He'd seen the fear on my face. "Is that what you want? I'm an old man. I'll be dead soon. But I'll do it if you want me to. I'll kill myself."

Then he added, "Besides, what happened to you is not such a big thing. When I was a child, it happened to me."

Thirty-One

I am running out of time in Louisiana, spending my hours in the cave of the file room and driving across the same flat vistas Ricky crossed, back and forth between Iowa and Lake Charles. Past the high school, past the Friendly Home Center, where Ricky worked briefly as a teenager, past the banks of the Calcasieu River, where he once dreamt of a life that would belong to him. Everywhere I look, I see traces of the people in the files. Alcide with his cap curled in his fist, standing on a dirt road in Hecker, his girls at his feet. Bessie adjusting the crutch that bit into her armpit, then bending to make the children's beds before they came home from school. And now Bessie and Alcide under concrete, in the ground. The heat has strangled the fields and driven everyone indoors. The land has the feel of a ghost town, a place a story passed over and blew through.

But I still have not found the house where Jeremy died. A simple, almost maddening problem: The addresses in the records contradict themselves. The police reports list the address as Route 1, Box 204. That's what Ricky gave the police, but no one referred to it that way; they called it Watson Road. "But it don't really got a name," said Ricky, and the police had so much trouble finding it. Sometimes the landlord is referred to as Watson, sometimes Ardoin, but the man named Ardoin quoted in the newspaper didn't mention being the landlord. The paper never gives the Route 1 address; in-

stead it sometimes says the house was on Ardoin Road. That's definitely a mistake; Ardoin Road is much larger. Sometimes the paper
says Ardoin Lane. But Ardoin Lane curves the wrong way. I've
asked at the post office, the town hall, the fire department, the genealogical society, and the police station. No one knows.

It's maddening that there wouldn't simply be a map that shows
the old route numbers—and there may be out there somewhere
still, but if so the parish press office couldn't help me with it and
the maps office swore there wasn't and I never found it—but over
time it starts to feel appropriate, somehow, that I can't find the
house. The feeling is like chasing a memory that slips from your
mind just as soon as you start to grasp it. Sure, it's dangerous to
read metaphor into life; sure, it smacks of a desire to read meaning
into cold fact, but doesn't all of this? All the facts in this case slip
away from me the minute I try to grasp them. In the files Ricky is
sometimes referred to as blond, yet I have sat across from him—
we are not there yet—and can assure you that his hair is dark brown.
Lorilei once wrote a frustrated letter to the *American Press* newspaper complaining that the DA had constantly said that Jeremy
had blond hair and blue eyes, when his eyes were brown. Alcide
wanted Bessie to have an abortion when the doctors said the baby
would be so damaged, but Bessie, sick with grief, wouldn't do it.
Or Bessie wanted the abortion, and Alcide was cruel and wouldn't
let her. Alcide was a loving father, or he beat them. Lyle was a loving replacement for a father, the one Ricky was truly close to, or
he once beat Ricky so hard that Judy had to pull a gun on him to
make him stop. My sister Nicola decides to think of herself as
someone who was never abused, when I remember the shadow
my grandfather made as he leaned over her bed, the rustle of the
bedclothes under his hands. I have a scar inside me but I can't remember its cause. Ricky molested Jeremy before killing him;
Ricky didn't molest Jeremy but killed him; Ricky killed Jeremy
and then molested him afterwards; Ricky killed Jeremy in an effort not to molest him.

Three trials and even that would never be nailed down into fact. It seems right that a house would move, shift, vanish.

After Lorilei visits Ricky in jail, he stops saying he wants to die. He doesn't seem to dream of release—I have many notes written in his hand, but after Georgia, he never again mentions release— and seems to accept living at the jail. His status has changed. He was on death row. Everyone knows Angola, knows he did hard time in that place of legend. Now he has opinions about how the parish jail ought to be run. The man in charge of the correctional center is Colonel Bruce LaFargue. In July of 2002, LaFargue is walking by Ricky's cell when Ricky calls out to him and asks if the two of them can talk. LaFargue leads him into a private room. There, Ricky complains that he feels like with this new trial, he's being used as a guinea pig by his lawyers. They want to set new precedent with his case, he says. But he doesn't want to be released. He says he molested Jeremy and fears that if he gets out he'll molest other children again. This is what Georgia has given him: an understanding of who he is that he can trade like a bargaining chip. He says that in Georgia he was able to get therapy for being a pedophile and it made him think about how to help other pedophiles, how to stop people from offending. That's what he cares about now, but no one will listen to him on it. He believes that if he could just share that knowledge, he'd have something good to offer the world.

"Uh-huh," LaFargue says. Nothing happens.

In October, Ricky tells another jailer that he wants to talk to LaFargue again. The man brings him to LaFargue's office. There Ricky tells LaFargue that after Angola he has ideas for how the prison could be run better. He wants better toilet paper. He wants more time to smoke. And one more thing, he tells LaFargue. He still thinks he could help people understand pedophiles.

"Talk to your attorney about that idea," LaFargue replies.

Ricky writes to his parents. "I want to share with you what has made me so happy, no, so proud. Do you remember, Mom, that in one of my letters to you I said that something good will come out of this?" If you believe that the slant of his writing on the page conveys a kind of emotion, conveys a kind of truth, you can trace a line back to his Georgia prison days for this. If you believe him. If you think he understands and that he truly wants to help.

Clive and Ricky decide to hold what Clive calls a "seminar" for the officers at the jail, at which Ricky will explain the mind of a pedophile. Ricky seems to believe that the seminar is his own idea, but meanwhile Clive has been putting it in place. He has his own reasons: At the last trial, the jury sentenced Ricky to death in only three hours. Clive has to find another way to tell this story. The prosecutors won't be invited to the seminar—Clive doesn't even let them know that it's happening. LaFargue has agreed, Clive will say later, that nothing Ricky says is to be used against him and there would be no recordings of the day. LaFargue will say that, no, what they agreed upon was that Ricky wouldn't talk specifically about the murder. An agreement Ricky quickly broke. That nothing Ricky said would be used against him? LaFargue says he agreed to no such thing.

And it's hard to know how seriously Clive intends the secrecy. He'll tell everyone he invites that they are not to take notes, that none of the information given is to leave the room. But two of the people in the room are reporters. More likely he wants to control how the story's presented and make sure it's Ricky's version that gets the ink. The prosecutors will be spitting mad when they find out. They'll depose everyone who was there and call the whole thing illegal and improper. But they won't be able to undo it. Like a line that a lawyer says in court knowing it's improper, knowing that the judge will say to strike it from the record, but knowing, too, that what the jurors have heard will lodge in their minds, harder to expunge from their memory, Clive will have what he needs: a test.

On December 17, 2002, at about three in the afternoon, Ricky is led through the tile-sterile corridors of the Calcasieu Correctional Center with his wrists cuffed, dressed in an orange jumpsuit and having once again neatened his hair down with water. Likely he's excited. Likely he hasn't been able to sit still all day, or eat his lunch or even one of the ramen packets he squirrels away in his cell from the commissary shop. He's fresh-shaven, though, with a razor he bought there, his skin rubbed raw in his excitement. Now his wiry body springs up with every step, the nervous energy and twitch that shows up on confession videos here directed toward propelling him forward down the halls, forward to what he'll do, the chance he's waited for so hard he quivers with it. To tell his story. The officers lead him into a small room where Clive's waiting, and the two of them rehearse again. Is this where Clive reminds him that under the agreement he's not to talk about the murder? Or is this where he says, *never mind, talk about it?*

Outside the courtroom stand officers from the Sex Offender Tracking Unit, detectives from the sheriff's department, and other law enforcement personnel, about two dozen people total. The hallway is abuzz with walkie-talkies, chatter, the smell of weak coffee emanating from soggy cardboard cups, the muzzled energy of holstered weapons. One of LaFargue's assistants gestures everyone in. The judge's bench is empty, an American flag hanging wanly beside it. After people are seated, Clive leads Ricky to the small table at the front at which the defendant usually sits with attorneys. Now the chairs are on the opposite side, so Ricky and Clive can face the audience. Clive introduces himself, then goes around the room, having everyone give their names and their roles. Then he says, "This is Ricky Langley. Ricky is the reason we're here today. He's going to tell you his story."

When Lorilei heard Ricky's story from Ricky at the prison, something in it swayed her, something made her understand that he wasn't just the monster who had taken her child's life, but a man, and made her decide to fight for him. Somewhere in this story is the person Bessie knew. The people in this courtroom are sitting in front of real-life, flesh-and-blood Ricky. Small and scrawny in his chair, swallowed by his orange jumpsuit. He will tell them who he is. He will tell them how trapped he's been. Clive takes a gamble.

How it backfires.

Ricky begins to talk quickly. First, about Bessie and Alcide. Then—he can't help himself, the words are tumbling out of him— about the car crash, about Oscar, about his father cradling Oscar's head by the side of the road and singing to it; how clearly Ricky remembers that moment, the beautiful spindly sound of his father's voice. He tells them about the photograph of Oscar he carried in his pocket as a child, about talking to it while he ate lunch crouched under the canopy of a yellowwood tree, Oscar tucked carefully between the snakelike roots.

An officer shifts in his chair. Another crosses his arms. This isn't an introduction to the mind of a pedophile. These are one man's memories, or else his imagination.

Clive catches Ricky's eye and motions to prompt him. He should talk about what they've discussed. Ricky takes a deep breath. He must feel a strange mix of pride and shame now, all these eyes on him when he's supposed to tell something even he knows to hide. "I've been molesting children since I was nine years old. Doing it is easier than you'd think." The room goes still. Their raptness is his reward. "I just ask a child to sit on my lap. Children are always sitting on people's laps, and it's always children whose families I know. Then I touch them. I've even"—all these eyes on him, him who's never been listened to this seriously, he cannot resist a bit of bragging—"done it with their parents right in the room."

This is when, some in attendance will report later, they began to feel sick.

"There are three kinds of pedophiles," Ricky continues. "The first kind does it to hurt children. They're just bad that way. Maybe you even think they're evil. Then there's the second kind. They do it for control."

A young woman stands up abruptly. Her eyes down, she walks quickly out of the room.

Ricky keeps going. "You know how it is," he says, and it must be nice to be talking to them this way, as if they are on the same side of this problem and Ricky is helping them to understand people who are nothing like him. "They don't have control in their lives, so they've got to have it over the kids." He pauses. Perhaps he is remembering the therapist in Georgia, the careful questions she asked him: Was he frustrated in his life? Lonely? Depressed? The therapist thought his love for children was a replacement for something else. She didn't understand. "Then there are guys like me." He finally gets to explain. "I loved Jeremy. I loved him like a boy-friend/girlfriend kind of love. Jeremy was my true love."

"If you loved him," a man shouts, "why'd you kill him?"

The question seems to take Ricky aback. He's silent for a minute. Then he blurts out, "I didn't mean to. I thought he was Oscar."

Whatever Clive hoped, whatever he planned for this day, has failed. The more Ricky talks, the sicker people feel.

Clive stands, putting his hand on Ricky's arm to silence him. "This may have gone beyond what we intended. Ricky has had to struggle more than most of us. Despite the unfortunate thing that happened, Ricky tried very hard. I believe—and this may be hard for Ricky to hear me say, but we've talked about it and he knows I feel this way—I believe that Ricky is mentally ill."

Clive's career is based on his ability to read people. That's true of any trial lawyer. It was true for my father, and when it went wrong for him was when his pain and depression fogged out that ability. And it's especially true for death penalty defense lawyers, who must read a jury well enough to save their client's life. Clive is almost uniquely successful in this regard, one of the most famous and most successful death penalty lawyers in the South. The man who'll lose only six cases in two decades.

But he must not see the way an officer in the back row has curled up his lip. He must not see a woman's face shut like an iron gate. Clive, in this moment, doesn't seem to see what's happening. How badly the crowd's turned against him.

What he sees is the past.

"My father was mentally ill," he continues. "No one understood him; they reviled him. Even my own family didn't understand him. We have a chance now to understand Ricky. He's being so brave. He's working to face who he is. For that"—he looks down at Ricky, maybe he gives Ricky's shoulder an encouraging squeeze before he looks back out at the room, the room in which person after person will remember this last line and repeat it to the prosecutors verbatim—"Ricky Langley is my hero."

"There's a case in Arizona right now," an officer in the back of the room shouts, his voice hard as a bullet. He stands. "Maybe you've heard of it. A father found out that a man had molested his child and he hunted that person down and shot him again and again and every time he shot him he told him he wanted him to know what pain really was. If someone did that to you"—he points at Ricky—"would that stop you hurting children?"

Clive looks aghast, then flustered. Ricky stares down at the ground. Clive says, "I didn't want to kill my father. That's not how we deal with these cases."

The officer ignores Clive. "Would that make you stop?" Right now the officer is remembering walking down the wet leaves on the side of the ravine, clutching his hat in his fist, planting his boots carefully so as not to stumble, holding his breath as he shines the flashlight into the wet leaves. How he hoped to see a child's face, hoped though he knew that if he found the boy the boy might be dead. Then the strange mix of relief and despair that fogged his heart that night when there were only leaves. He told his supervisor he didn't want to come to this meeting. He remembers seeing the killer's face for the first time on the evening news and realizing the boy was dead. He told his supervisor he did not ever want to see that face again.

Come anyway, the supervisor said. He told the officer he could leave at any time.

But the officer can't leave. He sits back down, his chest heaving hard, his face flushed. He is screwed to the chair by the bolt of memory. He is rooted as a witness. They are giving attention to the wrong person here. He closes his eyes to shut out the killer and tries to fix in his mind an image of the boy. The school portrait he was given back then. The boy's blond hair. He offers that image in his mind like a candle.

Thirty-Two

With only two days left in Louisiana, I know what I've been avoiding. In the tens of thousands of pages I've gone through, the transcripts and serology reports and bodily fluid reports and the documents from Ricky's life, his mental health records from Lake Charles and then from when he was imprisoned in Georgia, the only photographs I've seen of Jeremy are the ones in which he's alive.

But that's not how his story ended. I have been driven all along by the belief that there is a knot at the heart of the collision between me and Ricky that will help me make sense of what will never be resolved. The way my body is evidence. The way I carry what my grandfather did in my body. I carry it through my life. All the records I've seen have made me imagine Ricky, imagine his family, begin to empathize with him. I can't not know—I can't not face—what he did. I can't allow even any part of myself to think that Jeremy remained the boy in his school photo. Unchanged and alive.

I return to the clerk of court's office on a gray afternoon. The woman at the desk is friendly but brusque.

"Well, I can show you the trial transcripts," she begins.

"I've already seen those."

"But the photographs are evidence. You can't see the evidence, not without a court order. It was sealed."

I stare at her. "When was it sealed?"

"I don't know, ma'am, but it's not just free for the viewing. What exactly are you trying to see?" she asks.

"Only the photographs." I think about what else would be there. Everything I haven't considered: the plastic bags of evidence taken from the scene, the blankets. Jeremy's white Fruit of the Loom T-shirt with the holes cut out for the semen samples. His BB gun, with its long brown plastic barrel. How much am I required to see to understand?

I wait. I watch the thoughts move across her face. Her name is in the files. Her signature on every stamped document, over and over again. Everything I am trying to see, she has already seen.

"All right," she finally says. "You can see the photocopies of the photographs. Mark what you want, and we'll send you them later."

She brings out five or six stacks of papers clipped together, each several inches thick. I lift the cover of the top stack and see a black-and-white copy of an aerial photograph. Blotchy woods, dense and thick with black. A few small houses, arranged in a row.

The house at the end is white and bigger than the others. The Lawson house. It is like being shown a photograph of the ghost that has been trailing you. I see it nestled against the thick black web of the woods and I understand instantly why it was so strange that Ricky didn't get rid of the body. The woods were right there, only a few feet out the back door, dense enough to make a tangled darkness of the page.

I gather myself a stack of paper clips and small Post-it flags and I mark the pages. When I reach the pictures of Lorilei's son, I flip through them so quickly I register only flashes. The sheen the flash made against his blond hair. The moist bulb of his lower lip.

That night, in my motel room, I pour screw-top wine into a plastic cup and channel-surf stations. The too-sweet red wine blurs my mind, but not enough. The motel room is strangely constructed, with a sitting room I can't see from the bed. Twice I get up and check it. I am checking to make sure I am alone. I know I am alone. I do not feel alone. I check the closets and try not to think of Jeremy's body. I check the bathtub. For years, whenever I walked into a bathroom that had a tub in it I would have to peel back the curtain and make sure there wasn't a dead body in there. After my grandfather's death, it became, more specifically, his body. Him dead. I felt foolish for the gesture every time, yet I had to check. I had just done so, secretly, in the bathroom at a house where my family was staying, and emerged to see my mother standing there. Sheepish, I told her about this quirk of mine.

She looked at me, stricken. She might have seen a ghost. "When you were a child," she said slowly, "you found your brother Andy unconscious and blue at the bottom of an empty tub."

The mind remembers. The mind mixes up. Everything repeats.

The next afternoon, on the plane back to Boston, the clouds through the window are an unrelenting gauze. They seem not beautiful but indecently sticky. I order more wine and gulp it down. The white of the bubble of wet saliva on Jeremy's lip in the camera's flash. The plush white ribbing of the cotton sock he chokes on as it spills from his darkened mouth. I turn away from the window and press my eyes closed. I try hard not to imagine what I have invited to follow me home.

The process by which the jury is selected—voir dire, from the French for "to speak truth"—is unique for a death penalty case. The jurors must be death-qualified, which means that they must avow that they would theoretically be able to vote for a sentence of death. Clive has successfully petitioned to hold voir dire in New Orleans. People there won't be as familiar with the case. The selected jurors will then be bused to Lake Charles. Each day, panels of prospective jurors pass a corded microphone back and forth among themselves as the lawyers and Judge Gray ask them questions. The microphone cord becomes a running joke. Clive says that it will strangle him. Gray asks the jurors not to strangle themselves. The joke is strange in its recurrence—its insistence—and in the fact that Jeremy was strangled, a deep score around his neck from the fishing wire. Gray has seen the photographs. So has Clive. Are the photographs haunting them already?

From the start, selection runs into trouble. The New Orleans murder rate is eight times the national average. The first day of voir dire, Gray announces that he'll make sure they end on time each evening, because he doesn't want anyone on the streets when the sun begins to set. Nine days in, the prosecutor, Cynthia Killingsworth, comments that it's the first day since they've been in New Orleans that there hasn't been a murder. Gray corrects her: There was a murder. There's been a murder every day. One juror's nephew was involved in two murders. Another's friend is on death row. A woman's half brother is serving three consecutive life sentences for murder. She couldn't impose the death penalty on anyone, she says, because he maintains his innocence and in case that's true, she wouldn't want him to die. One man didn't used to believe in the death penalty, but his best friend of thirty years was found murdered on the street two months ago, and now he's not sure. He's just not sure. Another's brother was murdered. A woman's daughter's friend. "They never found out who did it," she says. A man's son was murdered at seven. "I sat down here and I got forty years of memories coming back to me," he says. "I don't mind coming to do my civic duty, but this one's really tough for me."

Because of death qualification, it is arguably not that hard to get off a death penalty jury. You just have to say you couldn't impose a death sentence, no matter the crime. By a week into voir dire, roughly three-quarters of the prospective jurors are saying they don't believe in the death penalty. That percentage seems suspect. True, this is liberal New Orleans, but it's still Louisiana, part of the so-called fry belt—named for its old quickness with the electric chair—and still one of the most active death penalty states in the country.

So when one lady, asked if she could vote to impose death, says, "Oh, no, I couldn't do that," a lawyer finally presses her further. "Do you mean to tell me," the lawyer says, "that if we have the trial and the lawyers present their evidence and you're convinced on guilt, you could not consider the death penalty?"

The woman is flustered. There will be a trial? "I thought we were gonna vote on whether he got the death penalty today." She's excused.

Soon voir dire has lasted almost two weeks, with nearly two hundred people questioned. Clive is losing his voice and apologizes to the jury for it. Killingsworth keeps talking about the New Orleans murders. Gray is sick of the whole thing. "When this is all over," Gray says to a juror, frustrated, "I am going to come in here and I am going to look at you, if you are on the jury, and I am going to say, ma'am, stand up. Does Mr. Langley live or die? And you're going to have to say life or death. I'm not going to let you—I'm not going to let you write something on a piece of paper that says, well, I vote the death penalty. I am going to make you stand up and tell me, look me dead in the eye and look that man dead in the eye, and look the State dead in the eye, and tell me, does he live or die. Can you do that?"

She's shaken. "I don't know."

"OK."

"I don't know."

"It's tough."

"Uh-huh."

"Nobody said it ain't tough. My question to you is, can you make the decision?"

"I don't know. I don't know."

Judge Gray and the lawyers must find sixteen people—twelve jurors and four alternates—to try this case. The people face being asked to make an unimaginable decision. There is no other situation in which we ask a civilian to decide if someone will live or die. The closest analog is military, maybe: a drafted enlisted soldier, somebody who didn't intend to end up in the position of having someone at the other end of his or her gun and deciding whether to shoot.

In law school, the concept of the jury is taught through the metaphor of a black box. Into the box, evidence and the law go. Out of the box, a verdict comes.

But a black box doesn't have feelings.

"Being exposed to the things I was exposed to," begins one prospective juror—she was on a death penalty jury once before, and now, bad luck, she's been called again—"it was very traumatic. I would say I haven't gotten over it." There is a name for the way the decisions of war haunt people: PTSD. People who have served on death penalty juries speak of depression, of trouble with alcohol, of being haunted. Not everyone does, but—some do. The men and women chosen for this jury will live sequestered in a hotel together, cut off from their families, isolated each night with the images they have seen that day. The images will take root inside them. Each day, they will see Ricky in the courtroom. Each day, they will be pressed closer to having to choose whether Ricky lives or dies. In the future, will they be haunted by Jeremy's face, by knowing that with a not-guilty verdict they have said he will have no justice? Or will they be haunted by the image of the man they have sentenced to die?

On May 2, 2003, the men and women who will have to face this evidence are finally selected. Nine women, three men. Seven are black, five white. Three have family members who are schizophrenic; three have family members who are bipolar. ("It sounds like an epidemic," a juror says, shocked that the secrets in her family don't make her so alone after all.) Two are nurses. A heavyset, white schoolteacher named Stephen Kujawa is appointed foreman. "I teach eighth graders," he'd said when Killingsworth asked him if he'd be able to speak his mind during jury deliberations. "I'm not going to be shy of anything." Gray sends the jurors home to say goodbye to their families. Then they'll be bused to Lake Charles. The trial will begin.

Thirty-Three

"Murder is not simple, but the elements are." At roughly 10:00 a.m. on Monday, May 6, 2003—eleven years after Ricky Langley killed Jeremy Guillory, nine years after he was sentenced to death for that murder, and two years after a new trial was ordered—prosecutor Cynthia Killingworth stands at the front of the jury and begins to tell them the story of the murder.

Killingsworth is second counsel on this case. With her hair cut into a sensibly short shag, and the fatigue in her face, she looks something like an older and more moneyed version of Lorilei Guillory. First counsel is the assistant district attorney, Wayne Frey, prematurely balding, with a chin that echoes the roundness of his glasses and whose state bar photographs betray questionable taste in ties. Third counsel for the prosecution, Sharon Wilson, is the lone black lawyer in the room. Killingsworth and Frey specialize in the death penalty cases for this parish, and if anyone notices how right their names are for this job—Frey so easily pronounced "fry" in a state that once had the electric chair—there is no reference to this Dickensian rightness in the record. The prosecution's strategy is fury: Killingsworth is a mother, and she'll linger on the details of what Ricky did. She'll say the sock he put in Jeremy's mouth was dirty. Call Ricky evil. Frey is a crusader, a law-and-order man.

On the defense side are Clive, tall and jittery and intense as always, as first counsel, and Phyllis Mann, whose plainspokenness matches her plain brown hair and the plainness of her suits, as second counsel. Against the prosecution's barrage, the defense's strategy is earnestness: to speak always as though from the heart. Both Clive and Mann are skilled at that.

Ricky has been formally charged with first-degree murder. Louisiana law requires that two elements be proved: first, specific intent, meaning that Jeremy intended to kill Ricky. And second, to make the murder first-degree, an aggravating circumstance. A murder is considered aggravated if the person killed was under twelve. Jeremy was six. That's met. So the trial will focus on the first element, specific intent.

In response, Ricky pleads two things: one, not guilty, and two, not guilty by reason of mental insanity or defect. What he and Clive once promised Lorilei they wouldn't plead for. So Gray, before anything has begun, has instructed the jury that because of Ricky's insanity plea there are actually *two* burdens of proof in the case. Yes, the prosecution must prove Ricky guilty beyond a reasonable doubt if it wants to prevail. But the defense now has a burden, too. If it wants to succeed on the insanity plea, it must prove that Ricky didn't know right from wrong at the time of the murder.

All this framing, all this setup. By the time the jurors take their seats they have been given clues about what this man seated at the defense table between his lawyers did, clues doled out in bits and pieces by Gray and the lawyers over the past two weeks.

But today, Killingsworth tells them, "the speculation ends." She is the first to tell the story of the murder in this space. The first to tell here this story that has been told so many times. "Jeremy lived in a very remote area of Calcasieu Parish," she says. "There aren't that many houses out near where Jeremy lived, but there are some." In one of them lived Jeremy's playmates, Joey and June. On the afternoon of February 7, 1992, Jeremy knocked on the door of the white Lawson house, but June and Joey were gone. Ricky invited Jeremy in. "And you will learn in this case that the fatal error Jeremy made that day was going into the home where the defendant,

Ricky Langley, was." Jeremy walked up the stairs. He sat down on the floor and began to play.

Then, Killingsworth says, Ricky came up to him, inserted his penis into Jeremy's mouth, and ejaculated.

It is a bold move to begin the trial this way. Picture the courthouse on this morning. The jurors spent the night in a motel, hours from their homes. They were all assigned their own rooms— a splurge for the parish, but Gray made sure of it, he'd promised them during voir dire—and they bedded down away from their spouses and loved ones, knowing that in the morning a murder trial would begin. When their alarms went off, far too early, they tossed back the weak motel coffee, boarded the shuttle bus, and there they made awkward small talk with the strangers with whom, they began to realize, they would make the gravest decision of their lives. They noticed who among them was pushy. They noticed who among them was shy. They began to get a sense of where alliances would lie. Once in the courtroom, they noticed the man at the defense table, with his jug ears and thick glasses and pale blue shirt and mismatched red tie. This was the man whose fate they would decide.

Now they are being told that he ejaculated into the mouth of a child. Killingsworth has begun her story with the element that will be most difficult for the state to prove.

But likely that is not what the jurors are thinking, that she must still prove this. They have just been told a story. They are thinking, *Poor child*. Ricky was referred to as a pedophile many times during voir dire. They are thinking, *So that's what happened*. They are thinking of the murder as sexual. *That poor, poor child*. The white clock with the black hand on the wall ticks slowly. Killingsworth pauses dramatically.

Then she finishes the tale. Ricky killed Jeremy. First his hands, then a wire around Jeremy's neck, then a dirty sock in his throat. He carried the child's body to the closet and propped it up against the wall, fixed a white trash bag around Jeremy's head and shoulders, and piled blankets on top of him. Lorilei at the door; the long, fruitless search; Ricky's blurted-out confession; the arrest; Jeremy's body. "I'm sure that the defense is going to tell you that nobody in their right mind, nobody who could tell the difference between right and wrong would do this to a child. But listen carefully. Listen carefully to everything this person did. And listen to how he told police he took that child's life on February 7, 1992. And at the end of the trial we will come back again and ask you to use your common sense and find the defendant guilty as charged." She sits back down, leaving her words to linger. Common sense. Yes. That is what it must seem like now.

Phyllis Mann, the defense attorney, gets up and paces. Then she stops in front of the jury box. "The things you've heard from the prosecutor this morning are a small part of the whole story. Clive and I have represented Ricky for a while now. And today, with the beginning of this trial, we hand him over to you." She looks searchingly down the row of seated jurors. Some of them must meet her eyes. Some must look away. "So if I seem a little nervous, it's because I am. A terrible, unimaginable tragedy happened on February 7, 1992, when Jeremy Guillory died. We have never from the very beginning ever suggested that Ricky was not the cause of Jeremy's death. But what we will show you during this trial is that Ricky Langley did not, could not, intend to kill Jeremy Guillory." Ricky's life is in their hands now, she reminds them. She asks them to spare it.

On television screens all over town, KPLC-TV, the local news station, is airing coverage of this trial. The lawyers talking to the cameras. Lorilei and her son Cole huddling together, Lorilei looking pained and Cole slightly stunned by the camera light. Then one clip that repeats over and over: Ricky Langley, twenty-six and scrawny, his floppy brown hair as wild as a current's shock, sits in the police station in an orange jumpsuit and tells Lucky and Dixon the story of the murder. "And then I got a wire and"—he jerks his hands up to his neck. He pinches his fingers together. He draws the imaginary wire across his neck and pulls his hands to tighten it. Like he tightened the wire around Jeremy's. "I made sure he couldn't breathe."

Two seconds of tape, if that. When the news anchor returns to end the segment, a small photographic still from this moment hangs in the upper right corner of the screen. Ricky, his hands at his throat. Killing Jeremy.

"This is Jeremy Guillory," Mann continues. They've enlarged Jeremy's last school portrait and mounted it on cardboard. He wears a checked shirt, his hair parted neatly. He smiles, missing one tooth. "Can y'all see? As we talk about Ricky's mental illness I want you to know that we are doing that so we can learn why Jeremy Guillory died. He was an innocent six-year-old boy. He made no mistakes. Back in 1992, his mother, Lorilei, was pregnant with another son she'd name Cole, and she and Jeremy were living in Iowa, Louisiana. Iowa is about ten miles east from here. And just down the road from Iowa is another little town called Hecker, Louisiana. And that's where Ricky grew up with his mother, Bessie, and his father, Alcide, and his older sisters, Darlene, Judy, and Francis, and his younger brother, Jamie. But what happened in this case was first set in motion several years before Ricky was born."

Now Mann tells the story of the murder. She doesn't begin with Jeremy's grabbing his BB gun and running out the door. She begins before Ricky was born, and tells the story of his birth: the crash, Bessie in the cast, all the drugs, Ricky. "The bottom line," Mann says, "is that Ricky was destined to be psychotic, and the only question is what form that psychosis was going to take."

    ("Destined." That first taped confession, when
       Lucky interrogated Ricky:
    Q: Now, you've had problems with kids in the
       past.
    A: Yeah.

Q: You want to tell me about those?

A: It's just, I can't explain. I guess that's my destiny, okay, it's true.)

That's when Mann talks about Ricky's beginning to see Oscar
as a child. He's the form the psychosis takes. In the story Mann
tells, Ricky talks about the car wreck as though he were there. He
talks about Oscar and Vicky's funeral: how pretty the children
looked laid out in the caskets, the white ruffles on Vicky's dress
and the brush of Oscar's eyelashes against his cheeks.

(Has Mann forgotten that Oscar was decapitated, decapitated
even in Ricky's dream? The story is being told a different way now.)

The way Mann tells it, Bessie and Alcide once took Ricky to a
therapist when he was a child, but they didn't want him diagnosed
with anything that could trail him throughout his life. They wanted
their son to be normal. So they did their best to pretend that
he was.

It was *Ricky* who realized something was wrong. Ricky tried
to get help, but was turned away. He tried to kill himself, but failed
or secretly wanted just the help attention would bring, not really
to die. By the time Ricky killed Jeremy, Mann says, he was in a
long psychosis brought on by stress, the stress of being back living
with his family, the family that was so difficult for him, the family
with whom the past resided. He strangled Jeremy thinking he was
ridding himself of Oscar. Thinking he was getting rid of the past.
Only when the child was dead did he look down and realize whom
he'd killed.

Two stories. Two different meanings.

This is how the choice has been framed for the jury: Is Ricky
a bad person, an evil person who brutally murdered an innocent
child? Or has Ricky battled demons his whole life, battled who he
is, a battle that has left him psychotic and has resulted in the tragic
death of a child?

The prosecution calls its witnesses, including the 911 dispatcher who took Ricky's phone calls; Calton Pitre, for whom Ricky drew the search diagram; and the photographer who took aerial photographs of the scene.

"The state's next witness, please," Gray says.

"Lorilei Guillory."

Thirty-Four

The jurors must tense in their seats. Five of them are mothers. The prosecution hopes they'll see themselves in Lorilei. The defense hopes they'll see themselves in Bessie and be horrified by what she endured during her pregnancy. Overhead, the fluorescent lights buzz. The jurors' hearts quicken.

The mother has light brown hair, like the light hair of her son in his picture. She looks like any mother, not someone you would notice if her name hadn't been called. She's older than they were imagining, perhaps. Listening to the officers who searched for him, they have forgotten that the murder was more than ten years ago. So the lines around her eyes lend a new gravity. Ten years she's lived without her son. All their children, they told the lawyers during jury selection, are living.

Lorilei settles herself into the witness chair. The jurors stare.

Under their stares, she must look down at her hands, she must brace her shoulders. Eleven years have passed. She's been living out of state. She'd forgotten about the stares.

"Ms. Guillory," Killingsworth begins. Maybe her voice has a note of sympathy that wasn't there before. It's careful, a little mournful. Lorilei must have forgotten about this, too. The being handled with gloves. Of course the prosecution has Killingsworth doing the direct examination. A mother, talking to a mother. "Can you tell me the name of your children?"

"My first child's name is Jeremy James Guillory. I have a second son, Cole Innis Landry." She shifts in her seat. "I have a third child that I gave up at birth named Rowan Lovell, as far as I know."

"Jeremy Guillory, the little boy who was killed in this case, that's your son, yes?"

"Yes."

"When was the last time you saw your son?"

"The last time I saw my son was that Friday afternoon when he went outside to play."

"OK. And what was . . . ?"

"Alive." Lorilei's voice rises. "That was the last time I saw him alive." She describes going to the Lawson house and using the phone. She describes standing at the edge of the woods and yelling out Jeremy's name and the silence, the terrible silence in response. Then the police, the searchers, the dogs, and the boats.

"How long did the search continue?"

"Three days." There is again in the transcript the problem of the enormity of what Lorilei must convey. She tries again. "To me it was three days and three nights. Friday, Friday night. Saturday, Saturday night. Sunday, Sunday night." Likely she wasn't told to continue on past this point in the story. But she can't help herself. This is how it ends. "And then on Monday, sometime Monday, they told me they'd found my son. And I said, where is he? And they said he was dead."

Cole is the reason Lorilei never has to wonder how long Jeremy has been dead. How old Cole is, plus half a year: That's how long his brother's been gone. Cole's age, plus six and a half: That's how old Jeremy would have been.

Seventeen now, as Lorilei sits on the hard pew bench in the gallery. Two days have passed since she testified. On that first day after Lorilei spoke, the state called Pearl Lawson, who described meeting Ricky. Nothing about her son or her husband, nothing about whether she knew Ricky was a pedophile. Then Lanelle Trahan, Pearl's supervisor at the Fuel Stop, who described Ricky's blocking her way on the stairs, his face turning beet red. The next morning, the state began with the FBI agent Don Dixon, now chief of police for the parish. ("I got a ticket, Chief," Gray said. "I ain't too happy.") In the middle of Dixon's testimony, Ricky felt light-headed, and Gray adjourned for the day. He wasn't going to have a mistrial, he said. The next morning, Dixon finished testifying about the search and Ricky's confession, then Lucky led the jury through the photographs of Jeremy. By the time he got to the close-up of Jeremy's body in the closet, wrapped in blankets, his boots and his BB gun tucked at his feet, Lucky was crying.

Now it is day four, and they are just back from lunch after a very long morning. First the lawyers fought, and though they fought in whispers in front of the judge's bench, their suited backs turned to the audience like the hard shells of beetles, Lorilei knows part of what they were fighting about was her. Her here. How she went and talked to Ricky. What she wants to say about how she feels.

At the first trial, in 1994, when her grief was fresh and full of anger, the prosecutors were eager to have her in the courtroom. But now that she's met with Ricky, they've called her an unfit mother. A fit mother, they say, would never support her son's killer. And they have evidence on her, she knows. All those years of al-cohol and drugs, of trying to find her way before Jeremy came and gave her a purpose. Then more alcohol and drugs after Jeremy was taken from her.

But she has a purpose again. Mothering Cole, yes, but also, some-how, this trial. What this trial has become. The prosecutors paid to bring her and Cole here from South Carolina for the trial—they had to—but now they say that since they don't want her tes-tifying in the penalty phase if there is one, not if she won't say she wants Ricky killed, they won't pay to keep her and Cole here any-more. Like she'd go home before the trial's over. And Cole's started the school term.

Then there's the evidence they're fighting over. The judge has up at his bench a letter from Ricky to Lucky written in 1992 from his cell at the correctional center, offering to sit down with Lucky and an atlas and mark everywhere Ricky has traveled to so he can tell Lucky about all the children he says he molested along the way. Those stories come to Lorilei like the silk and seed a dandelion sheds in the wind. Only the hard knot reaches her. Though the courtroom is the neutral temperature of still air, the stillness feels too hot and tight around her, and perhaps she feels a headache coming on. She rests her head back against the bench and closes her eyes for a minute. How many children were there? Did they meet ends like her Jeremy?

Jeremy. Maybe she lets herself imagine him. Jeremy at seventeen like he would be now. Finding somebody with an ATV he could sweet-talk them out of or jack out of their yard when they weren't looking, and riding it out over the reedy swamp grass on the long, empty weekend afternoons, maybe running it too quick and jumping off—wouldn't matter how many times she told him it is was dangerous, in this story he wouldn't know what dead was—until he and his buddies were thick-covered with mud, laughing, alive. That BB gun he'd loved would be an air rifle, the walks in the woods longer. He'd be sweet on a girl at the high school by now, and when she asked him about her he'd redden from his chin to his ears. She knows his smile so well that her heart aches. Jeremy under the Christmas tree at six, wearing a red sweater, his blond hair gleaming in the lights, grinning so hard his cheeks bulged. That was two months before he died. Don't think about the way they ran that picture on the evening news; don't think about the way they're running that picture on the evening news all over town now. Think of his smile. She transposes it. Grows it up. Subtracts the roundness from the jaw, makes stubble appear above his lip. Seventeen.

The videos from this morning are the bad dream, the unreal thing. Ricky's leading Lucky through the dark, narrow staircase of the house. The toys on the floor of the bedroom, the beaten-up doll of June's, that doll the last thing Jeremy ever played with. She has watched that video before, but when they showed it this morning she hadn't seen it in years. Did her breath catch when Lucky touched the closet door? Inside the closet was her baby. The blond, downy hair she'd kissed and ruffled her palms through, smooth and cool. The lashes that had just brushed his cheeks, as they did when he slept. The horrible blue-black marks on his neck and the bloom of red spots around them, like freckles of blood.

This morning, after that tape and another, they'd played one more. A third tape, one that had been excluded from the 1994 trial. In this tape, recorded two months after the murder, Ricky had changed his story. He'd described molesting Jeremy. Before Jeremy was dead.

So she'd had to watch that. Her baby.

"Take the jury out. Ms. Guillory?"

"Yes, Your Honor?" The whole courtroom is looking at her, even the witness. She catches up suddenly. The witness is a scientist. He was explaining how they tested for semen on Jeremy.

"Ms. Guillory, come see me a moment."

Beside her on the bench is ten-year-old Cole. She squeezes his hand, then stands and walks to the front of the room.

"Good morning, Your Honor."

"Is that your child?"

"Yes, sir."

"This is the wrong place for a child. This is a murder trial. It's awful enough—I don't think this child needs to be in this courtroom listening to this." Gray's voice rises. "There's—there's stuff about what happened to his sibling and all that. I ain't going for it."

"Not open for—"

"You think a child should be in here?"

The courtroom is perfectly quiet. Everyone watches her. Cole watches her.

"Your Honor," Lorilei says slowly, "my son has experienced everything I have. If I see that it's emotionally disturbing to him, I will take him out."

Gray shakes his head. "All right. It's your child."

"He still has questions that are unanswered as well as I do."

Then—all at once—Lorilei seems to sink. Her shoulders drop.

Her voice sounds like a balloon with the air gone out. "I'm not really quite sure that this is the right—you know—but I really didn't have any other alternatives for today for him and for me to be here as well." Richard hasn't spoken to her since he learned she planned to testify for Ricky.

Gray takes his glasses off. "Talk to Clive and them and see if they can give you some relief. I have problems with this trial." He rubs his forehead. "I know damned well a child would have problems with this trial."

An investigator for the defense comes and takes Cole's hand to lead him from the courtroom. I think of Ricky as a child, talking to Oscar outside his bedroom window. I think of myself as a child, standing in front of the bathroom mirror, trying to make up the sister I never knew. I think of Bessie with her trunk and my mother with her filing cabinet.

Lorilei stays.

Thirty-Five

There is no known grave for my sister, no end for her story. When my father told me what had been done with Jacqueline's body, I felt foolish almost. Foolish that I'd beaten my head against the past with my parents. For every fight we'd had when I asked why I never saw them get angry about the abuse. *Well, if they could do that with a baby,* I thought then.

But they had two babies at home to take care of. We were both tiny, both premature. On my third day of life, my lungs collapsed and my heart stopped before the doctors revived me. My brother was born without his digestive system fully developed, and though he grew up to be healthy, in the years before the surgery he was in three comas and in and out of the hospital. Both of us needed bottles that had to be sterilized and diapers that had to be changed and to be burped and soothed and dressed and rocked to sleep at night. Both of us needed them. They needed to take care of their family.

In a way, the choices my parents later faced—the choices that drew me to Ricky's story—were the same. Burying my father's rages and depression, burying the fact of my grandfather's abuse, burying, even, my anger at what he'd done, my insistence that it wasn't right and that we acknowledge it—to bury those threats must have seemed almost easier in comparison. They kept going. They threw away the baby book they'd started for Jacqueline; they threw or gave away every item their friends had made for them with her name on it; they dressed me, they must have, in some of the extra little girls' clothes and gave away the rest. They stopped filling out the baby books for my brother and me, the ones with evidence of her, and left them in the white filing cabinet. "The twins," they called my brother and me, and they taught us to call ourselves that, too. They built a happy home, and they made sure the neighborhood knew it. There were summers on the island and Christmases under the tree and there were the six of us around the dining table as my parents lifted their glasses and toasted their good fortune. I have come to believe that every family has its defining action, its defining belief. From childhood, I understood that my parents' was this: Never look back.

But a year after I asked my mother about Jacqueline's body, I was sitting with her in a pizzeria in a small, desolate city in eastern Pennsylvania where I'd moved temporarily for a teaching job. Long ago, all the factories in the city had shuttered; it had never recovered, and now half the storefronts were empty. It was good to see her—I had missed her—and I could tell she was happy to see me. Still, we were being careful with each other, the ties between us always sinew-strong, but always, too, in danger of snapping. Until the words left my mouth I didn't know I was going to say them. "I'm working on a project," I said. I couldn't yet bring myself to say *book*. "I'm going to have to write about Jacqueline in it."

I expected my mother to be angry. I had the sense that I was choosing to yank off a bandage, that maybe if I reopened the wound early it would have time to scab and settle. I loved her but I needed to do this. I loved her *and* I needed to this. I was daring her and daring myself and getting something over with, hoping that there'd be time to heal after. I braced.

But she wasn't angry. Her eyes brimmed quickly with tears. She started to speak. "At," she said—but the tears spilled and her cheeks flushed. Gulping, she made a little waving motion in front of her mouth.

Then she put her hand down. She swallowed. She took the paper napkin from the table, twisted it, and dabbed at her eyes. She sipped her water. Finally, she was ready. "At least now there will be a record she existed."

For Ricky's defense, what the witnesses and lawyers tussle over is how to understand his story. Which version will be written into the record and become fact. The DNA expert who was testifying when Judge Gray stopped the trial to remove Cole was the state's last witness. The defense begins its case with a DNA expert of its own, who testifies that the pubic hair on Jeremy's lip did not match Ricky. Ricky's sixth-grade teacher testifies, then a friend who was with him that night under the stars when he tried to turn himself in. His sister Darlene refuses to say that Ricky was harmed by his childhood. He was loved, she says. They all were.

The next day, a defense psychologist describes everything Alcide would say to Ricky when he was angry. That Ricky was worthless. That he was queer. That Ricky molests children, the psychologist says, may be a sign that he was molested himself. Most pedophiles were molested.

That isn't true. It's repeated a lot, but it isn't true. Most pedophiles, like most other people, weren't molested. And there's no indication that people who were molested become pedophiles. What is true is that among pedophiles, a greater percentage were molested than the percentage of people in general who were molested—but even then, it's not a huge increase. I want to argue with this so badly—but I know why I do. Because I was molested. How damned, how damaged, am I doomed to feel? My grandfather's words come back to me: "When I was a child, it happened to me."

"I don't know how you guys feel," Gray interrupts. "Doc, here's an expert on this. I'm all right during the trial, but the minute I finish I can feel that 500-pound gorilla on me. I'm sitting at happy hour and it slowly goes away. Every time I have a gin and tonic, one hundred pounds goes off, absolutely. My wife just closes the door and says, 'All right, darling, see you in the morning.' "

A psychologist for the defense argues that Ricky was legally insane—psychotic, even—at the time of the murder; on cross-examination, the prosecutor points out that he's the only expert who thinks so. A doctor describes Bessie's pregnancy, lingering over the alcohol and the drugs and all the X-rays. But there's no proof that Ricky was harmed by any of it, says the prosecutor. Those are all just risk factors—and there are no records of Ricky right after he was born, nothing that would say whether he was normal or not. Then Ricky's oldest sister, Francis, takes the stand. But she won't budge in her story. Ricky was loved.

"Your Honor," Clive says. "The defense calls Lorilei Guillory."

The jury must be so confused. They've already heard from her. They've seen the pictures of what Ricky did to her son. One juror broke down crying, looking at those pictures. Lorilei testified for the prosecution. So far, the defense seems to be focused on his past. Why is the defense calling her?

Clive asks her if she has anything else to say.

Yes. "Even though I can hear my child's death cry, I, too, can hear Ricky Langley cry for help."

Lorilei has said that she came to empathize with Ricky because she saw herself in Bessie. She couldn't take away another woman's son.

But it was when she heard *Ricky's* story that she made that change. All this fighting about whether he was loved. All this fighting about the troubles he had. She is someone who has had to fight her whole life, who has been on her own her whole life, who has had to make her own way. It must take unimaginable strength to do what she did. It must take unimaginable drive.

This is the moment with which I had such trouble when I first learned about it. The moment Clive and others described as her having forgiven him, even as she said no, she hadn't. The moment that seemed a betrayal of her child, even as I admire her for it. Even as it made her a hero. But now I look at what she did, I look at what she said, I look at what she knew, and I realize.

Did she see herself in Ricky, too?

Thirty-Six

The morning after I confronted my grandfather, I was home alone at my parents' house, standing in the kitchen. Early summer light streamed in through the window over the sink. I could see the old tire swing, its rope now frayed and starting to rot.

The phone rang.

There were no words when I picked up, only his labored breathing. He'd done this before, calling the house and just breathing when he heard me pick up. "Hello?" I said. "Hello?" I was ready to hang up.

But this time he spoke. "I'm an old man," he said. "I'm going to be dead soon. I need your forgiveness to go to heaven. Do you forgive me?"

I remember the phone ringing. I remember the light through the window and the black plastic receiver, smooth in my palm. I remember the sound of his voice, wavery and gruff and old, and the way my skin pricked and my heart thudded to hear it. I remember his question.

I have no memory of how I answered him.

What I once loved about the law is that it doesn't let questions go unanswered. It finds answers for them. In life we'd call what happened to Helen Palsgraf as she waited for the train to take her children to the beach a chain of events. It would be clear that one thing had led to another: the young man running late, the porter trying to be helpful by shoving him, the package falling, the explosion, the scales, and then finally Mrs. Palsgraf suing the railroad. All of these events, we would understand, were tangled together— no one cause, no one beginning. Each time we told the story we might tell it differently, choosing to emphasize the young man's being late if we wanted to make a point about carelessness, or the explosion leading to the scales' fall if we wanted to say *you never can tell what will happen*. No one meaning.

But the law can't leave it there. The law must determine what the story means. That's what a trial's for. The actual Palsgraf case was disposed of simply. The court found that the railroad wasn't liable because the porter couldn't have known that the wrapped package contained fireworks. What the case is remembered for now, though, and why I'm interested in it, is the dissent, which said that the railroad should have been liable, because the shove was the proximate cause of Mrs. Palsgraf's injury. The question in *Palsgraf,* the dissenting judge said, isn't really about knowledge of the fireworks. It's where you want to start the causal chain. Once you decide that, you have decided the meaning of the whole story.

Palsgraf is a civil case. Proximate cause, as a formal named concept, doesn't exist in criminal law. Criminal law doesn't care where the story began. But how you tell the story has everything to do with how you judge. Begin Ricky's story with the murder—and it means one thing. Begin it with the crash—and it means another. Begin with what my grandfather did to me and my sister. Or begin when he was a boy, and someone did it to him.

No one else can solve how to think about my grandfather. But with Ricky, at least, I hoped the jury would decide for me.

There will be four closing statements. Because the main burden of proof is on the state, it goes first and last. Wilson will speak for the state, with Mann rebutting her. Then Clive. Then Killingsworth.

"You may begin," Judge Gray says to Wilson.

Then, the transcript notes, Gray stands and walks out of the courtroom.

"May it please the Court," Wilson starts. The room erupts in awkward laughter. The "Court"—the judge—is gone.

She thanks the jury for their attention throughout the trial. There is really only one question they have to deliberate on, she says. When Ricky Langley killed Jeremy Guillory, did he know right from wrong? The evidence, she says, suggests he did. He started taking an anti-psychotic medication only when a defense expert gave it to him for the start of the trial. "He's never had to be hospitalized for psychotic episodes. Friends around the time of this incident never noticed any odd behaviors. They never noticed anything. They just noticed someone who seemed normal to them." The idea that Ricky has psychotic spells and was psychotic when he killed Jeremy is a concoction for this trial, she says. "I submit to you that there are people who do things that are just so horrible, and they know when they're doing them that they're so horrible, but at that particular time they choose to do them. Ricky Langley is one of those people. Those people simply aren't mad. They're bad."

While Wilson has been talking—the transcript does not note exactly when—Gray has returned to his bench. Now Mann signals she's ready for her opening statement. "All right," Gray says. "I'll stay for 'May it please the Court.'"

"May it please the Court," Mann begins.

Again, Gray leaves.

"It's undisputed from the very beginning and continuing through today that Ricky Langley caused Jeremy Guillory's death." But what Mann wants to talk about, she tells the jury, is the burden of proof. She reminds them that during voir dire she and Clive asked them what "beyond a reasonable doubt" meant to them— and they answered "very high, even 99 percent." The prosecutors must meet that burden of proof to make the murder first-degree. They have to prove specific intent to 99 percent. And, she says, they can't.

That they can't is the only reason they're claiming Ricky sexually abused Jeremy. In the absence of evidence of specific intent, they're trying to move the jury with emotion. But pay attention, she tells the jurors: Ricky is a pedophile, but there's no evidence he actually abused Jeremy in that way. Ricky told Lucky and others the story of the murder eleven times, she says, and only *one* of those times did he say he molested Jeremy. (She means eleven times the jury has heard reference to. It never hears about Ricky's bragging to Jackson, or how he described it in Georgia. The story was told many more times than eleven. It has been told so many different ways.) The only other piece of evidence of molestation is that there was semen on the back of Jeremy's shirt, semen that matched Ricky—but can the state prove that didn't come from Ricky's bedclothes?

So they're back to specific intent. For that, she says, the state must prove Ricky "actively desired" Jeremy's death. "How do we determine whether a person has specific intent? We can't open up their head and look inside. We can't take a photograph of their brain right at that moment." All we can do, she says, is look at the circumstantial evidence. Ricky says he doesn't know why he killed Jeremy. He didn't get rid of the body, like he presumably would have if he understood what he was doing. He's never been able to give a reason for any of it. "It's hard to have specific intent if there's no reason at all. They ask, 'Why did you do this?' And he says, 'I don't know.' If he had actively desired he would have known it. Heck, he would have told them that, too.

"The state's only theory is that he killed Jeremy to hide sexual abuse. There wasn't any sexual abuse, so he didn't kill him to hide it." Please, she urges the jury, use your common sense. This isn't a man who was capable of specific intent. And if they do find specific intent in the moment of Jeremy's death, it's only because Ricky didn't know right from wrong then.

Gray comes back long enough to call for a ten-minute recess. Then it's Clive's turn.

He begins—and Judge Gray walks out again.

Reading the transcripts of this is incredibly frustrating. No one acknowledges the strangeness of what Gray is doing. No lawyer walks to the front and objects. I suppose they couldn't—there was no one to object to, after all; Gray had left. But when he is in the courtroom, no one goes to his bench, requests a sidebar conference, asks for an explanation, reminds him that he's presiding over a capital trial, demands he stay.

And why is Gray gone? Does he just not want to hear this story again? He has said, over and over again on the record, in the lead-up to this day, that he does not want the judgment to be over-turned. That he's going to do it right so this trial is final. That's why he had four alternate jurors chosen, not the usual two, and that's why the alternates have been present for every day of the trial and have already been sworn in. He stopped the trial the day Ricky got ill from the new anti-psychotic drug the defense expert put him on. He waited for higher court rulings on minor questions in the case. He has proceeded with what anyone would call an abundance of caution.

Except for the comments he's made. Except for the jokes. Except for the times when, it seems in the transcripts, emotions have gotten the better of him. I look at him and I think of all the years I stayed away from the gray Victorian house. All the times I forgot Ricky's name, even when I'd just read it. How much my body tried to keep me away from this story, Gray will never serve on a death penalty case again.

But why don't any of the lawyers object to his absence?

About that last question, at least, I have a guess: The lawyers still don't know how this trial will turn out. Better not to do any-thing to disturb it if it could still go their way. That he's missing may be an escape valve at this point, one either side could use to appeal if it doesn't like the verdict.

"I've been doing this stuff for eighteen years," Clive says. "This is all I've ever done in my life, is stand up in front of juries on capital cases. And the day I quit getting incredibly nervous about it is the day I'm gonna quit doing it. This sort of responsibility really terrifies me. I'm sure some of you folks didn't sleep too well, and I hardly slept at all last night. And I hope you'll forgive me. I know I'm not going to get through this without getting all emotional."

He chose these jury members because of their personal experience, he tells them. Many have family members or loved ones with mental illness. Others are nurses or teachers. When they look at Ricky, he wants them to remember the people they know who've struggled.

Just as Clive remembers his father. His father is mentally ill, he tells the jury. "He's ruined his whole life, he's done some terrible things, some really terrible things." And yet, Clive says, "it would be very hard for anyone to prove that my father actively intended to hurt me when he was doing what he was doing, because he didn't. So they couldn't prove that under any circumstance, and remember that, because without specific intent"—proved beyond a reasonable doubt—"you can't find Ricky guilty of first degree murder."

"This is the poor child, Jeremy," Clive says. He shows the jurors the picture they've seen before, Jeremy at school. "This is Oscar Lee Langley." He shows them the portrait that's on Oscar's grave.

Stop here. This is the strategy Clive tried at the seminar: Talking about his father. Now let Clive hold the photos up for a long moment, as he does for the jury. The jury will never hear about the seminar—not with how horrified everyone there was at what Ricky said. Clive got that excluded. But still, Clive sees his father in Ricky. He can't not tell the story that way. So let him try to make the jurors do, in their minds, what he did with his father, and write the past onto the present. What he's saying Ricky did in his mind. What I know I did in seeing my grandfather when I looked at Ricky. In the photographs, both boys—Oscar in 1964 and Jeremy in 1991—smile gap-toothed grins. They wear short-sleeved checked shirts. Their hair holds gleaming parts carefully combed by Bessie and Lorilei two long-ago mornings. "Is it coincidence or is it evidence of Ricky's mental illness how similar these two pictures look?"

If Lorilei Guillory can see that Ricky deserves mercy, Clive says, then who is the jury not to? "In whose name is this trial going on? It's not the state of Louisiana, it's not me, this is for Truth. This is for the truth, the truth for little Jeremy Guillory. If Lorilei can see it, then we can see it, too. And Ricky is not just plain mean, Ricky is mentally ill, like my dad. Far worse than my dad."

It is, finally, Killingsworth's turn. One last time, Gray leaves the courtroom.

"Mr. Smith's father isn't on trial in this case. Mental illness is not on trial in this case. And when somebody comes up here and tries to convince sixteen individuals, sixteen citizens of this country, of mental illness that was made up in this case for your benefit, it insults me. You know, everybody can sit around and talk about oh, poor, pitiful Ricky Langley. Well, what about poor pitiful Jeremy Guillory? That's what we really need to focus on, Jeremy Guillory, this little boy whose life was taken away on February 7, 1992, by that man.

"Pedophilia is a disease. I'm not going to sit here and try to fool you or tell you that I don't think pedophilia is a terrible, terrible disease. It is. But pedophilia doesn't rob a person of their ability to make a decision between what is right and wrong. And that's what the issue is here." Ricky's choices in this case, she says, began when he first saw Jeremy. When he first realized that he wanted Jeremy. "He knew those choices were wrong. Because if he didn't know those choices were wrong why in the world would he be having this conflict in his mind?" He molested Jeremy. All right, she'll admit that they can't prove exactly when it happened, she says, but it *did*. That semen on the back of Jeremy's T-shirt—even if it transferred from the bedclothes, the stain would have had to be wet. "Use your common sense. What does that tell you?"

Ricky begins to shake in his seat, muttering to himself.

"That tells you exactly what you think it tells you. He had to ejaculate with that child."

Wilson, Clive, and an investigator rush to his side and try to calm him.

"If that's not molestation, I don't know what is."

"What's wrong with him?" Gray has come back in the room just as Ricky, who is now shaking violently, begins to shout.

"Unfortunately, what's happened is that Ricky can't deal with it," Clive says.

Of everything Ricky has heard in this trial, the semen is what finally sets him off. This evidence of who he is.

Thirty-Seven

After Killingsworth finishes, the trial ends.

The jury never hears about Ricky's prior convictions, as they did in the first trial. They never hear about the diary in which he described taking children into the woods. Were those stories dreams, or memories? They never hear about the classes he took in the Georgia prison; his struggles to understand religion and reconcile it with his life; that two social workers from the sex offender program paused the woman who came to interview them and said, their voices hesitant and nervous, "Remember us to Ricky. He touched our hearts, that boy." The jury never hears that it was *Ricky* who got himself into that sex offender program, that he asked again and again before he was eligible. They never hear that in those years, he pleaded never to be released.

They never hear that once he was released, and he killed Jeremy, he bragged to Jackson in that holding cell. They never hear him say he enjoyed killing Jeremy. Because they never hear about the seminar Clive held, they never hear about Ricky's belief in the three kinds of pedophiles. They never hear him say that Jeremy was his true love. So much is cast out and slips away nearly unrecorded, consigned to dusty cardboard banker's boxes kept in archive rooms out of view. It becomes the hidden thirty-thousand-page narrative of this case, the shadow narrative.

And so much is left unresolved. After the lawyers found Pearl Lawson and made her come back for the trial, they never asked where her husband and son were. No one asks her why, if a child was found dead in her house, and that child was her son's best friend, she is so tight-lipped on the stand. Whose pubic hair was on Jeremy's lip is never solved. What happened in that house will never be known.

Judge Gray sends the jury out to deliberate. After three and a half hours, they return. Lorilei is not there. "We the jury find the defendant Ricky Langley guilty of second-degree murder."

The death penalty is reserved for first-degree murder. Ricky receives a life sentence.

But Clive appeals. Not the prosecution trying again for a death sentence, but Clive. He wants Ricky declared not guilty by reason of insanity. Citing Gray's absence from the courtroom, he wins a new trial. The prosecutors do file for the death penalty again, but a higher court rules that because with this verdict Ricky has already escaped first-degree murder and a death sentence, they can charge him with only second-degree. The trial takes place in front of a judge, not a jury. Lorilei doesn't testify. Again, Ricky is found guilty of second-degree murder and sentenced to life. He is not found insane.

But none of that is what made me go to Iowa. None of that is what made me chase down the records of Ricky's life, or try to understand how I'd read my own into it. Instead it's what the jury foreman at the 2003 trial, the eighth-grade teacher, said later. After the verdict.

Ever since, in 2003, I first watched Ricky's confession and felt, in that moment, that I wanted him to die, I have always believed that it was Lorilei's words that had made the jury spare Ricky's life. That's how the media told it: The story of Ricky is the story of the power of a mother's forgiveness.

In the records, I've found that the truth is more complicated: She doesn't forgive him, but she doesn't want him to die.

But it's even more complicated than that. Because in talking about the decision to spare Ricky's life, the foreman never mentioned Lorilei. Instead he said: "I knew as soon as I saw him I wasn't gonna let them kill that boy."

"That boy"—Ricky. "As soon as I saw him"—voir dire, which Ricky was present for. Meaning *before* the trial. Before the evidence, before the witnesses, before the facts, and before the story-spinning by the lawyers, too. Before the foreman heard Lorilei say anything at all.

The foreman's brother-in-law was schizophrenic. The brother-in-law died well before the trial, but he lived with the foreman and the foreman's wife for years. They took care of him, and the foreman saw how much his brother-in-law struggled. He saw the pain that struggle caused his wife. He looked at Ricky. He saw his brother-in-law.

A few weeks after I see the photographs of Jeremy, I come back to Louisiana, because the archives division has found missing file boxes. Each day I look through more records, looking for answers. Each night I drive. I tell myself I'm driving to see the landscape: how the road stretches flat and faded in the sun, how the trees erupt in emerald profusions. But really I know I'm searching for the house.

Three hours before my plane back to Massachusetts, with the airport a two-hour drive away, I'm still driving back and forth on Ardoin Road in Iowa, looking. The house isn't here. I know that. I drove this road yesterday and the day before. It isn't here, and yet nowhere else makes sense. I have to leave. But leaving means accepting that I never will find the house. That this story will always remain unfinished inside me.

I pull my car to the side of the road, get out, and start to photograph the trees. Because I don't know what else to do. Because at least then I'll have that evidence of here. It's an unusually clear day for this time of the year, no clouds threatening rain, just the bright blue sky and the flat green grass for miles. The road is empty. The fields are, too. There's not a car I can see, not a person in sight. Not a bird in the sky. Before me, the blanketed fields; behind me, a thick wall of trees that abut a ravine, swallowing the horizon line. I lift the camera to my eyes and frame my shot: the long road that stretches the length of the viewfinder, the fields that stretch behind it like a memory. Maybe I never was meant to find the house.

And then I laugh. I have to. Because in the right corner of the camera's frame, at a spot I had passed at least twice before, is an entrance to an unmarked road. It is exactly where it was supposed to be, its placement exactly as it is on the aerial photograph. It is next to Ardoin Lane, which means I stood just yards from it on my last trip here and never once saw it. Something in my body kept me from realizing until now.

On the road's right is a one-story brick house with a purple foil pinwheel pitched in its yard. On the left, a white prefabricated house raised up on bare wooden stilts, a pickup truck parked beside it. Lumber and construction materials weigh down the pickup's bed, but the cab is empty and both houses are dark. Farther down on the left, just before the road truncates at a thatch of woods, there's one more house.

But that's it, nothing else. No more houses, only grass and then that mass of woods. The other lot is empty.

I park my car by the pickup. The high grass tickles my ankles. I trespass over the yards with impunity, to the empty lot, where a small shed stands. Did it once hold the washing machine outside the Lawson house, where Ricky washed sheets late on the night he killed Jeremy?

Behind it, the world falls off. The ravine. The one Jeremy liked to play in, propping up his gun as he lay on his belly in the soft earth, and the one the police dredged when he disappeared. It's deeper than I imagined, a steep sheer drop maybe ten feet down into dense brush and dark mud. A place where you could expect a child might have died, and where you would send out the searchers with their flashlights and the dogs with their noses and the helicopters that whirled and the ATVs, while all along his body rested fifteen feet behind you in a white house, wrapped in Tweety Bird and Dick Tracy blankets.

Fifteen feet. I turn and I walk to the spot. It's just a patch of green now. The air clear and still and scented sweet from the grass.

All this time, all this searching. I have finally found the scene of the crime.

And it's gone.

Thirty-Eight

When I get home to Boston, I climb the stairs to my apartment, open the door, and crouch to pet my cat when he runs to greet me. I push aside the mail the cat sitter has left on the floor, hang my keys on the rack, and walk through the entryway.

Then I see them. Three white boxes, each four inches thick, stacked on my bed. The photographs.

I drag them off. Before I do anything else, I drag them off. Each one weighs as much as a child.

The next morning, armed with coffee, I sit at my desk and open them. Inside the boxes are the pages I marked. First, aerial photographs of the house. The woods I just stood beside, the thin lane I now recognize. Then Bessie, the one photograph that exists of her in the cast. She is a pale face in a sea of white: white hospital sheets, a white nightgown pulled over the white cast. She looks frightened, or maybe just tired. Around her, her girls have piled onto the bed, wearing their Sunday best. Only the youngest—only Judy— looks at ease. Her older sisters, Darlene and Francis, hold their shoulders stiffly, a little away from their mother, as though they are trying to keep this new reality at bay.

But Judy? She is on her mama's bed, she can hardly remember her differently. Her mama has always lain this way. Her mama has always been so still. It is not so difficult to reach around the cast and hug her. The next photograph is the cast alone, against a flat black background, its empty white carcass the shape of a ghost or a haunting.

Then Jeremy.

He sleeps. That's what the first photograph looks like. I can't not write it that way, as sleeping, and I can't leave it that way. The flash of the long-ago camera lights up his blond hair. His eyes are closed, his lashes thick. His nose is the stub one of dolls.

For the next photograph the camera has moved lower. From his mouth there comes a white tube sock with stripes, dirty at the bottom. Jeremy in this photo does not look dead, he still might only be sleeping. His skin is still plump, his mouth still the bow bud of a child.

It's the sock that looks limp, lifeless. The sock that means Jeremy is dead.

The string around his neck has been removed for the next photograph. A ruler, a horrible basic wooden school ruler, presses to the gouge in Jeremy's neck, measuring the bruising. Around the bruising bloom black splotches. That word, that word that now haunts me: petechiae.

I steady my breath. I keep my pen moving. I try to describe each photograph. Through my open window, I hear music from a car radio. A woman laughs on the street below. When I finish one photograph, I move on to the next. I try not to feel. I just record.

It is the gun that does me in. Jeremy's BB gun. The photograph is of the open closet door. In the closet is a mound of blankets. I can't look too directly at the blankets—I know this is really a photograph of Jeremy's body, not of blankets—so I focus on a small dark shape in the blurry photocopy. The shape is a vertical bar. I can't make out what it is.

Then. The barrel of a gun, poking up from where Ricky tucked it. My own cry startles me. My sobs.

What I fell in love with about the law so many years ago was the way that in making a story, in making a neat narrative of events, it finds a beginning, and therefore cause. But I didn't understand then that the law doesn't find the beginning any more than it finds the truth. It creates a story. That story has a beginning. That story simplifies, and we call it truth.

Helen Palsgraf was on a beach outing with her children when her life changed forever and became a parable for where stories start. But there's something else about the case, something I didn't find out until years after I left the law: No one knows whether she was actually injured. She claimed mental injury; there doesn't appear to have been any evidence. The judges said they'd assume she'd been injured, so as to reach the more interesting legal question.

But that's an asterisk on history. To look at the reenactments law schools stage of the case, in which the scale crushes Helen, or the animations online to illustrate it for their study sessions, you'd never know that. Whatever happened in the past, the story wrote right over it. The story became the truth. What you see in Ricky killing Jeremy, I have come to believe, depends as much on who you are and the life you've had as on what he did. But the legal narrative erases that step. It erases where it came from.

For years I thought the lesson in the jury's second-degree verdict was that they didn't want to face the question of whether Ricky should live or die. A first-degree conviction would have meant proceeding to the penalty phase of a death penalty trial, in which they'd have to directly confront the question of what should happen to him. A second-degree conviction allowed them to escape that. Ricky would automatically serve life.

That was the only explanation I could think of. Otherwise, the verdict made no sense. Jeremy was under twelve. There was no debate that Ricky had killed him, so if the jury had found specific intent the murder would have to be first-degree. They'd been instructed that under Louisiana law, if Ricky understood the "reasonable consequences" of his actions he had specific intent. For someone *not* to understand that strangling a child would kill him, that a wire pulled tight around his neck would kill him, for someone to stuff a sock in a child's throat and then pinch his nose closed against air—well, I thought, the only way someone wouldn't understand death as a reasonable consequence was if they were legally insane. And the jury had turned that down.

The verdict was a legal contradiction.

So I thought that, faced with the question of whether Ricky should live or die, the jury had refused to decide. But I have realized that I am trying to rescue a place for the un-neatness of everything that happened. Lorilei didn't forgive Ricky, but she still didn't want him killed. My grandfather did everything he did, and he was still my grandfather. The law—with each side's relentless pursuit of one story—has never known what to do with this complicated middle ground. But life is full of it.

I see the jury's verdict differently now. While the verdict the jury voted is legally incoherent, what strikes me now is its elegant, human beauty. It says what cannot be true in law, but can only be true in life: that Ricky is both responsible and not. The law the jurors were presented with didn't have room for this middle ground. They created it, as though they opened up space in the law, inventing a category that doesn't exist.

Ricky.

Thirty-Nine

I make the trip to my parents' house on an early August afternoon when they're away on Nantucket. Only my parents' two dogs are there, large mutts they adopted when I was in college. My girlfriend, Janna, has come with me, and when the two of us arrive at the door the dogs come slowly. They are great beasts with heads nearly as high as my waist and long fur that is losing its color. Once they had barreled chests of muscle, but now one is blind and deaf and the other so riddled with fatty tumors that his skin rolls and spreads like a loose sack of apples. They are a portrait of age and time and when I gather them in my arms I can feel how they used to squirm as puppies. They lick my face and arms in their simple, welcome love. I beam and look up at Janna. "Meet the boys," I say. What is complicated about my relationship to my parents' house is that it has never been uncomplicated. It's always had pain. It's always had love.

While Janna settles in the kitchen to read, I work quickly. The white aluminum cabinet my mother kept when we were children, the one that reminds me of Bessie's trunk, or Bessie's trunk reminds me of it, is still in the long playroom we once played in. I have not seen my grandfather's face since he died—I have no photographs of him—and the photographs must be in there.

Instead I find pictures of my family. When my mother was pregnant, she wore her hair parted down the middle and tied into two low braids, so different from the stiffly sprayed style I've seen my whole life. She wears a green T-shirt, her hair parted and tied back and a smattering of freckles bridging her nose. My mother as a young woman is as distant to me as Bessie, as inconceivable and in need of being imagined. I can picture her giving birth to us only from the way I've been told the story. The doctors, worried that she can't take anesthesia, have kept her awake for the cesarean and given her grain alcohol intravenously instead. She is draped in a blue cloth from the waist down, she can't see what's happening, but, drunk, she sings as the doctors pull first my brother, then Jacqueline, then me from her. She sings us into the world. Her voice is free, full-throated. We are unknown; we are so tiny; we are just beginning. There is no one for whom she must be self-conscious yet. No one for whose memory she must arrange the story. The scene is no more or less real to me than what Ricky believes he remembers of Alcide's cradling Oscar's head, singing to the boy on the side of the road.

I find the chart I saw as a child, the one that listed Jacqueline's eye color as blue. Then—a bright yellow piece of paper folded in half—my missing birth announcement. "Hail, hail, the gang's all here!" Our three names listed, "in order of appearance, between 8:03 and 8:06 p.m." How tired my parents must have been and how sad, the two of them at home with Andy and me, boiling our bottles in aluminum pots on the stove, or trying not to be frightened when the hospital called with news of Jacqueline. I find a picture of my father, tanned and smiling on a beach—and think of him as he cradles the emergency phone in the airport. Alcide sitting in the truck stop with his coffee, then standing up and walking out and leaving the crumpled pamphlet of lots behind. It will be a long time before he gets his wife back. If he ever gets his wife back.

In another photograph, we are all seated around a dinner table in Nantucket, our cheeks sunburned, our hair wet. My grandfather isn't with us—I'm too old in the photograph for it to be the summer my grandparents came with us—but looking at the strangers who are my parents, I can only picture them as they lie in bed on another Nantucket night, the night they had just learned what my grandfather had done. They have just brought us to bed at the end of a long and frightening day, and they have smoothed the covers up over us. It's summer, but the East Coast ocean air is chilled and now my parents find each other under their sheets. They listen for my grandfather, who has gone to bed with my grandmother down the hall. They listen to make sure he doesn't rise again in the night. But the silence persists, and they settle. My father's body is warm and my mother squirrels herself against his chest, listening to the drumbeat of his breath and heart. They've made it through years. They'll make it through years. Everything has changed, but—nothing has.

Outside their bedroom, the secret sits, to wait out the night like a ghost.

I find love letters between my parents and fighting letters, reminders that we are all mysteries to one another. Once I was riding in a car alone with my mother, her driving, when our conversation turned to this house. She wanted to move, she said, but the finances had been difficult since all those dark raging years of my father's. The house had fallen into disrepair; now only developers showed any interest. "Of course, they'll only tear it down."

A moment, a hitch, a hiccup of time passed before I spoke. A moment I was only barely aware of, in which I made the decision not to remain silent. I have never been very good at remaining silent to spare her feelings.

"My therapist says," I began, but found I was out of words. Even to say this word, *therapist,* is a risk in my family. I tried again. "My therapist says that if the house is torn down I should get to drive the bulldozer."

She cut the engine. Wherever we were going, we'd arrived, but neither of us moved. The air in the car was suddenly thick, viscous with silence. When my mother spoke, her words came slowly. "I get to drive the bulldozer."

No one story is simple. No one story complete.

After two hours of searching, it's almost time for Janna and me to leave. We have to catch a train. But I cannot find a photograph of my grandfather. Hundreds of photographs in the cabinet, but not a single one of him. I keep wanting to think that when they told me it didn't haunt them, it didn't. I keep wanting to take the past, and my anger, at its word.

Yet someone went through this cabinet. There are photographs of every cousin, every aunt and uncle, of both of my grandmothers. Of relatives who died before I was born, and some I even recognize as of my grandfather's siblings, taken at the party for his and my grandmother's fiftieth anniversary. Someone removed the photographs of him. Not to keep him from display—this cabinet hides its contents. But to scour him even from here, the left-behind part of the story. And I don't believe, I realize, looking at all the photographs, that they did this scouring right after they found out about the abuse. Whoever did it, did it later. When they realized the hurt.

In the doorway, Janna appears. We will miss the train if I don't hurry.

"Five more minutes," I say.

Then I realize. My parents' wedding album. They keep it in the living room, on the bookcase opposite the couch that replaced the couch I lay on as a sick child. All the games of checkers I played there with my grandparents in the winter, when it was too cold to sit on the porch. All the Sundays and Christmases we spent here. As I sat cross-legged with the board on the floor, my grandfather would lean far forward on the couch to see where my checkers were landing. He'd laugh at the eager jokes I told, and ask me how school was. Above us the whole time, waiting, was the staircase.

The album is what I've come to the room for. But next to it is something unexpected. Another album, broad-faced and slender, that was once white. I run my hands over its vinyl cover. From its bottom, half a rainbow blooms. It was meant for a child. I flip through the pages, expecting it to be empty. Most of the albums on my parents' shelves are empty.

But suddenly, there is my family. We stand behind the house, on the lush lawn, its green as vibrant as I remember from childhood, the green my father tended from his tractor. I can almost hear Vivaldi's cellos and violins race from the speakers my father strung up. The photograph is labeled FATHER'S DAY. My siblings and I stand in a row, my sisters and me in dresses, my brother in a navy blazer and pants. Beside us, on a bench, sit my father's mother and my mother's mother. My parents stand behind them, and then— there. My grandfather.

His sport coat is gray, as are his slacks. His shoulders slump, his lips are parted just slightly. He stares directly into the camera. He is younger than I remember him being, but what is age to a child? The unexpected thing is how much a stranger he is. I would pass him on the street and think only that there, with a head of gray curls and his pants high around his waist, goes an elderly Italian man.

That's what I think, at first. But as I hold the album and study the picture, I feel the tremors start in my body. The bristle of his hair prickles. The wet murk of his mouth. The deep nausea and the grief and the shock and the fear. No. I might not know, I might not know consciously who I passed on the street, why I recoiled. But my body would know. My body remembers.

The girl in the photograph, standing to his left, is eight years old. She has brown curls brushed into gently waved frizz held back by a thin white headband. She loves Nancy Drew mysteries, and I know, looking at her, that right now though she holds her lips in a half smile she is off somewhere behind her eyes. She smells the grass; she hears the violins; she feels the weight of her family beside her. She feels everything she cannot yet understand. And she has escaped in her head, dreaming up a world that will live inside her, with characters who feel as real as her own.

A memory comes: I sit cross-legged on the living room carpet, my grandfather on the couch above me. I am sketching an oval on a drawing pad—the shape of a face. "Good, good," he says. He leans down to take my pencil. He shows me how to section the planes of the face into quadrants. He marks where the eyes go, the nose, the mouth.

"I have to go to my grandfather's grave." I have found Janna in the kitchen, seated at the white Formica table, and I realize that I am telling her we are going to miss the train. But I have gone to Jeremy's grave, I have gone to Bessie and Alcide's and Oscar's. "We have to go to his grave."

Forty

I say goodbye to the boys, kneeling down next to them to bury my face in their fur. Then we drive through Tenafly, down the hill and past the old apartment building, over the railroad tracks. The cemetery is a ten-minute drive away, nestled on a street framed high by elms and oaks.

Janna waits by the car while I walk toward the trees. "Marzano," I say to the caretaker who sits in a small office at the entrance gate, and he points me up an embankment, to a deep gathering of graves. As I climb, I pass headstones of gray and glossy black. On one, an engraved sun hovers over water, setting or rising, there is no way to tell. Above, the canopy is thick with leaves. Fall is coming.

I see the gravestone's back first. Rose granite.

I walk around to its front.

My grandmother is a young woman. In her wedding portrait her face is round and unlined, a white veil of Spanish lace laid over her hair, a wide bouquet of flowers spilling over her arms. Beside her stands a young man. My grandfather's hair is dark. He wears a crisp black suit, his white shirt collar starched into high points ringed by a black bowtie. He stands upright, no cane.

I remember this photograph well. When I was a child it sat on my grandmother's vanity table at their house, and I liked looking at it. How unimaginable the people in it had seemed then. But I see the picture differently now than I did as a child. Now I look at them and I see how young they were. I see love, and I see fear, and everything the years will take. They have so much ahead. They have no idea what is ahead.

They were young, then they were old, now they are dead.

The feeling strikes me unmistakably. The feeling strikes me as a surprise. *Now they are dead.* They are dead. I am alive.

What I feel standing on the grass of their grave isn't release, not exactly. It's grief, but not a bad kind. I can hear the cars pass on the road below. Janna's standing down there, likely watching the wind rustle the elms. She will wait as long as I need to stay, I know that without even asking, and when I am finished we will drive away from this place.

But it's not that action that will take me away, not the physical leaving. And not her, no matter what the future holds for us. I have learned that by now.

Instead it's all this. This telling of the story.

My grandmother is buried next to a secret. My grandfather died with the fact of who he was. I can't say that I forgive them. Only that forgiveness is too simple a word. They helped make me. They did such harm.

"I have to go now." My voice sounds strange, tremulous in the quiet. I have always found the dead in the stories they leave behind. Not in the stone-cold fact of the grave. But I never got to say goodbye while my grandparents were alive, because every goodbye I ever said was really just words that stood in place of all I couldn't say.

"I'm going to go finish telling this story."

There. Now they know. I am telling this story.

I mean those words to be my last to them. That where there was silence, there will be speech. That where there were secrets, I will make way for the complicated truth.

But I can't move. I stand on the grass and I listen to the quiet, to the small animals making their way through the blades at my feet, a world of a scale I don't know and can't imagine, and above me in the branches of the trees, the world of the birds, the wind and the sky that never touch down. The late summer leaves are just starting their turn to color. The grass around me is a sprawl of lives, the earth beneath me holds the dead, and each one is marked by a name that means everything and nothing. A placeholder for the story.

"I have to go now," I say again, and I hear how my voice has risen in pitch. I am saying this as much to myself as to them, I am trying to get myself to go, but as I say it I feel in my stomach the inkling of an idea. The inkling of an emotion, of what it is that I really need to say. What the complicated truth requires, too. Why I am still standing here.

The thought surprises me. I hold it inside me, wary, and study it. Can this be true? Must I really say this?

Yes.

"I love you."

The day I met Ricky was bright and blue, as clear a morning as visits Louisiana. Hurricane season had begun, but if trouble was coming, it wasn't visible yet. I was twenty-five. I had just watched his videotaped confession a few months before. You could say that the day I met Ricky was the real beginning of this story, its proximate cause. Or if the story began much earlier—in my childhood in the gray house—you could say that meeting him was a kind of end.

When I left New Orleans the sky was dark, but on the drive light broke over the leafless trees of Lake Pontchartrain, the streaks of brown where mud had mixed with water and the clear teal where it had settled. The white tombs of Metairie Cemetery, in their orderly lanes of houses for the dead, gave way to tangled mangroves. Fields stretched long and languid in the morning sun. I drove as if encapsulated by a shadow only I could see. I could not remember the name of the man I was driving to meet, only what he had done. And the face of the blond boy he had killed, the boy as he smiled for his last school photograph.

One road reaches the gates of Angola, the Louisiana State Penitentiary, the one road that is also the only road out. With thirty miles to go to the prison, the road splits off the highway at a sharp right angle. From there it is narrow and nearly unmarked, a path you take only if you know your destination. The town of St. Francisville, with its fast-food restaurants and its convenience marts, cedes to trailers set into the dirt. A single beauty parlor, housed in a shack with a hand-lettered sign. One kindergarten. Five churches.

The road dead-ended at the prison gates. Just beyond them, yards away, stood the white octagonal building that was once death row, before it was moved deeper into the prison grounds. I got out of my car and stood in the heat, watching the light strike its high walls. Dragonflies circled me, the sun knifing off the brilliant blues and yellows of their bodies. The prison grounds, once stitched together from old plantations, are larger than the island of Manhattan. Angola has lush fields and streams that burble down embankments. It has thick woods and thicketed bushes; wild pigs, rattlesnakes, and bears. Named for the homeland of the slaves who once worked its fields, for decades it was so violent that the federal government took it over from the state. With its size, its terrible beauty, and its terrible history, comes inmate rumor that a moat rings the prison, stocked with hungry alligators ready to eat anyone who tries to escape. Never mind that every inmate who arrives here does so through the gates I stood in front of, and is then driven through the fields. Never mind that they'd have seen there was no moat. The myth blotted the memory out.

At security, a guard patted me down, and I boarded one of the old school buses the prison uses for transport, white with ANGOLA STATE PENITENTIARY stenciled on its side. We drove through fields of long, swaying grass, to a building painted peach. Then another guard led me down a corridor of fencing to a door. Through the door was a gray-walled room with small, round tables and plastic chairs. Along one side of the room ran a series of Plexiglas partitions to which chairs had been pulled up. "Sit," the guard said, and pointed to a chair.

What happened next is a memory as vivid as anything imagined.

Through the Plexiglas I watch as a man walks through a distant door, turns to the guard, and holds his hands out for the cuffs to be unlocked. The man wears the same chambray shirt and blue jeans all the inmates do—Angola blues. He is older than he was on the tape. His glasses still just as thick. His ears jut out from his head, the mark of Bessie's drinking so long ago.

He is thirty-seven that day. But as he walks down the corridor toward me in my memory I don't see him as thirty-seven. He is the baby being lifted from a slash in his mother's stomach, lifted through the cut-out moon in the cast. He is the brown-haired boy with freckles and buckteeth, who crouches over the roots of a yellowwood tree and talks to a black-and-white picture he holds in his grubby hand. He is eighteen, sitting in his friend's pickup truck, the stars an explosion outside, and he sucks on the sweet glass neck of a bottle of schnapps and tries to get up the courage to walk into the mental health center and speak the name for what he knows he is. He is twenty-six, and his arm goes tight around Jeremy's neck. Jeremy's legs kick so hard in the air his boots fall off. Then the boy's body falls limp, and as the boy dies the man becomes a murderer, who he now will always be. He is forty-nine and he writes the last page I have in the files, a note so new it hadn't yet been put into a box like the others, but was handed to me loose by a clerk. It is a letter to a judge. "Well you know I do family research and I greatly enjoy it!" He has spent many years finding his ancestors' records, he writes, but there are still holes in the story. Can the judge please help him dig back further?

I know that need. If he goes back far enough, maybe he'll understand.

In this memory, I wear my too-heavy suit. I am twenty-five in the visiting room, but I am also three, and my grandfather's fat palm slides over my mouth. Eight, and my hands stick together from the swing-set polish and I laugh. The air smells of turpentine and cut grass. I am twelve and I close my eyes and rise onto my tiptoes to make my dress twirl—and when I open my eyes, my grandfather is watching me, staring frankly. Sixteen with a can of black paint, trying to write myself a new life on my bedroom walls. Thirty-seven and standing for the first time on what used to be the crushed shell of the Fuel Stop, determined to go where the past is, go there so I can leave it behind and find my way home.

Waiting, as the man walks toward me, I flick my tongue over my lower lip. An old habit. I do it, I feel my lips wet—and then I shudder in recoil, the same way I do every time. Because I know this gesture I do unconsciously. It's what my grandfather did when he was concentrating on a drawing. I watched him do it when he taught me to draw. I carry the memory somewhere inside my body I can't control, can't even access to reach inside and edit the memory out. I still want to edit it out. I still want to be free of it. But I know I'm bound in ways I'll never see, never understand. We carry what makes us.

Across from me, Ricky sits down. The problem of this day, the problem of this meeting, the problem that starts this story inside me and the only way it can end it is this: The man who sits down across from me is a man. He'll never be all one thing or the other. Only a story can be that. Never a person.

So I try something new. Not turning my back to the past, not fleeing it, but extending a hand. I say to the past: Come with me, then, as I live.

"Hello, Ricky," I say.

Sources Consulted

TRIAL TRANSCRIPT, 2003

Darlene Langley: They told mom and dad that because of all the medications that she was taking and you know, having surgeries, that he would probably be—

Prosecutor: Objection, Your Honor, unless she has personal knowledge.

Judge: Oh, I don't know.

Defense attorney: Your Honor, it's not for the truth of the matter asserted, but base—this is family lore that they had been raised with all their lives, that everyone has repeated and been told. Whether it's true or not, it's what everyone acted on.

Judge: Objection overruled.

For the sections involving my family, I have relied on my memory, and have at times confirmed dates with family members or had conversations with them about these events. For the sections from Ricky Langley's life, I drew mostly from court records and newspaper articles, as outlined below. That said, the specifics needed to bring the scenes to life—what people were wearing, where they stood, etc.—I sometimes imagined onto the scaffolding of the documents. At times, I needed to imagine what people were thinking or feeling, and there, whenever possible, I drew inspiration from other things they said or did that were documented.

CHAPTER ONE

This description of the murder comes from a mix of Lorilei Guillory's testimony in the 2003 trial (her 1994 testimony differs slightly) and the transcript of Ricky Langley's February 10, 1992, confession, which was the confession I watched in 2003. Two confession tapes were made that day; this was the second, though other details in this account come from the transcript of the first tape. The timing of when he possibly molested Jeremy Guillory—whether before the child's death, after, or not at all—is presented differently in the different confessions, and here I have chosen the simpler version, while also indicating the dispute. I have chosen to indicate that he gave three confessions because those are the meaningful videotape transcripts I have, but, as referenced elsewhere in this book, he told the story of the murder many different times and ways.

CHAPTER THREE

I have based my description of Lorilei Guillory's search for her son on her 2003 trial testimony, though I have tried to imagine her feelings, drawing from her 1994 testimony and the play *Lorilei* by Thomas Wright, which has been performed in the UK and internationally, and aired on the BBC. It was written in collaboration with Nick Harrington, who conducted research for it, and relied in part on Lorilei's own words. More about the play can be found in Clive Stafford Smith's piece "From Hatred to Forgiveness," published December 11, 2015, on TheNation.com. For her surroundings, I have drawn upon photographs published in the *American Press* and taken on my own trips to the area. The photograph of Lorilei and Jeremy Guillory referenced here was published in the *American Press*. Transcripts from the 911 calls were destroyed over the years, but I used 911 records custodian Gary Hayes's testimony during the 2003 trial to reconstruct their content. The description of Ricky Langley's bringing Lorilei a drink on the porch is drawn from the play *Lorilei*. Upon the bare information about the drink in the play, I have layered my imagination of what the moment must have been like. That said, the drink does not occur in other descriptions of the search, and should be considered disputed. My description of Lorilei's past comes from *Lorilei*, the *American Press*, and court records searches. That Jeremy was on a school trip to the science museum comes from Lorilei Guillory's testimony in the 1994 trial.

CHAPTER FIVE

This description of the search is based on Deputy Sheriff Calton Pitre's testimony in the 2003 trial, articles that ran in the *American Press* at the time of the murder, and KPLC-TV and KYKZ-96 transcripts that are in the court record. That the Fuel Stop donated coffee is from Lanelle Trahan's testimony in the 2003 trial. That the woman I have called Pearl Lawson knew Ricky Langley was a child molester and told him to leave that night while the search was happening is based on the transcript from Ricky's second February 10, 1992, confession, though I have imagined the conversation's specifics. That Ricky's parents asked him whether he was involved with Jeremy Guillory's disappearance is also in that transcript, but again, I have imagined the specifics.

CHAPTER SEVEN

This chapter is based on Lanelle Trahan's testimony in the 1994 and 2003 trials. The description of the motorcycle crash is based on the accident report, which is in the court record.

CHAPTER NINE

Don Dixon described the goose-hunting trip he and Lucky DeLouche took in his testimony during the 2003 trial. The phone call the probation officer makes to Lucky is a composite of many different phone calls and meetings that took place between the probation officer Elizabeth Clark, Dixon, Lucky, and other law enforcement personnel. Accounts of these phone calls and meetings vary. In Dixon's 2003 testimony, he says he and Lucky interviewed Lorilei Guillory first, before talking to the probation officer. Clark gave a much longer and more complicated description of events in the 1994 trial. The account presented here is closer to that in the play *Lorilei*. In all versions, it's consistent that they learned about Ricky Langley because of the probation officer's putting clues together, though he was not formally under her charge. The account of the arrest here is taken from Dixon and Lucky's testimony in the 2003 trial, though I have omitted a third law enforcement officer at the scene, Neil Edwards. I have imagined what Ricky was thinking in the police car, though that he covered his bedroom windows in foil is in the court record. The account of finding Jeremy Guillory's body comes from a February 10, 1992, videotape transcript. Again, I omitted other law enforcement personnel who were at the scene. The deputy who did the videotaping was not new to the job, but that information is in the 1994 transcript, not the 2003 transcript. I have retained my initial imagining of it and flagged it as imagined in the text.

CHAPTER TEN

The domestic violence incident described here is a simplified and imagined composite. On March 29, 1993, the *American Press* ran an article stating that the father of the boy I've called Cole was arrested for trying to run over a woman and her baby. Based on the address where the incident took place and its timing, I believe this woman to be Lorilei. The DA later dropped the attempted murder charges because the woman refused to cooperate with police, saying that she had no other means of support for herself and her baby.

CHAPTER ELEVEN

This description of the crash—and the note that the lawyers transposed the time of it—is based on opening statements in the 1994 and 2003 trials, as well as newspaper accounts from 1964. Minor conflicting details exist, and where I have not highlighted the conflict I have chosen among them. Notice of Oscar Langley's birth, before he had a name, ran in the *American Press*. For my description of Charity Hospital, I have drawn upon the opening statements from the 1994 and 2003 trials, Dr. Robert Maupin's testimony in the 2003 trial, and the book *New Orleans' Charity Hospital: A Story of Physicians, Politics, and Poverty* by John Salvaggio, MD. Throughout, I have also drawn upon Ricky Langley's sisters' testimony in all three trials. I have compressed Bessie's hospital stays for clarity and narrative flow. During the period after Christmas, she came home for stretches, and Ricky was born at Lake Charles Hospital.

CHAPTER THIRTEEN

The scene of Ricky Langley's helping his father build the house is imagined. I have built Ricky's dream of being led by a ghost to the scene of the crash from a 2003 statement by Heather Regan, a reporter for the *Southwest Daily News,* who was present at the 2002 seminar described in chapter thirty-one. She recalls Ricky's saying a ghost led him to the crash site; other attendees understood Ricky to be saying that Oscar Langley was that ghost. I have chosen Regan's account for clarity. Ricky's seeing his father cradling and singing to Oscar's head at the crash site comes from other occasions in the court record on which Ricky told psychiatrists of his vision of the crash. Ricky has repeatedly told psychologists, psychiatrists, and law enforcement officers that he began molesting children at the age of nine or ten, and in the statements taken after the 2002 seminar people remember hearing him say this. Other descriptions of his childhood are drawn from his sisters' testimony in the 1994 and 2003 trials, the opening statements in both trials, 2003 testimony by his sixth-grade teacher, Josette Melancon, and elsewhere in the court record. The night he tried to get treatment at the Lake Charles Mental Health Center at eighteen, but was turned away, is from Patrick Vincent's testimony in the 2003 trial. I have simplified the scene by having Ricky go in alone. In the text I have used the words *boys* and *teenagers,* but they come from the imagined point of view of the worker looking out the window at the car. Vincent was in his thirties.

CHAPTER FIFTEEN

This chapter is based on Ricky Langley's records from the Lake Charles Mental Health Center and testimony in the 1994 trial, in particular that of Dr. Paul Ware. The allegation that Judy once had to pull a gun on the man I have called Lyle comes from Dr. Ware's testimony, but has not, to my knowledge, been corroborated by the parties. What Ricky says and feels here comes from notes taken by caseworkers in those records, though I have imagined the scene with the unnamed female caseworker. The "approved visitor list" is from Angola State Penitentiary. The list is in the court record but is not dated, though it appears to date from before 1997.

CHAPTER SEVENTEEN

The Indiana portion of this chapter is based on Ruth McClary's testimony in the 1994 trial, though again, I have imagined many of the details. The Georgia portion is based on Ricky Langley's records from the prison and on testimony by Rick Hawkins, Dr. Clark Heindel, Jackie Simmons, and Dr. Ware in the 1994 trial. The Langley family history book referenced at the end of the chapter is *The Langley Family of Southwest Louisiana: A Genealogical Study of Some Descendants of John Langley (II) and Marie Willan* by John Austin Young.

CHAPTER EIGHTEEN

The description of Ricky Langley's crime in Georgia here is based on the victim's testimony in the 1994 trial. Ricky's description of it is based on documents in his Georgia prison record.

CHAPTER NINETEEN

This chapter is based on Ellen Smith's testimony in the 1994 trial. I have imagined the socioeconomic status of her family, the circumstances of her relationship, and the details of the party. The information about Ricky Langley moving back and forth, and whom he saw in Georgia, comes from the court record, as does the imagined exit interview scene. That Ricky's parents believed he had molested a family member comes from Dr. Ware's testimony in the 1994 trial.

CHAPTER TWENTY-ONE

The exchanges between Ricky Langley and the woman I have called Pearl Lawson are drawn from statements made by Ricky in his confession videotapes and by Pearl in the 1994 and 2003 trials. Those accounts are minimal and conflicting, however, so I have imagined the details of the motel and television exchanges and have highlighted some aspects of their conflicting accounts in the text. Based on statements from the 2002 seminar, Ricky also told attendees there that he babysat after returning to Iowa—he must have meant the Lawson children, since there was no one else he babysat or claimed to have babysat—and that he had first told the parents of those children that he'd molested children in the past. The various retellings Ricky gives of the murder are in the 2003 court record. The event that takes place with the inmate I've called Jackson is based on a February 10, 1994, statement by Larry Schroeder that is in the court record, as well as his testimony in the 1994 trial. Several attendees at the 2002 defense seminar described in chapter thirty-one recall Ricky's claiming there that he strangled Jeremy Guillory while thinking he was killing the ghost of Oscar Langley, and the same account appears in the notes of the defense psychiatrist Dr. Dennis Zimmerman, which are in the court record. The death row portion of the chapter is based on Ricky's Angola records and John Thompson's testimony at the 2009 trial. The exchange between them in this chapter is a composite, drawn from juxtaposing events in Ricky's records and Thompson's descriptions of his interactions with Ricky over time. The quotes by Clive Stafford Smith are in the court record, as is the appellate decision. Here and throughout the book, I have drawn some of my thinking about Clive's feelings toward his father from articles he's written and interviews and talks he's given, such as "My Father, Mental Illness, and the Death Penalty," a TEDxExeter 2015 talk. The description of Clive's house is based on my recollection from 2003. For other details in this chapter, I also drew upon *Nine Lives: Mystery, Magic, Death, and Life in New Orleans* by Dan Baum.

CHAPTER TWENTY-TWO

I deduced that the man who answered the door was John Thompson based on my recollection and statements he made at the 2009 trial about the work he did at the Louisiana Capital Assistance Center, then called the Louisiana Crisis Assistance Center (LCAC), during that period. The videotape described is the second one taken of Ricky Langley on February 10, 1992, and the description here is based on the transcript.

CHAPTER TWENTY-FOUR

The funeral and march scenes are based on articles published in the *American Press* and transcripts from KPLC-TV and KYKZ-96 that are in the court record. Ricky Langley calling to the guard is a composite moment, drawn from multiple statements in the court record that he would often try to speak with Lucky DeLouche and other officers while at the Calcasieu Correctional Center. My description of Richard Guillory is based on photographs that ran in the *American Press* and other photos available online. The editorial referenced was published by the *American Press*. My description of Lorilei Guillory after Jeremy's murder comes from *Lorilei* and Clive Stafford Smith in a hearing transcript. Her thoughts upon hearing that Ricky had been sentenced to death come from *Lorilei*.

CHAPTER TWENTY-FIVE

The pretrial-hearing transcript is in the court record. I have imagined the circumstances of Lorilei Guillory getting ready for this date, informed by *Lorilei*. Documents about Judge Alcide Gray's recusal from further death penalty cases and the briefs Clive Stafford

Smith filed to get the 2003 verdict overturned are in the court record. The Waiver & Agreement referenced here was signed by Lorilei,
Clive, and Ricky Langley on June 7, 2002. On May 8, 2003—
well after Lorilei met with Ricky and decided to testify for him—
the three signed a second Waiver & Agreement, which did make
clear that Ricky and Clive would push for a verdict of not guilty by
reason of insanity, or NGRI. Though I cannot be certain that
Lorilei and Ricky formally met at the high school, it was a small
school that they attended at the same time, as the next chapter makes
clear, and so it is a reasonable supposition that they did.

CHAPTER TWENTY-SEVEN

This description of the meeting between Lorilei Guillory and
Ricky Langley is based in part on *Lorilei*. I have also drawn on a
letter written by Lorilei and published in the *American Press* on
May 25, 2003, in which she talks about her thoughts and feelings,
though not the visit. Finally, I have imagined some of the details
necessary to bring the scene to life. The statements about Bessie
Langley's absence are in the 1994 trial transcript. In crafting this
chapter, I have also drawn upon Ricky's records from the Georgia
prison, a 1993 defense mitigation memo that is in the court record,
and the 1994 trial transcript.

CHAPTER TWENTY-EIGHT

I drew upon Eula Buller's pamphlet "Hebert Cemetery 2007" in
preparing this chapter.

CHAPTER TWENTY-NINE

The song "The Rose" was written by Amanda McBroom. The
description of the motorcycle crash that killed the father and son
I've called Terry and Joey Lawson is based on the police report,
which is in the court record, as well as an obituary published in the
American Press. The motion and brief referenced are in the court
record. That the motion was denied and that the family said they
would file a complaint with the Louisiana State Bar Association's

Disciplinary Board over the motion comes from an article published in the *American Press*.

CHAPTER THIRTY-ONE

The letter by Lorilei Guillory referenced here was published by
the *American Press*. The conflicting statements and descriptions are
from the 1994 and 2003 trial transcripts. The letter written by
Ricky Langley to his parents here is a composite drawn from several letters. This actual quote is from 1992 and was read aloud by
Clive Stafford Smith during Lucky DeLouche's testimony during
the 2003 trial; Ricky was referring to his desire to help others understand the minds of pedophiles. Descriptions of the seminar, as
well as what Ricky and Clive said during it and what attendees
were thinking, feeling, or said, are based on statements given by
seminar attendees to prosecutors later. In some cases, however, I
have compressed two attendee accounts into one person for ease of
reading. Further I have imagined the room and people's physical
actions. These statements are in the 2003 court record, but were
not admitted at trial. The meeting between Colonel Bruce LaFargue
and Ricky prior to the seminar is based on LaFargue's January 2,
2003, affidavit. A December 12, 2002, fax from Clive to LaFargue
asserts that nothing Ricky said would be used against him; in the
January affidavit, LaFargue says he never promised that and that
he responded to Clive's requests for that assurance only by saying
that they were in agreement that Ricky wouldn't talk about the
murder. In crafting this chapter, I have also relied upon testimony
from the 1994 trial.

CHAPTER THIRTY-TWO

The voir dire section is based on transcripts in the court record.
Judge Alcide Gray's and Cynthia Killingworth's comments about
there being a murder every day occurred on different days of voir
dire, but I have compressed time here for narrative flow. My esti-
mate of the numbers of jurors questioned is approximate. In thinking about this chapter, I drew upon *On Killing: The Psychological*

Cost of Learning to Kill in War and Society by Dave Grossman and *Jurors' Stories of Death: How America's Death Penalty Invests in Inequality* by Benjamin Fleury-Steiner.

CHAPTER THIRTY-THREE

The courtroom scene is drawn from the 2003 trial transcript, though I have imagined the lawyers' physical actions in the courtroom and what the jurors were thinking. The 2003 KPLC-TV clips are not available, but clips from the 2009 revisiting of the case include sections that were played in 2003, and I've relied on those here. It is worth noting that the aerial photographs of the woods were not taken at the time of the murder—at this trial, the photographer clarified that the helicopter had been unavailable then—but in the spring of 1993.

CHAPTER THIRTY-FOUR

The dialogue and trial descriptions in this chapter come from the 2003 trial transcript. The descriptions of the videotapes come from their transcripts. I have imagined the jurors' and Lorilei Guillory's thoughts and feelings. The Christmas photograph of Jeremy Guillory comes from the KPLC-TV clips referenced in chapter thirty-three. That prosecutors called Lorilei unfit appears in many statements given or articles written by Clive Stafford Smith, for example an October 10, 2008, opinion piece on the *Al Jazeera* Web site, "Death Penalty 'Utterly Barbaric.'"

CHAPTER THIRTY-FIVE

The trial portion of this chapter is based on the 2003 trial transcript. My thinking about whether most pedophiles have been abused is based on "Does Sexual Abuse in Childhood Cause Pedophilia: An Exploratory Study," K. Freund et al., *Archives of Sexual Behavior* (December 1990), and "Cycle of Child Sexual Abuse: Links Between Being a Victim and Becoming a Perpetrator," M. Glasser et al., *The British Journal of Psychiatry* (December 2001). Both articles are available online. By asking whether Lorilei Guillory saw herself in Ricky Langley, I do not at all intend to indicate that she saw herself in what he did. Rather, I am questioning whether she perhaps saw herself in some of the challenges he faced in life. In thinking about that possible connection, I drew upon the play *Lorilei*.

CHAPTER THIRTY-SIX

The trial portion of this chapter is drawn from the 2003 trial transcript.

CHAPTER THIRTY-SEVEN

The quote from the social worker is drawn from a 1993 defense mitigation memo that is in the court record; other descriptions of what the jury did not hear about are drawn from sources cited above in the chapters in which the events unfolded. More about the "dream diary" and the debate about whether it included dreams or confessions is in the 1994 trial transcript. That Lorilei Guillory did not attend the announcement of the jury's verdict for the 2003 trial comes from an *American Press* article. That Clive Stafford Smith appealed the 2003 verdict, and on what grounds he did so and what happened afterward, is in the court record. In 2003, I heard the jury foreman, Steven Kujawa, say what is quoted here in an event held at the LCAC office. The event was attended by LCAC interns who did not work on Ricky Langley's case, as well as community members who were not involved in the case. I have based my description of Kujawa's family circumstances on statements he made that day and in the 2003 voir dire transcript.

CHAPTER THIRTY-EIGHT

The photographs described here are in the court record.

CHAPTER FORTY

Some of my description of Angola is based on *God of the Rodeo*, a nonfiction account of the Angola Prison Rodeo written by Daniel Bergner. The letter from Ricky Langley to a judge referred to here is in the court record.

Acknowledgments

Sometimes good lightning strikes. I was fortunate that it happened twice during the writing of this book, when generous grants from the National Endowment for the Arts and the Rona Jaffe Foundation arrived at exactly the moments they were most needed. The financial support made the research for this book possible; the votes of confidence were invaluable. So, too, was time and space provided by the MacDowell Colony, the Corporation at Yaddo, the Millay Colony for the Arts, Blue Mountain Center, the Virginia Center for the Creative Arts, Vermont Studio Center, the Kimmel Harding Nelson Center, the Studios of Key West, the Djerassi Resident Artists Program, and the family of Alice Hayes, who funded a fellowship at the Ragdale Foundation.

Some of the sections in this book were published in previous form in *Oxford American, Bellingham Review, Fourth Genre, Bookslut,* and the anthology *True Crime.* I am grateful to their editors, Brenda Miller, Marcia Aldrich, Jessa Crispin, and Lee Gutkind, for recognizing promise in the material. A particular debt is owed to Wes Enzinna, then at *Oxford American,* who once called me at 10 p.m. about a verb. He was right, and that call taught me so much.

My agent, Robert Guinsler, was the best champion of this book I could have hoped for from the very first moment I told him about it. His belief has been unflagging, his agenting nothing short of wizardry. To agent fixer extraordinaire Calvin Hennick: Thank you, always. Thank you, too, to Szilvia Molzar.

To my editor, Colin Dickerman: Thank you for having such a clear and complex vision for this book, a vision that brought out what it could be. Thank you, too, to the team at Flatiron Books:

James Melia, Amelia Possanza, Marlena Bittner, Molly Fonseca, Nancy Trypuc, and Keith Hayes, as well as to Robert Ickes and Michael K. Cantwell. I feel privileged to be in such excellent hands, and in such excellent hands in the UK, with Georgina Morley and her team at Pan Macmillan.

Before this was a book, Douglas Whynott believed it could be one, and started teaching me how to turn it into one. For his mentorship and for the mentorship of Richard Hoffman, Megan Marshall, Pamela Painter, and their colleagues in the MFA program at Emerson, I am thankful. I am thankful, too, for the advice and encouragement along the way of Jonathan Harr, Sydelle Kramer, David Shields, Jane Brox, Joshua Wolf Shenk, Rachel Sussman, and Deanne Urmy.

At the Bread Loaf Writers' Conference, I am indebted to Michael Collier, Noreen Cargill, Jennifer Grotz, and Jason Lamb. There I met Ross White and Matthew Olzmann, who run the Grind, in which many pages of this book were written. At the Wesleyan Writers Conference, I am grateful to Anne Greene and the families of Jon Davidoff and Joan Jakobson.

Boston has one of the best writing communities around, and that is largely due to its organizations. I am deeply grateful to Eve Bridburg and Christopher Castellani for providing me with a home, for so many years now, at Grub Street, and grateful for the work of Alison Murphy, Jonathan Escoffery, Sonya Larson, Dariel Suarez, Lauren Rheaume, Sarah Colwill-Brown, and the many others who keep Grub running. I am thankful to the board and members of the Writers' Room of Boston, where much of this book was written, and in particular to Debka Colson. Thank you, too, to my colleagues at Harvard's Kennedy School of Government, and in particular to Jeffrey Seglin there, a great mentor, former teacher, and dear friend. To my students, past and present, in Grub Street's Memoir Incubator, other Grub classes, Cedar Crest College, and Harvard: Thank you for trusting me with your stories, and for teaching me through your bravery. Working with you is a deep honor.

In the middle of working on this book, I got an e-mail inviting me to join a writing group. Little did I know it was the best writing group that ever was. To the Chunky Monkeys—Chip Cheek, Jennifer De Leon, Calvin Hennick, Sonya Larson, Celeste Ng, Whitney Scharer, Adam Stumacher, Grace Talusan, Becky Tuch—so much gratitude and love. You are all basically the reason I still live in a place with winter.

The Reporters Committee for Freedom of the Press was a valuable resource. In Louisiana, Loretta Mince, Jeannette Donnelly, and Alysson Mills provided essential legal advice and assistance. I am thankful for the help of the staffs at the Southwest Louisiana Genealogical Library, the East Baton Rouge Parish Clerk of Court, and the Iowa Public Library, as well as the Bullers at Consolata Cemetery and Mari Wilson at KPLC-TV. A special thank-you to Sha Carter, Bethany Smith, and the rest of the staff at the Calcasieu Parish Clerk of Court criminal records division, for the endless photocopying, mountains of paper clips, and for finding me a comfortable chair.

The material for this book was often very difficult to write. For hugs and for bourbon, for pep talks and crucial feedback, thank you to Alysia Abbott, Howard Axelrod, Ned Baxter, Steven Beeber, Michael Blanding, Nicholas Boggs, Sari Boren, Lori Brister, Alexander Chee, Julia Cooke, Rebecca Morgan Frank, Ted Genoways, Michelle Hoover, Elin Harrington-Schreiber, Patricia Harrington-Schreiber, Hannah Larrabee, Ron MacLean, Richard McCann, Nicole Miller, Mary Jane Nealon, Shuchi Saraswat, Mike Scalise, Linda Schlossberg, Kat Setzer, Justin St. Germain, Rachel Starnes, R.J. Taylor, Laura van den Berg, Robin Wasserman, Sarah Wildman, Alexi Zentner, and Ann Zumwalt. I cannot say my thank-yous for this book without saying one to my late dog, Lada, who made the days of my early work on it so much softer. Thank you, too, to the staffs at Diesel Café in Somerville and 1369 Coffeehouse on Mass Ave. in Cambridge for all the necessary coffee, and to Zoe Keating for her music, the soundtrack for so much of my writing.

It cannot have been easy for my family to be supportive of me writing this book, but they have been, and for that and for so much else I am profoundly grateful. Every family is complicated, but it has been a deep blessing to know that ours is glued together with love.

Janna and I had our first date the evening it became clear this book would eventually be published. Some months later, she became a character in it. To her: Thank you for making the material of this book easier to live, and then easier to write. Thank you for your love, and for making a home with me where my memories of the past can live safely alongside my hopes for the future.